AMERICAN
SOLITAIRE

PALMETTO
P U B L I S H I N G
Charleston, SC
www.PalmettoPublishing.com

Copyright © 2024 by Craig Martin

All rights reserved

No portion of this book may be reproduced, stored in a retrieval system, or transmitted in any form by any means–electronic, mechanical, photocopy, recording, or other–except for brief quotations in printed reviews, without prior permission of the author.

Hardcover ISBN: 9798822954519
Paperback ISBN: 9798822952249
eBook ISBN: 9798822952256

AMERICAN SOLITAIRE

MY EXPLORATION OF AMERICA AND MY MIND

CRAIG MARTIN

*This book is for my family.
No matter what, I love you all*

CONTENTS

Opening		1
6/28/23	Day #1	9
6/29/23	Day #2	13
6/30/23	Day #3	20
7/1/23	Day #4	25
7/2/23	Day #5	30
7/3/23	Day #6	35
7/4/23	Day #7	42
7/5/23	Day #8	47
7/6/23	Day #9	52
7/7/23	Day #10	57
7/8/23	Day #11, Riding #10	62
7/9/23	Day #12, Riding #11	66
7/10/23	Day #13, Riding #12	71
7/11/23	Day #14, Riding #13	76
7/12/23	Day #15, Riding #14	80
7/13/23	Day #16, Riding #15	85
7/14/23	Day #17, Riding #16	90

7/15/23	Day #18, Riding #17	94
7/16/23	Day #19, Riding #18	98
7/17/23	Day #20, Riding #19	103
7/18/23	Day #21, Riding #20	107
7/19/23	Day #22, Riding #21	112
7/20/23	Day #23, Riding #22	116
7/21/23	Day #24, Riding #23	120
7/22/23	Day #25, Riding #24	124
7/23/23	Day #26, Riding #25	129
7/24/23	Day #27, Riding #26	134
7/25/23	Day #28, Riding #27	139
7/26/23	Day #29, Riding #28	144
7/27/23	Day #30, Riding #29	148
7/28/23	Day #31, Riding #30	154
7/29/23	Day #32, Riding #31	159
7/30/23	Day #33, Riding #32	164
7/31/23	Day #34, Riding #33	169
8/1/23	Day #35, Riding #34	174
8/2/23	Day #36, Riding #35	181
8/3/23	Day #37, Riding #36	187
8/4/23	Day #38, Riding #37	190

8/5/23	Day #39, Riding #37	193
8/6/23	Day #40, Riding #37	198
8/7/23	Day #41, Riding #38	201
8/8/23	Day #42, Riding #39	208
8/9/23	Day #43, Riding #40	216
8/10/23	Day #44, Riding #41	224
8/11/23	Day #45, Riding #42	231
8/12/23	Day #46, Riding #42	237
8/13/23	Day #47, Riding #43	240
8/14/23	Day #48, Riding #44	245
8/15/23	Day #49, Riding #45	249
8/16/23	Day #50, Riding #46	255
8/17/23	Day #51, Riding #47	261
8/18/23	Day #52, Riding #48	267
8/19/23	Day #53, Riding #49	272
8/20/23	Day #54, Riding #50	277
8/21/23	Day #55, Riding #50	282
8/22/23	Day #56, Riding #50	285
8/23/23	Day #57, Riding #51	289
8/24/23	Day #58, Riding #52	294
8/25/23	Day #59, Riding #52	301

8/26/23	Day #60, Riding #53	304
8/27/23	Day #61, Riding #54	309
8/28/23	Day #62, Riding #55	313
8/29/23	Day #63, Riding #56	318
8/30/23	Day #64, Riding #57	322
8/31/23	Day #65, Riding #57	327
9/1/23	Day #66, Riding #58	332
9/2/23	Day #67, Riding #59	339
9/3/23	Day #68, Riding #60	348
9/4/23	Day #69, Riding #61	356
9/5/23	Day #70, Riding #62	365
9/6/23 to 9/11/23	The Drive Home	375
9/12/23	Home, New Holland, Pennsylvania	383
Dining Room Table, Apartment		384
From My Video		387
10/15/23	Wrap-Up	392
Thanks		398
About the Author		400

OPENING

So how do I start exactly? How do I begin to attempt to write a book? Just writing that question was enough to get my pen moving. Sometimes, I have learned in my life, when you're unsure how or where to start something, you just need to think out loud, start with something basic, something simple, and build off of that. So now I have already written the first three sentences and kick-started my writing.

I grew up in the middle of the Amish and Mennonite farming area in southeastern Pennsylvania. I've lived in Lancaster County my entire life. I like it out here mostly: it's quiet (in certain areas), has beautiful scenery and lots of great hiking in the southern end of the county, and we are lucky enough to have multiple great rail trails in the county as well. Plus, the road riding is very nice out there, mostly flat, with hills if you want them. With the Amish out there riding, the cars are used to bicycles, and generally it is a safe place to ride on the roads. With all the back road farmlands, there's a lot of great scenic riding out there.

I graduated from high school (Warwick, 2001), and college (Thaddeus Stevens College of Technology, 2008) in Lancaster County as well. I've had my share of self-induced pain and troubles in life, mostly caused by my past alcohol abuse, combined with some pretty nasty depression. It's taken me to places I didn't want to be, didn't think I'd ever be, and also taken away a lot in life, including my freedom a few times. That all culminated in my last night of drinking, a single car crash that should have taken my life on January 28, 2017.

Life didn't become easier just because I stopped drinking; it just became easier to manage. But, best of all, it cleared a lot of the negative thoughts and thinking about myself out of my head. It's certainly been a better life without alcohol, and I'm happy with where I am in that aspect of my life today.

I've always had a love for the outdoors. In high school, my core group of friends and I were always out hiking and usually camped on the weekends. That continued into most weekends from then until now, minus the friends. Weekends I'm almost always out on some kind of trail or out enjoying nature. I'd say about seven years ago, I discovered the absolute joy I'd get from riding my old bike, on these new things I discovered back then called rail trails. That passion very quickly grew, and soon I was driving hours away to ride other rail trails. It eventually led me to buying my first "good" bike, a Diamondback Trace Complete model. I loved it and was blown away by how much easier it was to ride my new bicycle compared to my old one.

That newfound hobby led to a new discovery: campsites along some of the trails I was riding. Now my mind was going, thinking how cool it would be to camp on a bike trip. I bought some gear and started on one-night trips. Strange, I can't remember off the top of my head, but my first trip was either the Pine Creek trail (Pennsylvania Grand Canyon) or the Great Allegheny Passage (GAP); most likely it was the GAP. I remember having a great time doing that, and from there it just grew. It became weekend trips, and eventually I was using all my vacation from work to go out on these adventures for a week or more.

The thing about me today is I live a pretty isolated life. Self-induced for sure, but honestly I'm not sure why. Life has been hard mentally for a long time now, mostly with depression, but lately I'm sure there's more going on upstairs. Either way, this trip is a way to get away from that and the other things that have happened recently in my life. I want to feel the freedom of being out on the road with no support, besides using my phone if needed. Really, I think I'm searching for something—that something is my identity, it's me. I'm sort of feeling lost and wondering what's next for me in life. I think secretly I'm hoping I get something extra out of this trip, some help with my character defects, help with my confidence, which I hide inside and lack.

There are a few things in my life that need attending to, that I feel like I've let go, in a way. I need to start caring, take back control, and try to lead the best, most joyful, and productive life I can out of what time I have left. I may not be happy today at times and may not have been happy in the past, but that doesn't mean anything about the future. All I need is the power, or probably faith in myself, to turn my life around.

I do think by going solo on this trip, I will gain confidence and regain some self-esteem and hopefully use what I've developed to make a better life for myself. But most importantly, I need those tools to save myself. I can be my own worst enemy too. I'm extremely hard on myself and usually demand perfection or at least 100 percent competency in what I do. I think that comes from my years working as a machinist, where things are right or wrong; 100 percent accuracy is needed in some aspects of my work life, and I believe that bled into my real life. I beat myself up for mistakes, and I let that fester, and then sometimes I start to believe the negative things I say. It can be a vicious mental cycle, but it's what my life has become, and I've grown accustomed to dealing with it.

I've sort of been all over the place so far in my writings. I'm writing this with no help. I wanted to see if I was capable of writing a book. I want to share my journey, air out my mental struggles, and most importantly show you that you are capable of doing amazing things that you might think impossible. A lot has to do with planning and just getting your body ready—that's it. Yes, it takes a lot of work to put together a cross-country trip, but if I can do it, so can majority of America. You have to put in the effort and most importantly try and really care about the steps to achieve your goal. If you don't have a solid foundation to start your goal, then the chances of failure are much greater.

Some things about my trip: I'm following the route of the Great American Rail Trail (GART). I'm starting in Washington, DC, on June 28, 2023, and ending in La Push, Washington, on the Pacific Ocean. I've been planning and mapping for weeks, close to a month. I need to have all routes, maps, and planned campsites done prior to leaving, mostly because I just want to ride when I'm out there; I don't want to have to plan my days on the road and every night at camp. Also, my anxiety goes crazy under such circumstances, and I would waste a lot of my ride wondering and worrying about my route tomorrow. I don't like unknown routes on my trips; I have to know where I'm going. I'm OK with winging it on day trips or short trips, but on long trips, I avoid it if I can help it.

I have 56 planned campsites/nights spaced out every 60 to 70 miles. I have 11 pages of my "route order," as I call it. It's a detailed record of every trail change or road section. If a trail ends and I need to take a road or different trail, I know when, where, how many miles, what's next, and any sidenote I might need for the area. I make it very easy on myself, or as easy as I can make it. The peace of mind I get from those papers is invaluable to me.

A while ago I came up with a saying: "Don't let yourself; take away from yourself; be yourself." I hope this book serves a purpose, besides me attempting something I've dreamed about. I actually sort of enjoy writing but feel overwhelmed trying to write a book. So I think of it as, all I have to do is write an opener, a closer, and tell seventy short stories (it ended up taking seventy days to complete my adventure). To me, it's easier to tell short stories than to write a book, so that's how I thought about it and wrote it. But it's all the same at the end of the day. When it comes to obstacles in life, or accomplishing dreams or whatever is overwhelming you, try to break it down into something easier to digest.

If I can shove away my dark thoughts and feelings to write a little at a time, then you can also make progress in your life on what holds you back from achieving your dreams and goals. It's difficult even to just go through the motions, but eventually it catches on. Then you've realized you've already written six notebook pages when you didn't even know how to start writing a book.

When I feel stuck in life, I usually can still turn to the things I enjoy, and sometimes it will pull me up and out of the mental downward spiral. And if it doesn't help, at least I'm doing something I like and not wasting away on the couch or my bed, further mentally fading away into a self-induced hell.

Get up, get out, push yourself, and go a little further each day. I can't say when things will get better, but if I stop trying and moving forward, I'll never find out.

✪ ✪ ✪

I'll describe some of my gear and my touring setup. On this trip I'm riding my Diamondback Haanjo 7C (carbon) and starting out with Kenda Flintridge 700 by 40 tires. I sleep in a Kelty Salida 2-person tent with a Browning sleeping bag I've had so long I forget what the rating is. For clothing, I packed light but at the time wondered if I had too much. I packed 3 T-shirts, 2 long-sleeve moisture-wicking shirts, 1 pair of old Dickies work pants, 2 pairs of mesh shorts (1 for riding, 1 for sleeping), 4 pairs of ankle socks, 1 pair of regular socks, 5 pairs of boxers, 1 beanie, 1 regular long-sleeve shirt, and a pair of thin pajama pants. Nothing that was really warm, but I figured it'd be hot in the East, and if I got cold in the Pacific Northwest, I could buy something out there. I actually wouldn't feel cold until Yellowstone.

Then there were the bike tools you'd imagine: I like to have three spare tubes on hand, a first aid kit, OTC pills (headache, muscle, allergy), lights, a headlamp, spare batteries, a Jetboil stove, and the other usual camping stuff. I don't ride in or even own padded clothing, and I don't use a sleeping pad. I actually don't mind sleeping on the ground. In the summer, when it's eighty degrees in my tent at night, the ground draws the heat from my body. With my back issues, sleeping on a hard, flat surface brings relief at night.

I have a cell phone mount on the handlebars, along with my CatEye Velo wireless bike computer. It's very simple, small, and only has one button but has everything I need; for me, it's perfect. I use Google Maps for all my trips, and when I refer to Maps, it's Google Maps. I follow the exact routes on the GART website. The only maps I make personally are for gaps on the official route. I also bought a new, more powerful power bank (Anker 26,800 mAh) having power for the phone or anything else you need to charge is important.

That's where my route order comes in; it follows exactly the order of the website's route, east to west. I then have every map saved in my phone and even note cards detailing every turn on every road map. I do this because there will be a time when I need directions and can't get a signal to load my map. I have around fifty of these maps/cards for this trip. I won't use majority of the cards, but I still feel a need for them. You must be prepared for anything and everything when traveling alone.

I planned on riding 60 to 70 miles per day but really planned around where I could camp. I only used campsites along the trail, campgrounds, hotels, and a couple Airbnbs. I tend to avoid people and stay to myself, so I never used warmshowers.com or anything like that. I'm not sure why, but for some reason I avoid closer encounters like that.

I wish I knew why—is it fear of acceptance, feeling like I don't belong or fit in, or another reason I just don't see? I do enjoy a nice, quiet, peaceful night under the stars and when no one's around, sleeping without the rain fly on.

I will travel through twelve states and Washington, DC. I already did parts of this trail a few years ago. I rode from DC to Pittsburgh, and then later that year, I started in Pittsburgh and rode to the Indiana-Illinois border then up to Chicago to catch the Amtrak back to Pittsburgh. Also, a month before this trip, I rode the Ohio to Erie Trail both ways, so I'm very familiar with Ohio and some of Indiana.

I'm most excited about the Pacific Northwest. My grandparents used to live in Port Orchard, Washington, and I have a couple memories of the place. Also, I want to experience the trees, rain forest area, and general peacefulness of the place. Of course, I can't wait for Yellowstone National Park (YNP) and the three days I have planned there. I'm really interested in seeing the West and its mountains.

In my mind I know there's nothing that will stop me from completing this. I don't know if I realize how much more difficult it will be alone, but I don't really care. (1) I don't know anyone who would go with me, and (2) I like having the planning and everything up to me. I can do it my way, and if I'm wrong, I know where or how I went wrong (usually). Still, I actually underestimated how mentally tough I'd have to be at times to keep everything together.

I also don't carry any weapon, only a pocketknife I always have on me. I don't have any fear of people on the trail but always mind what areas I'm traveling through. I don't stop very long, and in some areas, I won't leave my bike unattended. You've just got to be smart and use good judgment: even if locked, it can be stolen, not to mention anyone can go into my bags.

I eat ramen noodles most nights, but anything that can be cooked with hot water I can use. I have instant oatmeal and instant coffee every morning, made with my Jetboil stove. This is my first trip with the stove, and now I can't believe I went without it. I refuse to let myself go one morning anymore without coffee *ever* again on a trip.

✪ ✪ ✪

On a final note, one of the things I worry about in writing this book is that this is the only thing people will know about me. As you'll read, I went through some very tough times mentally. I just want to say that that is not how I've been the past few years. This is how a person can get when untreated depression escalates over many, many years, and one incredibly bad incident puts into question almost everything you have in life.

6/28/23
DAY #1

Miles—66.03; Time—6:10

Huckleberry Hill Hiker and Biker Campsite, Knoxville, Maryland

(free, primitive)

Today is the big day. I woke up feeling the anxiety but also the thrill of knowing what I'm starting today. In a few hours and 130 miles to the south, I'll start my cross-country journey on the GART. I probably set my alarm for around 5:00 a.m. My mom and stepdad will be here to pick me up around 6:15 a.m. I'm catching the Amtrak train in Aberdeen, Maryland, and riding that to Union Station in Washington DC. On some Amtrak trains, for an extra twenty dollars, you can bring your bicycle on board the train. The train departs at 7:40 a.m. and arrives in DC at 8:52 a.m. A good time to still get a somewhat early start, and it's Wednesday, so I don't anticipate many people on the trail outside of our nation's capital.

Loading my bike on this Amtrak train was the absolute worst experience. I've used Amtrak many times with my bike and never had an employee tell me there's no room and I need to find a spot for my bike. There were some more issues with this certain employee, but this will not start out negatively. I'll end it by saying his coworker told me to call customer service, so I wasn't the only one unhappy with him, I guess. His coworker cleared my paid bike spot, and all was good again. Then, when the train arrived in Union Station, I started to load up my bike for my ride through Washington, DC.

I'm all loaded up, and I realize I can't find my phone mount. I must've looked for ten minutes, but it felt like a half hour. I need a map from the train station to the start of the Capital Crescent trail. I eventually find it, and I get on my way. I've ridden around DC a couple times before, but I still enjoy stopping by some of the monuments and statues. My favorite one to see is the World War II memorial. Riding through DC around the White House and memorial area was a mess. There were multiple roads, sidewalks, and areas blocked off. I assume it was from them setting up for the Fourth of July festivities.

I get on the Capital Crescent trail after a 3.25-mile sightseeing tour of the capital. The first few days are all trail, and knowing this helps me transition into a more comfortable mindset to get myself ready for this adventure.

We had a very, very dry couple of months before I left on this trip. And then before I left, we had heavy rain for a few days, close to a week of steady rain. Anyone who has ridden the Chesapeake and Ohio trail (C&O) knows how sloppy that trail can get. I was surprised to see the first 20 miles from DC were very well maintained. I don't remember the C&O being like that before, but its been almost three years since I've been down here. After those miles, it goes to the rough and bumpy canal towpath that I remember. The trail had lots of big water puddles, and I had picked up a lot of dirt along the way. There is a very nice hiking trail off the C&O, close to DC, that leads to a bridge overlooking the Great Falls. It's just a few steps off the trail and a must-see along the way. The scenery on the C&O is very nice, and I usually see a good amount of the local wildlife.

I went to the chiropractor a couple days before I left and can feel the slight aching pain from my body readjusting to the realigned muscles in my back. It doesn't help that I always overpack on water and food to start. I started with 6 water bottles, 2 Gatorade bottles, a 12-pack of ramen noodles, a 24-pack of Clif Bars, oatmeal and coffee, and other snacks. I know there's not a lot on the C&O, especially with not using the water pumps on the trail for drinking. I knew I wouldn't need to stock up on food until close to Pittsburgh. Also, I was unsure on the water status at the pumps—most wells are untreated—so I packed extra water. I only cook with the pump water out there. Altogether my bags usually weigh 35 pounds each at their heaviest and about 25 to 30 pounds on average.

Going upstream, I'm climbing all the locks, and the surface is wet, all of which helped in making me work harder today.

I remember thinking I can't go on like this for the whole trip. I was in some pain at camp and feeling very tired. It's funny that on these trips, when I have hard days or I'm going slower, pedaling harder, I think there's something wrong. It has nothing to do with the weight I'm carrying or the fact that I might be riding uphill or on a slower surface. Nope, something's wrong with the bike or something is rubbing, causing some friction somewhere. It's funny how my mind works like that, like I can't just admit this is a tough area or hard day riding. No, my bike has to have an issue. I think it's just my brain making excuses for me working hard.

It was a good temperature that day, as I remember, but there was some smoke in the air coming down from Canada due to their wildfires. I personally don't feel like it affected me. I couldn't really even tell aside from the hazy skies, but I did see some people wearing masks. One of the things I do enjoy about the C&O is the remoteness of the trail at certain points. There's also a lot of free primitive camping along the trail—just be prepared with plenty of water or a filtering system.

I made it to Huckleberry Hill primitive campsite on the trail after 65 miles. A good distance for my first day. The campsite is located just across the river from Harper's Ferry, West Virginia. The other thing I like about canal trails is that when I'm on them, I'm always close to the sounds of water. On the C&O, one side is the canal, and the other is the Potomac River and West Virginia. I really enjoy riding along rivers because I feel it adds so much more, both good and bad. The wildlife the water attracts is an example of one of the good things.

I love taking off my shoes and jumping in the river on a hot day riding the trails. I always bring a quick-dry towel on trips; I *hate* wet socks. I'll go swimming almost any chance I can get or when I feel like it. The one bad part is, like Huckleberry Hill, the water also brings mosquitoes and other annoying bugs. This site was not immune to them; after I was done eating, and writing my daily journal (from which I draw most of my memories for this book), I couldn't take it anymore. I had to go in my tent for cover. This is another reason I packed light pajama pants: there were lot of nights at camp during which I had to cover my entire body if I wanted to stay outside, to keep from being attacked.

All in all, a very successful first day, and I'm feeling confident. But I'm also very familiar with this trail. I was the only one at the campsite tonight, a perfect way to end the day. I also used the water pump to wash all the dirt off my bike. That's another benefit of the pumps: cleaning out all the dirt from the gears, chain, and everywhere else that it has collected.

6/29/23
DAY #2

Miles—70.38 (136.41 trip total); Time—6:32 (12:42 trip total)
Cacapon Junction Campsite, Hancock, Maryland
(free, primitive)

I started day two around 8:00 a.m.; I like getting an early start. Plus, I usually end up seeing deer in the early morning hours. The rain has let up for a few days, but more rain is in the forecast in the coming days. The trail today was in a lot better shape as far as puddles; I only came across one spot all day. After running through gritty, sandy water puddles all day yesterday, I was thrilled to stay dry. I also started to notice more of a presence of the Canadian wildfire smoke. I can now smell a faint hint of smoke, and the sky has gotten hazier also. Add in the fact I'm riding north, and it all adds to the intensity. I can say it's certainly making people stay inside; I noticed that I'm not seeing many people out on the trail.

The surface of the trail varies on the C&O. At least it's smoother now; while it's still rough, I'm seeing fewer ruts and washouts. I remembered that the C&O, for some reason, has always given me some bike troubles. I've ridden this trail and the Great Allegheny Passage (GAP) trail a few times. The surface varies, consisting of crushed stone, cinders, hard-packed dirt, and concrete canal locks. The trail is wide enough for two, but it also goes down to a skinny one or two-lane stone with grass. It all makes for a changing and scenic ride along the canal.

I've ridden a few canal trails before, and the one thing is that, for me, riding them for multiple days can start to get stale. Only because a canal is usually very straight, flat, and has the same scenery for many miles. But here there are changes to sort of keep things fresh, plus I always see a lot of wildlife. I really enjoy seeing the turtles here; there is a nice variety of them around. I always see a bunch on the trails because of the canal water. But in the end, there are definitely pros and cons about canal trail riding for me.

My back was definitely feeling better after the ride today compared to yesterday. A lot of it had to do with the weight I was carrying.

Although I am going upstream and climbing the canal locks, I still felt better today. I'm also putting in a good amount of miles per day on the slow riding C&O. Because the surface is crushed stone, I tend to go a slower speed. I have to work harder to maintain a speed in the 11 to 12 miles per hour range. Riding at around 10 miles per hour is also common on a trail like this for me with the weight. Really, what reason is there to rush?

I don't necessarily rush or ride fast to get done sooner; I usually just get moving at a comfortable pace and go with that. The bike I ride is very efficient with pedaling, at least from my perspective. I have only a very basic understanding of gearing: little gears / fewer teeth means harder pedaling, more output, and bigger gears / more teeth means easier pedaling, less output, and these 48/32 up front and 11-34 in the back are phenomenal.

I do also know I'm probably riding more miles than I need to daily. But here's where I wonder about the physical versus mental aspects of riding. I train for these trips, but I'm not in the greatest shape. I push myself when things get tough; I can push past safe lengths to achieve a goal if needed. I feel I'm at a point with my body where I can shut my brain down when it tells me I can't go on and I continue past that mental roadblock.

On a trip as long as this, I should consider fatigue and burnout, but I don't. I will continue to ride through any extreme condition. I've continued riding when I get goose bumps in the heat and I can feel my brain and body slowing down. This isn't an every-time thing by any means, but if I have a goal in mind, I will accomplish it by any means necessary. That's my mindset: there is no quit. I feel like a machine sometimes, just powering through what I aim to accomplish. On day trips and one-nighters, that's OK, but not now. Out in the West, there can be very severe consequences for not taking things seriously or being unprepared. While I do respect the conditions out there and the potential dangers, I'll leave all this for when I actually get out there. I just have to consider whether I will burn out if I continue at this pace.

I have to realize I'm 40, not 25; I'm going to have to learn in the not-too-distant future that yes, I do have limitations. Or at least I hope I realize that. But my point is, I guess, I can't accept failure. If I plan on riding 60 to 70 miles a day for two months, then I will do what I need to do to accomplish this goal. I don't know why my mind works like that, but it does. I see a challenge and say "I can do that," then I have to follow through. The fear of being a failure or failing, I think, drives me to push past pain and sometimes logical thinking.

I'll talk about one part of my life here that might shed some light on my thoughts and actions. In my deep, dark times, when I physically want to feel pain or hurt, I use unconventional methods. I don't do self-harm, and no matter what I say in the heat of the moment, I have very strong thoughts on suicide. When I want to hurt, I put my body through extreme challenges. I've done 100-mile century rides, I've hiked from dawn to dusk—anything that requires an extreme energy output that will test my body and make me push past the pain to finish. A healthy exercise but in an unhealthy way. Which is scarier, self-harm or opening up yourself to the world?

Getting back to the physical-or-mental question. After so long, the body gets used to your riding position (as long as you repeat the position) and the pains and aches start to stop. I've heard before that bicyclists get stronger as the ride goes on, and I 100 percent believe that. But eventually, it will all add up and you'll need to be mentally strong to ignore the physical pain and fatigue. I believe in the power of the mind, that you can convince your muscles to keep moving when you're past the point of exhaustion and or fatigue. That you can go into a mental autopilot where you take yourself out of the physical element and everything becomes a mental challenge. In that mode my body is going through involuntary motions, sort of like breathing. Unless you consciously think about it, the body automatically takes over. I guess it's like the runner's high I hear about people experiencing at high physical outputs.

I do believe in a lot of Buddhist philosophies; I'm not a Buddhist and don't profess to know a lot about the religion, but what I do read about has helped me tremendously in my life. The power the mind holds is incredible, and if you can get in tune with that and your body, I feel you can achieve so much more. I don't pretend to know a lot about all this; it just makes the most sense to me in the realm of religion but mostly philosophy. Without an open mind in some of these ways, well, I would not be in tune with my mind at all and I'd be even more lost in life. I also believe you can continue well past what you think you're physically capable of. You just have to be able to ignore pain and let the mind go blank.

Getting back to the riding, there is this very cool area north of Sharpsburg, Maryland. I believe it is called the Big Slackwater area. The trail moves away from the canal and borders the Potomac River, and on the other side are cliff walls. It's fun riding on the concrete trail scattered in between the grassy areas. There's a good drop-off from the trail to the water. This continues on for a few miles and is a good change of scenery. There are some long stretches where the views of the river, rocks, and trail are beautiful.

This day on the C&O was pretty desolate and deserted. I only passed two small towns for supplies, basically water, and those both required a short detour. Another reason I packed extra food to start.

I'll use pump water for cooking and coffee since I boil it. I don't mind buying water on short trips, but going this long a distance, I'll need to think of ways to conserve money. Filling up water bottles when I can is a very easy way to save cash. I eventually carried three 1.5-liter bottles in my bags, which was plenty; I never ran out. I just need to fill up bottles when I get a chance on the trail, and almost every campsite has water, so starting off fresh isn't usually a problem.

After a good second day, I made it to Cacapon Junction trail campsite in Hancock. A nice, free primitive site by the looks of it; all the sites along the trail are pretty basic and the same. I read the Google reviews about the train noise, so I knew ahead of time, plus I had stayed here before. Trains don't seem to bother me, and I've never had trouble sleeping with them in the background. I ended up hearing about five trains in my first two and a half hours of being there. Thankfully that turned out to be the busy time, and it quieted down after that.

I also had two visitors at the campsite. Just as I was getting dinner ready, I saw a deer casually walk into the campsite area and just start munching on some grass. It occasionally looked at me while going back to the grass. A good dining partner but lacking in conversation. It eventually turned and walked away after about ten to fifteen minutes. I always enjoy having such visitors. Not so much my second guest, though. While I was sitting in my chair, I caught a glimpse of something from my side vision in the trees on my left. It was a raccoon walking past me, and it kept on going, so I left it alone. Later it decided to come back toward my camp. I sprung up out of my chair fast, yelled, and stomped my feet as I ran toward it to scare it away. It took off without making any sound. I've seen the carnage raccoons can cause, and they'll take anything they can carry away.

I kept my shoes in my tent that night, ha ha. I didn't get woken up by a raccoon or a train during the night. However, I'm sure both made an appearance while I slept.

I'll end with the ending of my journal entry from that day: Doing good but feeling OK. It's starting to sink in just what I'm attempting to do. It amazes me and sort of blows my mind. Why not? Why not try? It'll probably crush me if I fail at this, but I can't be scared of failing at trying to fulfill a dream of mine. I just got to keep my head up, slow down, and not burn out. Enjoy the moment and stay mindful of everything I'm experiencing out here.

✪

6/30/23
DAY #3

Miles—52 (189); Time—5:00 (17:45) [note these are estimates as I did not record numbers]

Ramada, Cumberland downtown, Cumberland, Maryland ($110)

The day started off like any other day on a bike trip; little did I know what was in store. A nice-weather day and my final day riding the C&O trail. Up next was one of my personal favorite trails to ride, the GAP. Before I left, I made a video on using my Jetboil stove. This is the first time using it, and I can't believe I didn't bring it before. It's so convenient, easy, a real time and money saver. I can have coffee right away and any time I want during the day. But best of all, I don't need to throw away money every day on coffee at a store, stopping after I just get going, or worse, find myself with no place to get coffee in the morning. I've encountered these scenarios on all my prior trips.

It's like eating. Part of the fun is eating at new places and places I'll probably never go to again. Every day for a week or weekend, OK. On a two-month cross-country trip, however, you just can't financially do this. Well, I can't at least. On a trip like this, the Jetboil stove is an absolute necessity and will now be a fixture on all my future trips.

But here's another absolutely frustrating way I've seen my depression wreak havoc in my life. I've had that stove for over a year, maybe two—I honestly have forgotten. I got a case of being lazy, and I can't even remember why, but I just felt like having to use it, learn it, buy fuel was too much—I was basically looking for any pitiful reason to not use it—with having to plan everything else. It's like I feel overwhelmed by this, and it sounds incredibly stupid, I suppose, trying to explain myself, but maybe someone out there understands my madness. It sat on a shelf in my apartment unused. An amazing, easy, not to mention over-one-hundred-dollar device just sitting around because my depression/anxiety was telling me I had enough to deal with at the moment. But the moments continue, and one just leads into the next. Absolutely crazy, and for the life of me, I still can't explain it. I wish I could.

Back on the trail, I was coming up on the Paw-Paw Tunnel in Oldtown. I was told by a fellow rider that the tunnel was closed and I had to use the detour up and over the mountain. All the rain the week before my trip created a mudslide (I guess) that clogged up the tunnel, and crews were working to clear it. When I got to the tunnel, I soon remembered how big those mountains are. The detour was a hard, steep, 1.5-mile switchback trail up and over the mountain. I passed a few other people walking up and down with their bikes. It sure seemed like more than a mile and a half, though. This was steep even for a hike, let alone pushing my bike uphill with sixty pounds of gear. The views along the way were some of the best I saw in the beginning of my trip. When I could see through the trees, the lookouts were awesome. I love the views of the Appalachian Mountains, the trees, and water; all make for a pretty scene.

After scaling this detour, I finally made it to the top. The hike down really wasn't any easier, having to hold my brakes, or really, hold the bike to prevent it from taking off down the hill. It went faster but not easier by any means. I tried riding a little but couldn't ride long enough for it to make sense as I tried to navigate my way down the mountain. Eventually my hike came to an end, and I was back on the trail.

I knew the trail was bumpy, and my bike was taking a lot of jarring around. Every time I've ridden the C&O, I have felt like my bike's not running like it was prior to the trail. Not that it's the worst trail ever, far from it—it's a very good one. But there's something about it and me, I guess. I'm riding, and I start to feel this bobbing up and down of weight coming from the rear. I look behind me at my tire and see the problem. My pannier bag is doing the bobbing up and down on one side. I stop and inspect the rack and am not really thrilled obviously. It's then I see why I felt that: the bottom screw from my rack to the bike had snapped off! Of course, the screw body is recessed into the frame. Not a good thing three days into my trip at all. I knew I was coming up on Cumberland, which is a city with a bike shop on the trail.

It's also where the C&O trail meets the GAP trail. It's actually a big biking area because it's where these two long trails connect. Also, there's a Amtrak station there, so people can get a bike pass and only use one car for a long-distance bike trip. I've left my truck there before, when I rode the GAP to Pittsburgh on a few-days-long trip. It's a very good place to start/stop because of that.

I got to the bike shop, Wheelzup at Canal Place, and showed the mechanic my problem. It was getting close to their closing time, so I got a hotel in town. Here's another cool thing about the guys at the shop: they let me keep my bags in the shop overnight, which was a blessing, because that way I didn't have to make multiple trips to move all my things the three-quarters of a mile to my hotel. I just grabbed what I needed for the night in one pannier bag and headed out. I forgot my journal and some other things. I was rushing because of my anxiety and left stuff I would've liked to have had. In no way were the guys rushing me, but I still felt the anxiety of just packing a bag for the night! I had what I needed, and everything was in line for tomorrow.

One cool part of riding the C&O is it's littered with history. Especially lots of Civil War sites. Today I rode past a couple interesting-looking sites. I noticed a small single headstone off the trail near the Oldtown trailhead. It was still being maintained with flowers, a flag, and a mowed single lane to the marker. I couldn't read any of the words on the grave, though. It was an American flag, not a

Confederate one. Maryland was in the Confederacy, so most of the flags at graves are Confederate flags, sometimes with an American flag as well. I also saw a memorial site for two Confederates, the Pollocks. Not much to see, just a neat preserved historical area. I really like the American historical sites and reading about what happened years ago on the same ground I'm currently standing on.

I saw some more wildlife as well. I saw two different black snakes and some more turtles, of course. It's pretty cool seeing the turtles all lined up on the branches sticking out of the canal. Some branches are completely covered with turtles getting some air and sun.

7/1/23
DAY #4

Miles—95 (274.35); Time—6:38 (24:23) [these numbers are estimates]
Stewart's Crossing Campground And Adirondack Shelters, Connellsville, Pennsylvania (free, primitive)

I was at the bike shop a little after they opened up at 9:00 a.m. They had a quick fix before me, and then my bike was up on the repair stand. I was a little worried because this was going to be a drill-out job, which always runs the risk of thread damage. I know from experience that the threads at the end are stripped already. I imagine watching the mechanic working is like watching a surgeon on a family member. It's painful to watch, you might even squirm around, but you know it's all for the better. You clench your teeth and deal with it.

He got the broken screw out with minimal damage around the hole. I was happy with the work, considering the circumstances. The mechanic also noticed the sounds up front I was hearing. He found a cracked compression tube in my headset. Like I said before, all-star shop here—I went away very happy with the service. Finding the part, though, was a different story; I'd soon realize how few stores have spare carbon parts in stock. I left the store at 10:30 a.m., not bad at all, and all for a fair price too. I definitely recommend this place if you're in town.

Because of this late start, the rain in the forecast, and the fact that I wanted to make up miles to get back on track with my camping itinerary sheet, I knew I'd have a long day ahead. My itinerary sheet is a daily list of planned campsites, daily estimated mileage, towns I'll encounter, trails, and map numbers. I don't intend to be die-hard in following it; it's more of an aid so I don't have to search for stuff out here while riding. I have fifty-six planned days, but these are just provisional plans—like I said, just to make it easy for myself, like a quick cheat sheet. But of course, with the way my mind works, this turns into an itinerary that I strive to keep up with. Sometimes I hate the fact my mind tells me I need to keep up this pace, but a problem in my life is I can't slow down. This will come up again a few times over the course of the trip.

I'm on the GAP, and it's my favorite trail to ride. It also has my favorite state park to ride through, Ohiopyle State Park. The first 25 miles are all uphill, until you reach the Eastern Continental Divide. The last 5 to 7 miles after Frostburg, Maryland, are a little steeper, but it's not too bad; after all, it's still a rail trail. It's a beautiful ride still, and something new I don't remember from my prior trips on the GAP. On the old train tracks, they have these frames with steel wheels for the tracks and seats all welded together. They're two-person carts that people pedal down the hill, on a one-way trip. The trail itself is almost always in such great shape, and its packed small-chip surface is good rolling material. Plus, after the divide, it's mostly all downhill to Pittsburgh.

There are a few tunnels to ride through, and the Big Savage Tunnel is the longest by far of the bunch. Located in Meyersdale, Pennsylvania, this tunnel is just short of thirty-three hundred feet long. The tunnel is only dimly lit, so a light is a very good idea. It's flat, paved, and provides a very nice, cool ride on a summer day. There are also a few bridges to go over, with most spanning a valley below the trail, which then produces some just incredible views, adding to the beauty of the GAP.

Right before the Big Savage Tunnel is the Mason-Dixon Line. Half that distance farther is the Eastern Continental Divide and the end of the climb. There are usually people stopped here as it's a good resting place and a way to escape the sun if needed.

I stopped for a short time to get a few pictures and catch my breath. I had a lot to cover yet, but the route would be mostly downhill. The downhill elevation, compacted surface, and my pushing a little all combined to make my riding a little easier. I averaged probably 14 to 15 miles per hour the rest of the way, which really helped me get to camp before it got too late. Plus, with the weather, I was rushing. I ended up getting soaked twice during my ride. The rain was certainly something I'd be dealing with a lot in the East and at the start of this trip.

I still enjoyed my brief time in Ohiopyle, even though I rushed through it. I did stop, like I always do, and sat by the Casselman River for a little bit. No swimming this time—I was already wet. Just sitting, thinking, and really just enjoying the moment for everything that it was. The scenery, trees, the Casselman River, the trail surface, and everything else just combines to create this perfect blend of gifts for the senses. I love it out there, rain or shine.

Another reason I was rushing was the campsite situation. Stewart's Crossing in Connellsville has four free Adirondack-style shelters, rain was coming that night, and it was Saturday as well. I desperately wanted one of those shelters that night. I also had 90-something miles to ride to get there. Starting at ten thirty, I knew I'd need to pick up the pace and have some luck. As luck would have it, I got the last shelter available! These shelters are great: three walls and one open side, with a few places to hang my wet clothes.

I was cleaning my bike—it got loaded with dirt again from riding through the rain. I was trying to take off the rear rain guard but ended up breaking the plastic mount. Luckily there was a couple, probably in their early thirties, next to me, and I started talking with the guy. He gave me a few zip ties to hold my rain guard to the bike rack. Very cool people, and I was thankful for his help. I'd see over the course of my trip that a lot of people love to help.

People enjoy hearing and seeing people on these trips, I'm learning, and generally like to help out if they can. Generosity and caring people are not things that I'm used to, either because I don't put myself out there or because of my isolation, most likely. There is also a big grocery store next door to the camping area to get food for the night or anything else. All in all, a terrific place right on the trail. There were fireworks that night, but most of them were blocked by the trees.

I'm definitely glad I'm encountering these obstacles early in my trip. Between my rack and the rain, its showing me this isn't easy. That there will be unforeseen obstacles to overcome. It also shows I'm able to adapt and roll with what comes my way. Every day I seem to be gaining more confidence about my trip. Perhaps I was getting ahead of myself, as it was only day four, and little did I know the challenges I'd face up ahead. The problems are easier to deal with when I'm in a populated area and in places I'm familiar with. Soon enough I would have to work through and see what real problems and difficulties look like.

It was a long, hard riding day, and it 100 percent took its toll on me. At camp I thought I had a tick under my skin, so I tried digging it out with my knife; it wasn't a tick. Not sure what it was, maybe dried blood from my metal pedal biting into my ankle earlier. I was ready to go to sleep after that; it was a late night with the fireworks. With the rain forecasted overnight and into the morning, I didn't set an alarm. I know, especially on camping trips, that I don't sleep late. If I sleep past 7:00 a.m., I consider it sleeping in. I usually wake up before my usual 6:00 a.m. alarm anyways.

7/2/23
DAY #5

Miles—74.85 (349.20); Time—6:30 (30:53)
Sleep Inn and Suites, Pittsburgh, Pennsylvania ($100)

Today started out with rain in the morning. Rain again—rain has had something to do with every day so far. You can look at it from many different views, but ultimately you've got to find a way to cope with it. Can't change the weather, and all I can do is just try to find cover when I need it. I'm not sure what time I left, but I do remember sitting around a few extra hours waiting for the rain to stop so I could start. I was in the Adirondack shelter, sitting in my chair and enjoying my coffee and listening to the Grateful Dead channel on the SiriusXM app on my phone. At least I was enjoying the morning and relaxing. Although, I feel my anxiety rising about the time and getting a late start. Those rushing feelings, I constantly fight them, but I've grown semi acclimated to them now. The rain has either stopped or is just a light mist at this point, so off I go.

After riding over 90 miles yesterday, I only had roughly another 70-ish to finish up in Pittsburgh today. As much as I love the GAP, I don't love riding in the rain or staying wet all day. Once again I was waiting out the weather, but it was just a messy day all around again. The trail had seen multiple days of rain, and it was sloppy in certain areas. As for me, I got to avoid the rain, but the mist and slight showers gave me a daytime shower anyway.

I did see lots of flooding in the little creeks and streams, with the usual brown, muddy-colored water. The river was even flooded by then and had risen higher than I'd ever seen it while out there. It also added to the small trail side waterfalls; they were flowing heavier than usual. There are also two different-colored mini trail waterfalls. One is a red waterfall between West Newton and McKeesport and is colored from the iron and sulfur coming from the coal mining. The other one is a silver-looking waterfall a little farther up, heading north, also colored by the minerals in the earth from mining.

The day was cloudy all day; there hasn't been much sunshine so far. A lot of rain and not a lot to help dry it out. The GAP trail does a good job of absorbing the water, though, considering how much there's been lately. Even with the weather and gray skies all day, at least it wasn't a miserable riding day. Just a little messy, but by this time I'm getting used to it.

I'm washing my bike out at my breaks and at the end of the day.

After starting in more of a nature setting, it starts to transition to more of an urban setting as one gets closer to Pittsburgh. There are a couple amazing bridges to cross on the trail, some with some great views, before Mckeesport, mostly while crossing the Youghiogheny River; the trail will cross the Monongahela River too.

I always stop to take a few pictures and just enjoy the landscape and moment. I got through Mckeesport at a quick pace, it's all road and goes through some sketchy parts of town. I must say I have never had any problems or issues. I look for the trail signs throughout the town as the trail has a few turns.

After climbing a hill, I came up on the outside of Kennywood Amusement Park. Just something fun to see along the trail. I also passed a big water park, with a lot of long, winding slides. I crossed another large bridge spanning this huge rail yard, just past Kennywood. As I'm interested in mechanical things, I always stop by this *huge* gantry crane. It's no longer in operation, but the sheer size of it blows my mind. I guess that's one of the things I really enjoy, seeing the mechanics of how absurdly big equipment works.

After passing the Pittsburgh Steelers and Pittsburgh University Panthers football training facilities, I made my way to Pittsburgh. The GART used to go through downtown, then the North Shore, and finally to the Montour Trail. I took the new southern route because I'm a strict follower of the original route. Since my last time riding out there, the trail changed routes, and honestly I don't think it's nearly as good. The old route passed Point State Park (confluence and start of the Ohio river), PPG Paints Arena, Roberto Clemente Bridge, PNC Park, Acrisure Stadium, and a very nice waterfront trail and then transitioned to a not-so-bad road ride to the Montour Trail. Trail riders following the new route miss all this. Now it's a shorter 11-mile road ride from the Three River's Heritage Trail to the Montour Trail. I missed seeing the Penguins arena, something I always make time to stop by. I'm a *huge* Penguins fan, have a Penguins tattoo, and enjoy going there for games.

Before my planned campsite, I stopped by REI in South Shore, Pittsburgh, to see if they had the part I needed for my bike. I told the one mechanic it was a carbon tube and not alloy and that I needed a carbon part. I was basically repeating what the Cumberland, Maryland mechanic told me. The REI mechanic said front tubes usually aren't carbon that I should wait for the other mechanic to install the part. After waiting an hour, they tell me they don't have that or, really, any carbon parts. Now I'm kind of mad; I understand stuff happens, mistakes are made, but I told him it was a carbon tube. It should've been as quick as "Yeah, that's carbon; we don't carry carbon bike parts," and I should've been on my way. Leaving pretty frustrated, I got back on the road.

While riding and waiting at the store, I was weather watching. More rain was on the way that night, and I just didn't want to deal with rain. I got a hotel for the night. It was right off the trail, or so I thought. On Google Maps it looks like the road to the hotel crosses the trail. However, when you go to the "terrain" view, it's clearly an overpass road to the hotel, damn it! Not bad but a busy road and an extra hill to climb. Hopefully a lesson learned in Maps. It ended up just pouring that night again, so I was glad I ended up getting the hotel.

I made a video in the morning while waiting out the rain, and I'll kind of sum that up. Before leaving on this trip, I know I didn't fully understand how enormous of a trip it really was. Even with the months of planning, it was very hard to fully comprehend the trip as a whole. Encountering some problems and adversity early was, in a way, good for me. It's completely different anticipating problems versus having to actually work with or around them. And you have no idea how you'll really react until you're in one of those situations.

Having some problems early reminds me that this isn't just a vacation joyride that will be problem-free. I will encounter issues that need to be addressed and/or fixed by me. How do I react to issues on the fly? These problems will happen. Will I let them beat me down, make me miserable, potentially end my trip as I encounter them? Or will I keep my head up, keep going, and keep the mindset I currently have, a positive one.

My mind and feelings can go south real fast if I choose to let them and give up fighting. I know how hard it is to pick myself up and wash my self-hate away. Sometimes it's impossible to push those feelings away. Staying positive for me is more important than I could ever describe. As you'll see later on, I struggle with this more often than not.

★

7/3/23

DAY #6

Miles—64.43 (413.63); Time—6:00 (36:53)
Harrison State Forest And Campground Jewett, Ohio
(free, primitive)

It certainly ended up being a good choice to stay at the hotel last night. The rain was very, very hard and heavy. It would've most likely flooded under the tent, soaking everything. I got on the Montour Trail at eight thirty because there was more rain coming in a few hours. While I won't log many miles today, I know I have a lot of climbing today according to my road maps. The miles are split almost evenly between trails and roads, at a little over 30 miles each.

To start, I finished up the Montour Trail. It was a cool trail going through some nice, quiet, tree-filled areas. The creeks all along the trail were severely flooded over their normal levels. The fine stone surface was wet, and these little things loved getting into all the spots on my bike they could cling to. There were a few good hills to climb, but I got to end on a downhill ride. The storm caused a couple trees to block the trail, but they were relatively easy to navigate around. About 13 miles later, in MacDonald, I connected to the Panhandle Trail for the next 20 miles. It's a very easy, well-marked transition between the two trails.

The Panhandle Trail has similar scenery to the Montour, but it is paved. I usually don't have a preference between a paved trail or a hard-packed-stone or dirt path; I never complain about a paved trail, though.

Even as gray as my days have been, with all the rain, I still have lots of green to see. Green grass, leaves—at least everything on the trail is alive and thriving in a serene, seemingly flourishing terrain.

After crossing into West Virginia, or a little before then, it started to slowly rain. I made it to the end of the Panhandle in Weirton, West Virginia, and luckily I had shelter there.

At the end was the Route 22 overpass, which I used for cover from the rain. It was coming down hard at times and was forecasted for about an hour. I got my chair out, got comfy, and sat there for forty-five minutes. Waiting out the storm, I made a video since I had some time to kill, and think I was pretty on point with it. I made a sort of video diary, I guess you would call it, in which I really talked about stuff going on in my life with no restraints. I'm not sure if anyone will ever see these videos, since I don't keep anything back, but I do also use some of the content in this book. It's not that I hold back in this book, but I still have a life to live through, and I feel I have more than enough about my thoughts and feelings already in this book.

I was frustrated with the rain today; I got soaked twice and wet once more. When I considered this in combination with rain-related issues from the other days of my trip, I was ready for some days of sunshine.

Waiting long periods of time, I probably needed the video outlet more than I knew at the time. The real issue the rain causes me is time; I feel the need to rush from the rain, to try to squeeze out as many miles as possible before the rain starts. It compounds my issues because I can't slow down. I wish I could, but I can't; I don't know how. If there's a plan in place, I feel a need to get it done. I'm just going to keep on going until I do it. Sometimes it's detrimental, and sometimes it's beneficial, but it's always stressful as hell. And I'm feeling it. I'm stressing about stuff that is part of the trail experience, and feeling like my mind is twisted up like a pretzel doesn't help. It's overwhelming and I think compounds other issues.

It can put me in a foul mood in which I'm stressed out and overloaded instead of being happy. A feeling like there are a million things I need to do but I don't have the time to finish them. Then that creates this nonstop laundry list of things I need to get done, but on that long list, not many items are important or even really matter. Still, in my mind, I need to get them all done. I can't slow down, but it would make life a lot less stressful if I could.

I did find my part in Columbus, Ohio, after calling a few places a couple days ahead. So that's all taken care of at least—one less thing on my plate. Here ended my video and the rain, for the moment.

The road section from Weirton, West Virginia, to Jewett, Ohio, is incredibly hilly, with not a lot of options for riding to my campsite. Before I get too far, I want to mention this section of the trip will always have both negative and positive experiences and feelings for me. Three years ago, I was piecing together the GART in sections, in the summer of 2020. One trip was Pittsburgh to the Illinois-Indiana border and then north to Chicago for the Amtrak back to Pitt.

On this section of road, about 5 miles from the campsite, I was given a choice. I had ridden nearly 90 miles that day, and it was close to 8:00 p.m. It was going to be dark soon, and I'd been on the bike since, probably, 8:00 a.m. Also, it was my first day, so I probably drove the 3 hours to Pittsburgh as well, which meant, most likely, a 4:00 or 4:30 a.m. wake up.

I got to a road on my map, and I was in the middle of a rural farming area. I could take one road that would add time and a few miles or take this rocky gravel road. The gravel road was definitely not suited to my bike and the gear I was carrying. You have probably already guessed which way I went.

I already had a minor crash once today on a questionable road, and this would be no different. The second time I went down, that was the one that hurt—I actually went down twice on that road, meaning I had done this three times total that day. The bike was OK—it was scratched, and the chain jammed in the chain rings—but I took the worst of the crash. I wasn't going fast at all, but my rear wheel gave out. These crashes were more like falling over going about 5 to 6 mph. My hands, ankle, and knee were cut up and bruised pretty bad. I could handle the cuts, but my left shoulder was hurting the worst.

I was going maybe 7 miles per hour when I went down. My foot and leg got caught in the frame, and my arm went out to brace my body. I think I stretched out my shoulder or extended something in that region, based on how I felt. That was really the reason I stopped, but later X-rays revealed nothing; I was just sore for a while.

There I was bloodied, bruised, not really having a clue where I was, but I knew then that I needed some help. If I did not get help, it would be a 5-mile walk to camp all busted up and unable to pedal my bike (although at the time I didn't inspect it). Amazingly there appeared this woman on a small all-terrain utility vehicle with her daughter. I asked her for help and she stopped; I told her what happened and asked her if there was any way she could help me. This was the first real instance of human kindness showing up on the trail, or any trip of mine. She told me to hold on, that she was staying at her parents' and would return with her Dad. Perfect, exactly what I was hoping for. I could keep going here, but I want to emphasize what a true help and generous family this would turn out to be.

They returned, we talked, and they loaded me up after I asked for a ride to the campground. The campsite was less than 5 miles away. I got the drop-off and some help with the lights from the guy's truck to set up my tent. By now it's dark, and it would've been a pain to do it with only a headlamp. When I was all set up, I thanked them, and then they left. I sat in my tent, hoping nothing was broken, in a good amount of pain.

I was a roughly six-hour bike ride from my truck, so I was unsure how to get back to my truck in Pittsburgh. But after my day, I'd deal with everything the next day.

After I woke up, Hillary and her Dad reappeared to check on me! I couldn't say how much them coming back meant at the time and still can't today. I told them where I was parked, and her Dad offered me a ride to a nearby town. I packed up and went with them. We went to their house, and they welcomed me in like family. They were farmers and fans of International Harvester (IH), so since I worked as a machinist in the prototype shop of the agricultural manufacturer that owns the IH brand, we got along great and conversations weren't hard to have. In fact, I sat there for a while, maybe close to an hour, drinking coffee. The mom actually asked if I wanted breakfast! I don't think she meant simply pouring me some cereal, but I kindly said no thanks. I'd feel bad saying yes even if I was hungry; I get a guilty feeling—it's just the way I am. This family took me into their home and just showed me incredible generosity. This certainly wasn't what I was expecting that morning, but it was exactly what I needed.

After talking with me, I guess Hillary felt comfortable enough that she offered to drop me off at my garage in downtown Pittsburgh. She was going to that area anyway, but still, to offer a stranger a ride with your daughter along—wow, I was very grateful. I'll never forget this story and how just a little time out of your day can completely change someone else's. I got the drop-off, and we said our goodbyes. She wouldn't take anything as payment. I tried—gas money, lunch—she wouldn't accept anything for the help. She just told me to do the same when someone was in need of help.

That is why any time I complete this road section, it's a huge win for me. I healed up a little and got back out there a couple months later the same year and completed that section. There are a lot of steep climbs out there, and if I'm remembering right, I had to walk over 5 times, and 3 seemed like a quarter-mile to half-mile walk. Maps had it at a 2,000-foot incline and almost 1,800 decline total, over 32 miles. It's maybe the toughest road map in the East and the hardest that I've ridden personally. I started listening to music a little while, pushing my bike; it helps me stay in a good mood, hearing music.

I don't get scared, really, while I ride. I won't put myself through too dangerous a situation but have little to no fear of injury or death from riding. My feelings are if something is going to happen, it's going to happen; I can only prevent so much. I've also accepted what may happen out here; I'm mentally prepared and accepting of my fate. If I die out here, so be it; if I get hurt, well, that comes with the challenge. As part of the experience of this adventure, I've accepted the potentially grave situations I will or might encounter.

I crossed the Ohio River in Steubenville on the Market Street Bridge. There are no bike lanes, and the surface is open metal grating the entire 0.3 miles. With the rain and wet surface, it literally felt like riding on an ice cube. I felt my back tire slip badly twice, and both times I thought I was going down. This scared the hell out of me; I was breathing heavy and white-knuckling my handlebars so much my hands hurt and I had to release my grip a few times. There was also a long line of cars behind me. Thank God, I think the person right behind me saw me swerving and was probably as scared as I was.

If I could've closed my eyes and just been anywhere else but there, I would have taken it. In my mind I wanted to stop, freeze, hold the railing, and wait for the cars to pass me. But that wasn't an option—I had to ride it out, no other choice. I haven't been scared like that since; well, it had to be a high peak I was hiking to. But this—this made my body shake and not just my legs. It took me a while to compose myself after finishing this challenge. I've been on this bridge before, and it's not bad at all if it's dry.

I made it to the campsite, and it's a really nice spot with maybe six or seven spots. It's also free and primitive, my favorite.

I'll wrap this up with some journal stuff. I needed a victory like today, after the first few semi deflating weather days. The weather and rain had put me in a bad mood and mindset. I felt like I needed to rush through my day to beat the rain. Rushing gets my anxiety going, and then that snowballs into other stuff. I need to learn to work around the rain, not try to beat the rain.

That's a good metaphor for a major problem in my life. I need to slow down, but my problem is I don't know how or how to maintain it over a long period of time. I can slow down temporarily, but then ultimately it always goes back to the ways of rushing. It seems like I need to do what I do in order for everything to work smoothly in my life. When I don't, things compound, snowball, and build up quickly. Then I get out of sorts mentally, running around trying to balance everything out. I think, as funny as it sounds, maybe I need to also learn how to relax.

7/4/23

DAY #7

Miles—69.57 (483.20); Time—6:37 (43:30)
Ohio & Erie Canal Towpath Trail Campsite Franklin, Ohio
(free, primitive)

Today was supposed to be my first day of not having any rain in the forecast, and of course I was very much looking forward to that. I started my day with a 5-mile road ride to the Conotton Trail. With a tough hill to start, I actually had to walk a little bit up this steep road.

I had to manage my water last night—I ran out between cooking and drinking. There was no water at the campsite, and I assumed there would be. With that being said, I always think about that and save some water just in case. In times like that, you'll be glad you did save some for camp. I wasn't hurting from it; it was just not good planning on my part yesterday. With a quick stop in Jewett this morning, I was resupplied again. It was good to get the water early, especially because it would get hot out that day.

The Conotton Trail is a mostly paved 11-mile route from Jewett to Socio, Ohio. It's a very scenic, quiet trail and a great way to start off my day. I also really enjoyed all the cool covered bridges I got to ride through. They're all newer but still fun to see. The Conotton even has a couple tunnels to ride through, a little bit of everything. I really like this trail, and I'm glad I got to ride this for the second time.

I enjoyed the trails today, and I sort of figured my 21 miles of road would be a traffic-heavy nightmare since it's the Fourth of July. The riding still had some good climbs, and once again I had to get off my bike a few times. I ride as far as I can, then walk my bike while recuperating. I will then get back on my bike and try to make some more progress. With the gearing, I can start riding again after walking a little bit in the low gears while still going uphill. I can walk between 2.5 and 3 miles per hour, according to my readout, which, depending how long I have to go, can mean that hill takes a very long time to walk. I try to pedal until I drop below the 4-to-5-miles-per-hour range, unless of course I'm almost there, in which case I try to tough it out.

I was right, there was a lot more traffic out there today. I encountered more RVs and trucks hauling boats today as well. Like I said before, to do this kind of trip, a person absolutely must be able to ride very close to very fast traffic. Not every place has shoulders or is bike friendly. Only a very small percentage of drivers on my trip, I'd say, were completely inconsiderate. I feel if I do my part and get over as far as is safe for me and generally stay safe out there, so will the drivers. Bottom line, 99 percent of drivers don't want to injure or kill someone out there, but yeah, it can get scary riding sometimes. I wear a neon green reflective vest every time I get on the road, along, of course, with my helmet and a mirror attached to my helmet.

I wouldn't think of getting on any road on this trip without all of those things. If I expect the public to help keep me safe, then I need to do my part as well. A big part of that is just being visible. Like I said before, I can't ride recklessly out on the roads and also hope for a little room when being passed. Further, it didn't help that I was on Highway 212 West for 16 miles today with heavy traffic.

After my road riding was over, I rode from the Conotton in Socio to the Zoar Valley trail in Dover. I rode that trail for 5.5 miles and then another 2.5 road miles to the Ralph Pegula Trail, which is part of the longer Ohio to Erie Canal Towpath trail. I rode this trail for 27 miles to my campsite. This is a good riding trail with fine crushed stone as a surface. It is another great trail to ride as it is flat, minus the canal locks, and offers some more of the green, quiet landscape I've been enjoying in Eastern Ohio.

It was such a nice day; I saw a couple groups of people out tubing on the Tuscaroras River. I'm also very familiar with this area as I was just there a little over a month ago. I rode the Ohio to Erie trail from Cleveland to Cincinnati and then back to Cleveland. That trip included some parts of the ride I'm currently on; I'll be on the same route for almost two days.

Along the trail I stopped to fill up my water bottles—I was carrying three 1.5-liter bottles at that point—and noticed a bike shop. To my surprise, they were open on the Fourth of July. They were also right on the trail and did some river outfitting, I believe, as well. I asked if they might have the part I needed, and their mechanic came out for a look. What luck, the guy told me he had the exact parts from the assembly in his toolbox. He didn't have the entire assembled part, but he had the part from it I needed! What kind of crazy good luck was that? It really makes you think, Are little things like this supposed to happen? To top it off, he only charged me five dollars.

I was talking with an employee about my trip while waiting—the gear was a giveaway I was on an overnight trip somewhere. It's funny to me, or strange maybe, to have people take a general interest in what I'm doing. I guess because riding is just a fun hobby of mine, I usually don't think much about my bike trips. But it's always nice talking about my adventures with people. I'm seeing a lot of people have done cross-country trips and I remind them of a past adventure they were on. A special thank you to Ernie's Bicycle Shop, off the trail in Massillon, Ohio. Just a great experience here, and some real caring, cool people too.

After getting my bike fixed up, I only had a short ride to my primitive trailside campsite for the night. It's a really cool campsite for a few good reasons. It's right off the trail, just a short walk to a three-spot campsite. It's quiet, but I did hear a couple trains throughout the night. Trains almost never bother me overnight, though. It was a free site but had no water supply. I camped there years ago and remembered how it was. I had plenty of water this time, though, knowing that prior to arriving. The worst thing about the place was the mosquitoes. They were everywhere and made me make an early retreat to my tent. I bought these bracelets off Amazon that were supposed to ward off mosquitoes, and they actually worked. I didn't get one bite on my skin that was covered by the bracelet.

I deal with bug bites, poison ivy, and what I'm certain are blisters from the sun or humid heat. I get these red dots in random areas of my legs, from the knees down, and some on my arms, though those are not as bad. These little blisters are concentrated in one area but spread like wildfire overnight. Literally overnight, it can go from a few little spots to having these spots wrap around my leg. They start out red and eventually get a whitehead on top. There are so many it pulls my skin tight, and just moving my hand over them causes a slight pain. Nothing OTC helps; calamine lotion does start to dry them out, but they stick around a few days after. I have no idea what causes it, but my self-diagnosis is the humid air and sun. It's mainly on my legs, which aren't covered; I don't get them out West where it's dry, and this only happens on trips where I'm out in the sun, exposed for long periods of time. And yes, I apply sunscreen multiple times a day. It starts to go away if I wear pants instead of shorts for a few days in a row, another giveaway it's related to the sun.

Today was the first rain-free day, and tomorrow is supposed to be dry as well. But the rain comes back for a couple days after that. Hopefully I'm getting my rain days out of the way early—yeah right. From being wet and slowly drying, in addition to sweating and not taking a shower everyday, I have begun to be able to smell myself. I'm starting to stink; I need to take some time soon and do my laundry.

7/5/23

DAY #8

Miles—88.63 (571.83); Time—7:37 (51:07)
Bluebird Barn (Airbnb) Mt Vernon, Ohio ($80)

It's such a different start mentally for me when the weather is good for riding. Especially now, after all the rain I've had so far. Not that I get off-center right away, but the sun just has a different feel for me than the clouds. The sun is the good, the light, and the clouds are the bad, the darkness, and obliviously bring the potential for bad weather. I do believe in the yin and yang, the need for balance from the light and dark. I see biking as a way for me to balance out the turmoil in my life, a way for me to get away and let my problems go temporarily. My bike is a big part of me getting the balance right in my life. I know it's just a mental thing for me, but I do notice the slight changes. I will be meeting up with two new friends I literally ran into a month ago on my Ohio to Erie Trail (OTET) trip. It'll be good to see some people I know and do a little riding with them.

I really enjoy riding in this area. The path starts in Holmes County, which has a high population of Amish. I live in the Amish area of Pennsylvania, Lancaster County, which is also the heavily farmed eastern part of the county. So being out here just reminds me of home. The fields, farming, even the smell of manure feel like home to me. I know I'm home when I pass by the fields after they fertilize them or any chicken farm. I've been around that my whole life, so those things are all just another day to me. I also like how it seems a little more slowed down out here. A sort of less-hustle-and-bustle-type area, my preference for sure.

I was on the road more today than in the prior days. There are a couple gaps on the Heart of Ohio trail. I had a total of 4 road maps today, totaling around 35 miles. I had about 28 of those road miles to start the day. I didn't have much traffic, and it was a good thing because I didn't have a lot of room on the shoulders to ride on. The streets were nice, and with all conditions being very good today, I was able to maintain a good speed on the road. The bike's gearing combined with the fast tires, I could average on flat roads anywhere from 16 to 20-plus miles per hour. If I'm on a road, I have no problem riding a little faster than normal, depending on where I am. I don't mind road riding at all, but (1) on a long trip like this, you need to take advantage of what you can, like a nice paved road surface and (2) my riding room and the scenery play a big role as well in how long I want to be on that road map. But ultimately, I want back on the trails. This stretch of road was flat, and I connected back onto the Holmes County Trail in Fredericksburg.

As I've mentioned, along this trail I had plans to meet with two friends, Karen and Larry. About a month before, on the OTET, I was riding down the trail at about 15 miles per hour and came upon two riders. They were riding side by side with a space in the middle. I said, "Passing left," but I've realized that I'm too quiet in announcing myself. Also, I was going faster than I probably should have been given that I was trying to pass.

Anyway, here I come, and that middle space is still open. I thought they were letting me go through the middle; I've had that happen before. Wrong! As soon as I'm between them, one moves over and bumps me, which pushes me over, and I bump into the other rider. Both of the other riders go down, but I'm still going.

Of course, I stop and go check on them. Feeling absolutely horrible and completely at fault, I go to them, and prepare myself for whatever they are going to say. Fortunately for me, it seems they feel the same as me, or at least they said so.

After a little cleanup and a minor repair, we were talking and later became friends. I contacted Karen to see if she and Larry would be interested in a ride when I came through. We rode around 10 miles together and then stopped for a packed lunch they had brought. It was nice meeting up with people to ride with; it's not something I'm used to. I always ride alone; I don't have anyone at home I call to go out riding with—isolated life, remember?

After saying our goodbyes, we parted ways and I got back on the road. Eight miles and one big hill awaited me on the section from Killbuck to Glenmont. The hill in Glenmont is right at the start of the trail. All my road maps are named either Trail Gap [number] or Missing Gap [number]. They directly correspond to the GART map on the official website; it makes it super easy for me to keep everything in order as well.

The hill was a good climb for 5 to 7 miles, but after that I was done with climbing for the day. Glenmont has a Holmes County trailhead, so I continued the paved trail here. The trail has a couple names, either trails run together or one ends and a new one starts.

I will also ride the Kokosing Gap and Heart of Ohio trails on my way to my Airbnb tonight. The trails out here are all paved and double-wide. I call it "bikes and buggies" since both are allowed on the trail out here. One lane is for bicycles, and the other is for buggies. No motorized vehicles are allowed. It's a very nice, easy area to ride, and everything about this place is just like home. I do like it out here.

Along this trail is the Bridge of Dreams. Three years ago I came upon this for the first time. I can't explain it, but this place immediately felt special to me. Something I can't see, feel physically, or hear draws me in. I sat here and just, well, dreamed a little my first time. I guess it's more of a spiritual connection to something bigger here, a quiet place to let the mind drift.

On my OTET trip, I met a group from Wounded Warrior, and they were riding on a sponsored GART ride. Talking with one guy in the morning, I knew I wanted to finish my own GART trip. Coming back on my return to Cleveland, I stopped and thought about it all at the Bridge of Dreams.

I knew with what happened last summer, the time was now to do a full ride on the GART. Life only gives us certain chances to do the things we dream about, hopefully, and when that time comes, you must absolutely take advantage of it and accept it. You never know when, or if, life will provide another opportunity. And now the time is right for me.

Tonight, I'm staying at the Bluebird Inn in Mount Vernon. I stayed here three years ago and got completely soaked on the way here. Pamela, the host, offered to dry my clothes and even got my shoes dry! I'll always stay here when I'm in the area. Her property abuts the trail and is easily found with a sign by the trail. It's three separate rooms converted from a barn. It's very nice, and I 100 percent recommend this place. There is no AC, but garage-style screen-covered openings on both sides provide more than enough fresh airflow to keep it cool. I was the only one there, so I aired out all my clothes and let everything get dry. Thank God for the airflow because, whew, that smell was strong!

I also at that point realized I left a long-sleeve shirt at a hotel; I was down to one regular and one quick-dry long-sleeve shirt. Pamela has the fridge well stocked with cold drinks and good food options. The place is always clean too. This host and property have a good vibe and provide a great, quiet night.

I enjoyed today, my second day of no rain. The sun was also out in the sky, and it started to get pretty warm outside. Tomorrow I'll be back to weather watching and having to be on the lookout for rain.

✪

7/6/23

DAY #9

Miles—71.98 (643.81); Time—6:10 (57:17)
Prairie Grass Trailhead, London, Ohio (donation—bathroom, Wi-Fi, electricity, water)

I left my window open overnight, and a bird singing woke me up around 5:45 a.m., which wasn't a bad thing as there was lots of rain forecasted for today in and around Columbus. Pamela had the fridge stocked with a few good breakfast options, but with my rushing ways, I skipped cooking eggs. I decided on some quick cereal and one of those microwave cracked-egg things. Really my morning was fast-paced so I could get as many miles in before the first rain came in. There was a good amount of time today during which it was supposed to rain on and off. I figured I might have to just ride when I could and take cover when needed.

The day started nice and sunny and then flip-flopped to dark, cloudy, and rainy. By the end of the day, it was nice and sunny again; it was an on-and-off-rain day. I first had to finish the Heart of Ohio trail. Around 15 miles in, I passed the marker for the high point of the Heart of Ohio. Anytime I pass a marker saying high point, it's a feeling of relief, tired or not. At that point at least I know my highest hill to climb is done with, not to mention I normally get to go downhill then too. That part of Ohio, which is easy to ride and relatively flat, has less of a negative mental affect on me. I guess because I'm not working as hard and physically feeling better.

I also passed through Centerburg, the midpoint of the OTET and basically the center of Ohio (or very close to it). The farms out here are very different from the ones back home. Back home all the farms are smaller, and most owned by Amish or Mennonite families. Out here there are miles and miles of fields of crops. The size of the fields and of the enormous silos amazes me. I won't see anything this size until the Nebraska and Iowa farming fields.

The trail is still all paved and an absolute pleasure to ride. I definitely would recommend biking out here if you can.

After that was a 1-mile road ride to the Sandal Legacy Trail. Three miles later, I came to the end at the Hoover Nature Preserve in Galena. I've stopped here three times now, and every time it's been closed. I thought three years ago it was closed for bird migration but could be wrong. Now I think it's been closed down because it's unsafe to walk on and in need of repairs. It looks like such a cool area, and I'd love to walk that long boardwalk on the water but maybe another time.

Then I came to my next longer road map: "Through Columbus." In the Westerville area, I came across this really cool park on the trail. The first thing to catch my eye was the roller hockey rink. Hockey is my favorite sport, and I still enjoy playing when I can. These sorts of things immediately grab my full attention. I don't care how old I am; I hope I always have the adventurous inner childlike spirit and youthful energy to do these sorts of things. It was a BMX dirt course with hills and 180-degree turns, and my adventurous side would not just let me pass this by. Of course, I had to try it, and of course I didn't want to take my bags off either, LOL.

Off I went on my first set of moguls, and I sounded like I was guiding a horse at every crest of a hill. "Whoa, whoa," I was saying, ha ha! Into the first banked turn, I was very glad I took the low part of it. I thought I was going down. I made it through the second set of moguls and turned onto the home stretch. I started to get excited, I guess, and hit the last hill a little too fast. I thought I was surely going to blow out my front tire coming up and over the last hill. I made it, and with about sixty pounds of gear loaded on still.

Man, I love doing things like this when they come my way. You have got to have fun on these trips, and if you want to do something, do it; who cares what anyone else thinks? I'm sure the ten-to-fifteen-year-olds there were more than impressed with my bike skills, but like I said before, it doesn't matter what anyone thinks. I had fun, and that's what counts. I also made a video while riding this course; it makes me laugh a little watching it.

After that I was just on the outside of Columbus, and the clouds were starting to turn gray. The first rain was on the way, but at least I was near the city. One good thing, even if you don't like city riding, is in bad weather, you can always find an awning or some type of cover. Riding through Columbus is easy, and it's basically all trails, bike lanes, or huge sidewalks. I actually enjoy riding through big cities and seeing the sights. I'd much rather ride through a city than drive through or to one. Not waiting in traffic and instead just passing it is way better.

Not long after I got into Columbus, the rain came. I started on the Alum Creek Trail, which is loaded with great scenery all around, while getting more into an urban setting. Lots of bridges crossed the muddy and severely flooded Alum Creek. After that was the fun city riding—the 670 Bikeway through downtown. I could feel the drops starting, and I started looking for a good, quiet spot to stay dry. I found a park on the Scioto River with this large canopy overhead. I got my chair set up, took a few snacks out, sat back, and waited for the rain. When it came, it was an absolute downpour. I was very happy to be where I was as I had a very nice city view to complement my dry area. This first rain lasted about forty-five minutes.

After the rain stopped, I packed up and headed to the Arena District. I love hockey, as I've said, the NHL and try to detour to a city's pro sports stadiums when near them. I had to swing by Nationwide Arena on my way out of Columbus. Being a huge Penguins fan, of course I don't like the Bluejackets. I've been to a couple games here with my dad and I've stopped here on past bike trips, so I didn't stop this time.

Then came the second rain, during which I ended up getting a little wet. I was only able to move for a little before I got caught in the light part of this rainstorm. The rain wasn't what my issue was this time; it was where I got stuck. I just happened to stop at a homeless hangout. The awning protecting us only hung out about two feet, and it was keeping me and five to six other people dry.

My desire to immediately leave started when I looked down and saw a needle by my foot. Near me some guy was yelling about something I couldn't understand, and all I could think was "Please, please, rain, stop so I can get out of here." It was not that I didn't feel safe; I really just wanted out of that atmosphere. I've seen enough erratic drug abuse ruining lives, and I don't need to see anymore.

Eventually the rain slowed enough that I could take off and leave. I got about 15 miles from the end of my day and ended up getting wet. Not soaked, but my clothes were wet. Soon enough, I came to a Circle K gas station. There were no benches or seats, but I was out of the rain and now dry or at least not getting any wetter. Eventually the last rain stopped and I got to my campsite for the night.

I really, really like this free (donations accepted), no RSVP "primitive" campsite. There are two platform sites and four leveled pad sites. There is a big pavilion with plenty of benches and tables, an electrical outlet, the cleanest campsite bathroom you'll find, Wi-Fi, and an overhead drip shower. The setup there is just phenomenal, and it is my favorite primitive campsite to stay at. The guy looking after everything, Dave, is just the nicest, friendliest person and caretaker. A++ job for sure here, in every respect.

Since the camp is on the outside of town, I went and got a sub from a pizza shop; it was good, but really I just wanted a change from the ramen.

Today was a lesson in how I need to slow down, relax, and breathe. I missed the first rain, semimissed the second, and ended up getting wet on the third. I immediately got mad because I had managed to stay dry all day and got wet at the very end of the day. It got me so off-center that I considered giving in and getting a hotel. Then, twenty minutes later, the sun came out, and it was a nice rest of the day. I put my clothes out in the sun at camp and dried them all out as best I could.

I don't know why sometimes I overreact to situations like that. I don't do it all the time. I think I was only mad because I more than likely pressed my luck and tried to get the most miles in before the rain instead of taking cover early. I know that's not a smart move, but I do it still and then get mad when I get caught.

I know this stuff happens, but I can't keep reacting the way I sometimes do. It's not good, and it only adds stress that doesn't need to be there in the first place. I need to learn to slow down, understand the how and why, take a second away from the situation, and just relax. Obstacles happen, and I need to learn how to successfully manage these bad/hard situations.

7/7/23

DAY #10

Miles—90.4 (734.21); Time—7:30 (64:47)
Travelodge, Richmond, Indiana ($85)

Today will be my last riding day in Ohio, and it's another state to mark off the list. The day started out with total cloud cover, but in a couple hours, it turned into a nice, clear blue-sky day. I started out with trails for the first 60-ish miles and would finish with close to a 30-mile road ride into or near Richmond, Indiana.

First up, it was back on the Ohio to Erie / Prairie Grass Trail for 29 miles to Xenia, Ohio. On my ride to Xenia, the weather really made a turn for the better as the sky was showing a pure blue sky. I could feel the warmth of the sun heating up my exposed skin from the morning cold. It's an easier riding trail with a few long, straight stretches.

That's to be expected out here with the farming and endless train track following the trail. Once again, I'm just amazed by the size of them. When I really think about having to feed America or even other countries, it's easier to comprehend all the long continuous miles of crops. I guess experiencing this stuff firsthand makes me think about it in the perspective of just how I'm barely a speck in size compared to everything out there in America alone. My eyes are opening to just how big America really is—among many other things I would experience for the first time in my life on this trip. Seeing things I've only read about and seeing the magnitude of things really makes me realize how much I was blind to, along with exposing myself to new experiences and, more importantly, new ways of thinking among American people from different regions. I now realize just how small I am in this now seemingly greatly expanded USA.

I arrived at Xenia, and I make a quick stop by Creekside Cyclery, looking for a front handlebar bag. I was thinking about weight distribution and wanted more space to store some things. All my weight was in the back, and I didn't have or want front panniers. Also, when at full weight, with my light carbon bike, I can't use the kickstand. My bike wants to do a wheelie from all the weight in the back, and I actually ripped up my handlebar tape from it falling over.

No problem—just get a bag. But I sort of make it into a problem or really more of a distraction. Now my mind is thinking a lot about the bag. I search on my phone for shops and make detours to go to them. It also takes me away from the scenery and can overtake my ride by being a semiconstant thought. Once again, it's my mind seemingly taking over and creating a new priority number one.

I talked to the two guys in Creekside Cyclery; one employee used to work out of Reading, Pennsylvania, and knew of New Holland. Reading is about twenty minutes away from me, and it's always fun meeting people from my area far away from home. No front bag, so I'm back on my way. Nice shop and workers, though. I would make one more stop that day at a shop in Dayton.

From Xenia I made my way west to Dayton on the Creek Side and Mad River trails. I was actually excited to get into Dayton. From my last trip, three years ago, I remembered how beautiful the trail was along the Mad and Miami rivers. Riding through the Riverscape Metro Parks, with the big open areas, statues, a fountain to cool off in—it's just a very well-planned and put-together park. Lots of people were out enjoying the park and weather. But when

I'm there, there's also always construction going on. I had my first of three detours there. In this case, the workers let me walk past. It looked like the water had washed out some of the bank leading up to the trail.

There was so much rain and flooding, I wasn't surprised to see these washed-out banks. The trail is only a few feet from the water when not flooded. All the waterways are muddy, fast-running, and flooded. In light of the detours, I managed to go a different way through Dayton than I took last time. I passed the Wright Brothers statue of the Wright Flyer 1, which I didn't see last time, very cool in my opinion.

After that, I continued on the Wolf Creek, Mad River, and Great Miami trails for a combined 8 miles. A short road ride took me to the last section of the Wolf Creek Trail to wrap up my trails for the day. Once again, all these trails are paved, and it's really an amazing network of both long and short trails weaving into each other. I would finish up at my planned campground, the Archway Campground in New Paris, Ohio. That would put me right on the Ohio and Indiana border. It was a nice road ride through the farms in western Ohio. The roads have little traffic here. In fact, in the Ohio farming area, I've gone over an hour riding without seeing anyone, something I was not necessarily used to in the East but would certainly grow accustomed to in the West.

The ride to the campground was a nice way to end my time in Ohio. I'm certainly ready to cross off my fourth state, in addition to DC, but always will enjoy the bicycle riding in the Buck Eye State. With the easy road riding, it's relaxing to just sort of let my mind drift away into not really thinking about anything. I try to push everything out, good and bad, and just casually pedal. Of course, I also keep an eye on my phone for my map and as always keep alert to any traffic. With no traffic though, it's easier to mentally wander into whatever I care to think about.

My ears are always open, though, and I look into my mirror to remain aware of my surroundings. I try to think about it like my mind is a clean, blank sheet of paper, empty of thoughts or writing. Well, that makes sense to me at least; I hope it does to you as well.

I have to talk about the experience I had at Archway Campground and its owner. I'll just say the Google reviews do *not* exaggerate. I also stayed here three years ago on that trip I keep referencing, and all was fine that time. I'll say I did know the place took cash and the fee was thirty dollars for a site. All the sites have electricity and water. Being on a bike, I don't necessarily agree with but have no problem paying RV rates, if they don't have separate primitive biker spots.

I showed up and thought I had a ten-dollar bill; turns out I was wrong. There is a self-pay station at the entrance. I called the owner and asked if he was on the grounds to break a twenty. He immediately flipped out, and told me, "No, and in eighteen years, it's never been a problem. Get my money or leave."

I told him to calm down, and he just kept going on and flipping out on the phone with me. I got sick of hearing it, so I just hung up while he was still going off. It is not that long of a ride to get to the nearest gas station, but it involves crossing a super busy four-lane highway. I didn't want to get back on the bike either, really.

The guy calls back yelling about me hanging up on him, asking me again to get his money, and finally tells me he doesn't care about anything but his money. I hung up again and thought about my options. I walked around the campground and asked a couple people if they could break a twenty; no one could. I thought about it, and my thinking was screw this guy; I'm out of here. Literally 1.5 miles down Highway 40, across the state border in Richmond, Indiana, there are a bunch of hotels.

It's a busy trucking area as highways 35, 40, and 70 all converge here. I packed up my tent and the rest of my gear, and I left for a hotel. I booked a hotel and got there without any more problems. Little did I know what a great choice this would turn out to be. The guy did call back again after my second hang-up, and I wanted to answer and tell him what I thought. I just hit the side button on my phone. Nothing good could have come from me answering, so I decided to drop it because it was over; it was history. Later I found a ten-dollar bill in another area where I kept money, ha ha.

No need to invite more stress and negativity in my life or this trip. In life and especially on a trip like this, I must remain vigilant and on guard at all times. There's no need or time to get caught up in the stupid little things in life. Angry campground owners, bad weather, bike problems—I *need* to be able to stay mindful of everything and how it's affecting me. It's an easy choice to either engage or not engage in any situation like that. I just need to relax, take a couple seconds, and do my own thing. Slowly breathe, analyze the situation, or just ignore it and keep on pedaling. Life will go on, and, yes, I do have a choice today.

7/8/23

DAY #11, RIDING #10

Miles—3.74 (738.05); Time—0:30 (65:17)
Travelodge, Richmond, Indiana ($71)

Today was my first zero day but not by my choice. Another full day of off-and-on rain. I was figuring I could ride maybe a couple hours, find a good cover for the predicted 3 to 4 hours of straight rain, ride another 3 to 4 hours, and then again find cover. Thinking about what I was saying about rushing around, trying to push too much on things—well, this was an example. Do I want to do this again with the rain? This time, though, I'd be stuck in the same place potentially for hours. And because of the amount of rain, I'd most likely get a hotel again anyway.

    I don't like camping after major rainstorms because the ground gets so saturated that it soaks through the tent floor. Then the entire floor is damp, not to mention my sleeping bag, pannier bags; everything on the floor absorbs the water, creating a mess of everything. I decided to stay put and do some much-needed things I haven't had time to do, which was basically doing some much-needed laundry.

    My clothes smelled so bad, it was starting to offend me. This would of course be the top priority of the day. I had a couple-hour window of good weather before the first rain shower. I looked at my phone and saw a Laundromat just down the road less than a mile away. I got everything together and was there waiting for them to open at 9:00 a.m. I also was lucky enough to have a Walmart across the street, so I could do a resupply trip while I was washing my clothes. My food still mainly consisted of ramen noodles and instant oatmeal in the morning. Even at big stores like this mess called Walmart, there just isn't much to buy that is cooked solely by hot water and also takes little packing space. I ended up buying ramen, oatmeal, Clif bars (my favorite is peanut butter banana), Nutri-Grain bars, instant coffee, Pop-Tarts, and a big bag of Skittles or gummy bears. Ice cream is my weakness, but since I usually don't have access to it at night, I get my sweet tooth satisfied in other ways. I managed to drop off my food and dry my clothes right before the first rain came.

I also bought a new Kryptonite lock at Walmart. It's a combination cable lock and weighs less than half what my current Kryptonite U-lock and cable do. That means less weight and an only one-piece lock, which now I have wrapped around the front of the frame. I also have a little more bag space, losing the cable.

It then proceeded to pour, with heavy rain, for the entire early afternoon. While sitting around, I saw there was a DICK'S Sporting Goods store next to the Laundromat I was at earlier. I also searched for bike shops in Richmond and found one in town 2 miles away. I contacted them, and they had front bags in stock; DICK'S did not. After the rain cleared, I headed out for the bike shop.

I made my way the couple of miles into the town of Richmond on some side roads that followed the main drive. I do remember having a dog give me a half-block chase in town—just some lady letting her good-sized pit bull loose in the streets to get some exercise, I guess. It didn't get that close, but I wasn't happy about being chased in the city by a pet. I do always carry a pocketknife on me, as I've mentioned; it's my only form of defense I have. The absolute last thing I want to do is hurt an animal. I will say if I'm going to be bitten, knocked off my bike, and/or attacked by any animal, I would consider using my knife. That's only if necessary, basically meaning it depends on what's attacking me and how aggressive it is. I wouldn't pull a knife unless I really felt my life threatened—absolutely a last resort. I don't want to injure anyone's pet, plus you never know how an owner will react. I'll stop by saying I will not let an animal, especially a city pet, end my trip.

I got to the shop downtown and didn't see anything that caught my eye, so I went back to the hotel via a different route, of course.

I was tired of going to places and looking for bags. It was starting to take away my focus from my adventure. I tried something new: I ordered ahead and used an Amazon Locker in Marion, Indiana. I ordered a front tube bag and a larger front cell phone bag for the rain. If I'm on the road and it's raining, I need to see my directions, so I use a front bag with a cell phone screen. I really hope it all works out; I've never used this feature with Amazon before. The delivery is scheduled for tomorrow, and I'll be there Monday, in two days. It'll be a huge mental relief to get these taken care of. I'm really trying to drop weight from my bags and distribute some up front. That would also free up a lot of space in my bags. It seems like no matter what, my bags are always full, though! I'll also be sending home my old lock and cable, the two bags I'm no longer using, some brochures, and papers.

I'm not sure why I feel this big need to do all this. I hope it's because I tried a new front bag (without the screen) and realized it's not what I wanted for this trip. I really liked the bag, but again, I must be able to see my directions in the rain. Hopefully things will all be settled and I can just get back to riding and enjoying my trip.

I feel like I started in a bad mood because of the weather and bike issues. Then the rain went away, my bike got fixed, and all returned to being great. Now for some reason I have this idea that I need those bags. I bought a phone bag at Walmart, but my phone didn't quite fit in the screen holder part. I've been looking for a larger one to replace that one.

When there's something in my head that I have a need for or I feel like I have a need for, sometimes I can't stop thinking about it. (I don't want to say compulsively but looking back now writing, is it?) I made a few detours every day for the past couple days, and it was really starting to bother me. Almost like I was feeling I needed these bags more than my ride. Fingers crossed this issue will be put to bed on Monday.

Today was a good, productive day overall. But it was so hard to stay here and not move. I had this feeling I needed to keep moving. It was so difficult to stay put for the day. Hopefully, tomorrow my head will be clearer and I can get back into riding carefree.

This may be a once-in-a-lifetime trip, and I need to make the absolute most of it. I can't let my bad attitude win. I need to slow down and just accept what comes my way and roll with it, no more fighting it. Also be happy, I'm going across the country fulfilling a dream. *Lighten up!*

I came up with a saying last year, while talking with a friend when I wasn't feeling like myself: Don't let yourself, take away from yourself, be yourself.

It's great advice but difficult to always adhere to.

7/9/23

DAY #12, RIDING #11

Miles—73.6 (811.65); Time—6:14 (71:21)
Super 8 Gas City, Marion Area, Indiana ($88)

I was eager to get back on the road again after being idle for the past day. I woke up late, around 7:00 a.m.; I was up late watching UFC on my phone. I knew that I had an easy riding day today. I started with a 5-mile ride into Richmond, Indiana, to start the longest rail trail in the Hoosier State, the Cardinal Greenway. An incredible trail that has a few road sections connecting it for 62 total miles.

It was a great day for riding, with the temperature in the low seventies and the sky switching from cloudy to sunny and back to cloudy to finish out the day. Richmond had some really cool painted buildings I passed before starting my trail ride. The first was a Ford Model T painted on the side of a building, but my favorite was across the street. It was a painting of a building fire, with people hanging out of the windows for help. Of course, the firetruck and firefighters are there, dousing the flames and walking up the ladder to save people, a wonderful painting! The trail is paved and has lots to offer. It has some terrific scenery, from farms to wooded areas and more. The greenway has plenty of places to stop, be it towns or rest areas, all with plenty of amenities if needed.

I could feel the temperatures slowly rising throughout the day, although it stayed in the low eighties as a high. I rode around 50 miles from Richmond to Gaston on the greenway before an 18-mile road trip to my campground.

I made it to a campground where I had planned to stay. But upon arriving, I was told the tent area was still flooded from all the recent rain. I was shown another area, but it was right off Interstate 69, in Gas City; it was incredibly loud there. When camping, I can handle trains and perhaps highways but not this super busy interstate traffic all night. If I wanted to hear that interstate, I'd go find a place to sleep under an overpass for free. I ended up at the hotel up the street instead.

I was doing a lot of thinking today while I was riding. I feel like I'm at a crossroads and not sure what I want to do. I've always enjoyed Lancaster County, although I've certainly had thoughts before about leaving. With everything recently and in the deeper past I've been through, is Lancaster, or even Pennsylvania generally, where I want to be? I don't know; it's something I need to think about. Another part of me is screaming I don't want to go home, I don't want to be in Pennsylvania anymore, and perhaps I don't belong there anymore.

I don't know if I can leave, though. I'm not sure if I can go because of my parents; I feel this huge burden of guilt for even thinking about leaving. It makes me sad because of their ages—I'm not sure how much time we have left. I have to say here that there is time, age-wise, there are a lot of good years left for sure. I feel like I need to be here for the rest of the time I have with them. With my isolation, they're also the only people I hang out with or even see.

It would be good to leave Pennsylvania, I think, but I just don't know if I can do it. It makes me feel like a piece of string all tangled up in a ball. There's a beginning and end, but the middle is a tangled mess. It ultimately becomes too much to think about; I end up staying put and feeling sad and guilty about both points. I've been through that cycle more than a couple times.

The other thoughts were of joy and happiness: Will I ever find lasting joy in my life? There are instances of happiness in my life, but happiness and joy are two different things. Joy is lasting, and happiness is just a feeling in the current moment of time. I want that happy feeling to be able to turn into joy and the feeling of contentedness in life. I feel like I get more depressed than normal, but I'm also sure everyone who suffers with depression probably thinks that.

What in my life do I need to do in order to attain a feeling of being content with where I am, not having to wonder about these things anymore? It's hard to stay content in my current life because I also worry about my future; sometimes it scares me. I've had a fun, good life that I do enjoy overall but not necessarily a fulfilling life, if that makes sense. Some things need to change because I don't want to live out the rest of my life the way I currently am, but at the same time I'm really not sure what to do. Certain things in my life contribute to this and some don't. It's something I need to figure out in my life, and I'm hoping this trip sheds some light on the subject of me finding my way. Do I want to go back to school or go back into the workforce?

I was in talks with a local college branch campus about doing a credit transfer to pursue my bachelor's degree in mechanical engineering. I have an associate degree in machine tool and computer aided manufacturing. That is a long way of saying I became a machinist in two years; well, I had the knowledge for a great start at least.

What I'd really love to do is be able to make money off my bike and just ride for the rest of my life or be a tour guide. I'd love to have my own company or just work for a place as one. I don't really see any of those things ever happening. It would be an absolute dream, though, to ride for a living or even somehow get a sponsor.

I guess it's just a matter of taking it day by day and rolling with it all. Just trying to make the most of every day, stay present, and be grateful for the current state of my life. My favorite saying is "carpe diem"—seize the day. It's something I try to remember, to remain mindful, and when I can stay in the moment, things tend to slow down for me. Obstacles seem to come less frequently when my moves are slower and deliberate.

I need to make some lifestyle changes too, but once again, I seem to draw a blank. How does someone make friends at forty? I usually avoid people, and I think I have developed a fear of being misunderstood or rejected. I think these are the two main reasons I avoid people. I don't know how much of this book I wrote then erased because it was nonsense. It was me writing out the whys (explaining myself). And why do I do that? Because I think I'll be misunderstood, so I tend to go into more detail than needed. The isolation makes for a lonely life, but sadly it's all I really know anymore. Maybe doing this trail will help me open up and be more comfortable and outgoing around people.

7/10/23

DAY #13, RIDING #12

Miles—99.32 (911.03); Time—8:03 (79.24)

Rising Sun Campground, Monterey, Indiana ($10, primitive)

What a beautiful day it was outside today; there was an endless supply of blue sky all day. I was very happy to be able to enjoy the weather. It was another early start, at seven thirty, and I also knew I had a long day ahead of me. My plan was to ride from Gas City to Monterey, Indiana, which would put me in the 100-mile range. First, I finished up the remaining miles on the Cardinal Greenway but made a couple stops in Marion along the way.

I stopped at the James Dean birthplace marker first. The memorial marks the location where he was born, but the building is no longer there. He's also buried south of here but too far out of the way for me. The other reason I stopped was to pick up my bags from Amazon. The pickup location was a cell phone store in town. All I had to do was complete an easy one-time activation on the Amazon app and then go to the location with Bluetooth turned on. I show up at the store, and I saw the big locker-style machine on the wall. As I came within a couple feet of it, a door opened up. My phone was telling me to get my order and close the door. It was just that easy to order off Amazon on the road. I don't necessarily like Amazon, but you can't beat the convenience.

I had ordered the bags ahead of where I was by a few days just to make sure they were delivered before I arrived, as I mentioned. I had three to four days to pick up my order until it was shipped back automatically. My cell phone bag was good—it was huge actually—but the handlebar bag was a little smaller than I thought. I ordered another one for an East Moline, Illinois, pickup in two to three days.

The Sweetser Switch Trail is one of my hidden gem trails. I've been on it a few times, and it's just a low-volume, nice, quiet, and fun trail to ride. The trail is well maintained, paved, and includes three to four covered bridges made by local craftsmen. The trailheads were also landscaped by local companies. The landscape was nice, pretty much all large-acre farms. I just wish it were a longer ride than the 6 miles it is.

After that was a mixture of flat and very straight roads. One thing I do really like out here is the way the streets are named. They have numbered roads, like N100 and E250. The first number is the mile, and the last two are the fractional amount. If I just crossed E100 (1 mile) and I need to get to E250 (2.5 miles), I know I need to keep riding another mile and a half, super easy. Since my career is staring at lots and lots of numbers in programming, this is very easy for me to navigate.

That brought me to the next trail on my list, the Nickel Plate Trail. In western Lancaster County into Lebanon county, there are the Conewago and Lebanon Valley trails, which constitute 20 miles combined. Everything besides the surface Nickel plate is paved, reminds me of the trail back home—farms, woods, and a few road crossings. This trail has a short 3.5-mile section on the road in Peru that connects the parts of the trail. I took the trail for the 28 miles into Rochester.

I needed to get on the road here in Rochester; I had another 25 miles to go to get to the Rising Sun Campground in Monterey, which would also put me very close to reaching the next time zone. Once again, my road riding was very enjoyable, flat and no traffic. I think the best thing I could report about a day was it ended uneventfully.

I'm the only person in the tent area tonight, so that means no rain fly. Hopefully there's not a lot of light at night here and I'll be able to see the stars while lying down in my tent. It's a very nice, quiet campground, and I have a perfect spot on the Tippecanoe River. My tent door opens to the river fifteen feet away. I've stayed here before, and it's a very good place to stay if you are biking or just wanting to get away in the RV.

Today was another day of thinking and analyzing my life back home. Why do I isolate and drift away from everyone? Well, from friends, mostly, but how and why have I become the isolated person I feel I am? Most importantly, how do I start to change my ways? I don't want to be around big crowds and do enjoy my alone time. But there's a healthy amount of time and an unhealthy amount. It's been a while since I had a few friends that I did stuff regularly with. Honestly, it's probably been close to ten years since I had a true hiking friend. I do miss the camaraderie and human contact, also the relationships both platonic and not. No woman, no pets, no kids—I've gotten used to the solitary life. I suppose I could go on, but you get the point, and there are only so many thoughts I'd share publicly as well. I know I'm not alone, but it's hard to shake that feeling away. I have family and friends; I guess I pushed them away, or more likely I faded away in the distance.

Sometimes my life feels like a room with a closed door. I'm on the inside and holding the doorknob so no one can come in. But secretly, inside, I want to let go and open the door. It sounds strange, but I'm not sure I know how to let go anymore. I hope this trip in some way can help with that.

I passed a sign today on the road; I can't remember where exactly. It was in the front of a church, the kind with individual letters. It read, "The truth will set you free." I want to feel free again. I don't feel free and haven't for a while. I feel a heavy weight holding me down, and even if not a weight, lately any sort of problem seems to have the potential for destruction in my life. What is truth? How do I know what the truth is anymore? When I feel like a stranger in a strange world, the truth can be muddied by my convoluted thoughts. Then the truth becomes blurred for me between some fake fantasy and reality and then I don't know what to think.

7/11/23

DAY #14, RIDING #13

Miles—82.62 (993.65); Time—6:43 (86:07)
Travelodge, Lansing, Illinois ($75)

Another early start, and honestly that's the new norm. I enjoy the early starts, which hopefully lead to earlier ends to the day. I don't tend to sleep in anymore; even at home I'm usually up by six or six thirty. Today I also gained an hour pretty early in the day by changing time zones.

It was a short ride into Monterey to get on the Erie Trail and North Judson Trails. All of the trails in the past couple days have been paved, and that's something I'll see more of as I continue into the Midwest. The trails here are like the past few I've been on. I start to feel like a broken record by describing everything I'm seeing along the trail. It's been a lot of the same type of landscapes and views from the trail. Not that it's a bad thing at all, but does anyone really want to hear me try to describe the woods, farms, and fields again? The trails today were in great shape, and they provided a pleasurable, smooth ride.

I followed that up with a road map I had made from the Erie Trail in North Judson to the Erie-Lackawanna Trail in Crown Point, Indiana, a 45-mile ride that would be a little over half my day. It's mostly flat, according to the map, on the back roads, with some Highway 8 mixed in. Somewhere along the way, I came to a detour. This detour was from a bridge being completely rebuilt, with no possible way to walk around either. Normally I'll try to walk around the detour, depending on how safe it is. If I can, I'll walk through if no one's working; you never really ever feel like backtracking. This required going almost 2 miles back to the next road. The bigger issue at that point was that there wasn't another bridge close that I could cross the river. It wasn't the worst thing, though; at least the closest bridge was west, the way I was going. The detour was 10 miles out of the way.

What can you do? I just rolled with it. These things will happen on the road, and in places where there isn't much around, some road detours can potentially get very long.

I need to learn to stop and take breaks on the road. When there's nothing around on a day like today, I'll literally keep going, like I did today. I was hurting most of the day because I didn't stop to take breaks. I only really stopped to fill up my water bottle. I sort of go into this mode, like a machine, and just push through obstacles and, if needed, any pain I feel. Today my back was hurting from the nonstop riding. "Just keep going and get this done." I can't have that mindset, especially when I reach the West. I only get that way on the roads, mainly because I don't have a place to stop besides a road shoulder. I don't do this on trails.

I had to dodge the rain again, got a little wet but nothing too bad. Then, around 4:00 p.m., I came into Lansing, Illinois, on the border with Indiana, and the sky quickly had a change for the worse. A surprise storm was coming, and judging by how fast the sky changed, it would be here very soon. Not long after, it completely opened up something fierce. It was coming down very heavily, and I luckily came to a building just in time. A towing garage and some specialty doctor's office shared the building. The towing place was closed, so I used their awning for cover.

As I was waiting outside, the doctor came out and invited me into his waiting room. What a nice guy. Of course I took him up on his offer. It ended up pouring for almost an hour. I was just sitting there and ended up having a conversation with some elderly woman waiting on her husband's appointment.

Doing some weather watching on my phone, I saw the rain was coming and staying all night. Given how saturated the ground would be, as much as I didn't want to book a hotel, it was looking like I had two choices: camp and most likely get everything wet or get a hotel room.

The doctor is now done for the day. I thank him and wait outside for a little longer before I just take off for the final short distance to the Travelodge. Yuck, I'll just say we all know you get what you pay for. Instead of going into details, I'll leave it at this: We've all booked a cheap hotel at some point to save some money. We have all dealt with all that comes with it, mostly dirty and disgusting rooms. With the weather that happened overnight, it was a smart decision even if hotel conditions were less than ideal.

Tomorrow rain is forecasted all day, so I'm not sure what's on tap for tomorrow just yet. I also know I need an attitude adjustment. I feel off-balance lately and like I'm trying to balance a lot to make my trip run smoothly. I do know I cause some of this feeling but also need to maintain what I do to provide accountability on this trip. I'm on my own, far from home; I can't just give in, get lazy, and let everything fall to pieces around me. I need to give a damn through this entire trip, not just when I'm feeling good.

Tomorrow I start completely new sections of the GART. I've ridden to just shy of where I am currently. So far the territory has been familiar to me. I've stayed at these campsites a couple times now, in some instances. It's more than crossing another state off my list. This marks for me the new start of my trip. Now I'm riding into uncharted territory, for me. Now's the time to see how good I am at my mapmaking and planning. How do I control myself in troubled times, alone, and probably with no idea where I am? I know my capabilities, and I'm confident in what I can do without my pride getting in the way. This is one aspect of my life where I feel confident—a bike trip.

Bike packing is what I do; this is me. I love all the challenges, from the planning to the climbing. I want to see how good I am at planning this trip by myself. I'm nobody special; if I can put the time in to plan this trip and complete it, so can a lot of people doubting themselves. It doesn't need to be about this either. All you need to do to accomplish something that seems impossible is to be dedicated to the cause. Do you really want it, or do you want to just dream about it? Dreams are for sleeping, not living. In reality, living out those dreams results in lifelong adventures and treasures that can't ever be taken away. It also requires real effort, drive, and a 100 percent pure interest in doing what you love and trying to accomplish it. It's hard to stop a person who fully believes and feels these powerful feelings inside. Follow them as far as they go and turn dreams into reality.

7/12/23

DAY #15, RIDING #14

Miles—64.73 (1,058.38); Time—5:50 (91:52)

Quality Inn Morris, IL ($130)

Today will most likely be a hectic weather-watching day, a rush to stay ahead of the rain and still make some progress. It will mostly be a day on the trails, so finding cover can sometimes be tricky. Having to ride waiting for a park or shelter along the trail in the rain isn't very much fun. It can be scary if there's wind; one big branch falling on you could be it.

This day I would make out pretty good on staying dry at least. The first rain of the day happened before I could even leave. I opened the door, and it was already coming down.

The very first thing I saw today on the road to my trail was a sign in the front yard of a church. It read, "Enjoy today. It is one of the good old days you will miss." *Wow*, what an incredibly powerful message and something I was very grateful to see on my trip. The message really hit me, and I even turned around after half a mile to return for a picture. It made me really think about rushing and getting ahead of myself. It was something I needed to see, for a reminder. I need these random reminders to slow down and enjoy what I'm doing in the moment. And for God's sake, lighten up and just enjoy the journey.

I finished up the Pennsy Greenway in Lansing and then went on a 2.5-mile tour through town to connect with the Thorn Creek Trail. Somewhere along here I had the first stop for rain. Luckily, I came upon a park with a gazebo I could sit in. I only caught the first few drops. This would turn into the shortest rain delay for the day, ending after 30 to 45 minutes. After the nice 10 paved miles, I picked up the Old Plank trail for the next 22. There were a lot of cool things along the Old Plank, with my favorite being the bridges and some of the waterways. One bridge in particular stood out. It's a regular bridge over a busy road. It has two support beams overhead close to the middle, with four cables coming down in the middle only. I also liked it for the peace and quiet it offered. It went through a lot of really nice places, offering some variety on the trail.

On the Old Plank, outside Joliet, I had my second rain delay, and this time I took refuge in an abandoned baseball dugout. It rained harder and longer. This one lasted almost an hour. Here I had time to make another video on my real, honest inner thoughts. As with my journals, I try to include most of what is in these videos or at least what I'm willing to share.

I saw a sign at a church today when I first started about the good old days, as I've mentioned. They say you see or hear things for a reason, and I think that was something I definitely needed to see today. Not that I'm not having fun, but I think I'm letting myself get taken away by trying to make this trip not necessarily better overall but instead focusing on something that will help out along the way. A perfect example was the bags and the time they took away every day.

I've been feeling flustered by the rain. It's frustrating, and I get frustrated with my actions sometimes in the rain. Sometimes I know the rain is coming, but I feel a need to squeeze out as many miles as possible before the rain arrives, which usually gets me wet, then possibly off balance with my choice to press my luck. For some reason I do this more than normal logic would let a person. I feel it starts taking away from my experience and why I'm out here. I need to remember I don't control everything, not literally everything, but rain and nasty weather happens; bicycle issues happen. It's out of my control; all I can do is just react to it. How will I respond to situations further along?

I can do better, and I will do better. I needed to see that sign this morning. I kind of feel like it was a sign placed there purposely, like somehow I was supposed to see it. Just confirming I need to practice mindfulness. Get back into more thinking about some of these Eastern beliefs and philosophies in Buddhism that have helped me in the past. And for the life of me, once again slow down to a regular life speed.

After my recording and a wait, the rain went away. There was more to come; I wasn't done with the rain just yet. I only had a short road ride to my next trail, and I needed some luck at the trail head. I was coming up to the start of the Illinois & Michigan Canal Way (I&MC) in Joliet when I started to feel the drops hitting me. So I kicked it into high gear. I started to get wet, and the rain was really starting to get heavier by the second. I get to the trailhead, but there was no shelter!

It was now a complete, all-out downpour, but as I got a closer view, I saw an informative sign shelter. The shelter had three sides with a covering overhead. I was very lucky for sure; there was nothing around, and it was raining so hard I couldn't see the trail up ahead. I backed my bike in and had just enough room to squeeze in and avoid the runoff water from up above. This was the longest delay and the fourth rain of the day. This was the heaviest by far and lasted 1.5 to 2 hours! It was a long time standing, but I was so happy to have a dry place to stay.

The bad side, of course, was that this was a canal trail. I expected crushed stone, a dirt surface, and flatness, not very good for draining water. I was expecting absolute hell in terms of trail surface, actually. Exactly the type of trail to avoid after a big rain, not to mention literally right after a storm. I was currently dry; I was happy, so all was good.

The rain stopped for the last time today, and I took off. I could see the trail was severely flooded from my viewpoint, and just knew this wouldn't be a fun ride. I had a hotel, so no matter how cold, gritty, and dirty I would be, I would have a hot shower later. It was all I thought it would be too.

The first 6 to 7 miles were the worst. There were literally 2 lanes of water, with marshy grass in the center. The water was up past my tire to my rim from the ground at some points. I rode in the grass as much as I could. I could hear the dirt and grit running through my drivetrain and everywhere else.

If this happens, there really isn't anything you can do. You're going to get soaked, and the rain guards only do so much to help. After a certain point it doesn't even matter anymore because you have to ride through it. After the first couple minutes, you get over it and don't really care as much about the mess. I'll let the hotel shower drain worry about it all later.

A tip for new travelers: the hotel shower can double as a bike wash. I do get a majority off prior and wipe down the chain. Dirty black grease from the chain will stain the shower floor, trust me. I've done this plenty of times, and especially today, I needed it. I got almost everything clean before in the parking lot, but all the little nooks and crannies needed washed out. Take the front wheel off if space is an issue. I also hit the 1K-mile mark today!

7/13/23

DAY #16, RIDING #15

Miles—67.05 (1,125.43); Time—6:42 (98:34)

Hennepin Canal Lock 6 Campground, Princeton, Illinois

(free, primitive)

My day started out very good: the hotel was nice, clean, and had a slight upgrade from the standard continental hotel breakfast, which has typically just been an automatic waffle maker at every hotel so far. Today was a spread of Jimmy Dean microwave sandwiches, SunnyD, juice boxes, and prepackaged muffins, not great but better than that waffle. I had a good breakfast and packed a couple things for lunch. Whenever I'm at a hotel, I always try to get to breakfast when it opens.

After breakfast I had a 4-mile ride through the small city of Morris to get back on the I&MC. I was wondering how the trail surface would be after the massive and pounding rain yesterday. I had about 40 miles to finish up and heard all kinds of bad things about the trail. How I should avoid it because it's going to get sloppy. Of course, I had to see for myself and I would end up riding the trail regardless of conditions like that.

When I do my trips, I try to follow the trail route as closely as possible. If I decide to skip trails for whatever reason, then this becomes just a cross-country trip. I want to complete the GART, so I follow the trail exactly as it is on their website.

It turned out the trail was relatively dry, with little to no big puddles. I was really surprised by the condition of the surface. It's a very interesting trail, with the surface going from a wide stone trail to a single-lane stone path and even just grass, all accompanied by thick trees. I passed under this really incredible-looking wooden bridge that was very interesting and looked different from any wooden bridge I've seen. It was a small bridge over the trail but all wood except for the hardware holding it together.

Along the trail, about one and a half hours into the ride, I came upon a guy walking his bike. I slowed down and asked if everything was cool. He said no, flat tire. I stopped and asked him what size tire he had. "Seven hundred" was the response, so obviously I then asked what width; he just sort of looked at me. So I asked, "Thirty-six to forty-three range?" He told me yes, and I informed him he was in luck today with his flat as I carried three spare tubes. I got out one tube, a multi-tool, and my pump. He took the multi-tool and went to work on his rear tire while I got everything else.

He had his back tire off, tube switched and was riding again in 15 minutes! I, meanwhile, spend 15 minutes fighting to get my tire over the rim. We were talking, and he had a ride coming, but it was over an hour away. He was also 25 miles away from his car. Even on single-day trips, always, always carry a tube and repair tools.

He asked if I had a GoFundMe or would take Venmo (whatever that is). I said no thanks, and I wouldn't take anything anyways. This was a perfect time to do something for someone like so many have done for me. He got everything put back together, and we went our separate ways.

Back to the I&MC. I was very happily surprised by the trail conditions. I was really amazed that I didn't see any standing water. But soon enough I would encounter trail conditions I've never dreamed or had nightmares of encountering. Somewhere near the end of the trail, I would say the last 5 to 7 miles, I ran into the worst muddy area ever. This was at least a quarter to half a mile stretch I had to manage through. I came riding into the area and immediately knew it would be trouble.

The entire trail was deep, thick, tire-grabbing mud, with little to no clean grass on the sides. I attempted to ride through, but the mud stuck to my wheels and wound up in my rain guards. Eventually it all built up and my tire seized up completely, 100 percent jammed with this heavy mud. My zip-tied rain guard was acting like a divider as soon as the underneath filled; it started going over the guard and getting into my rack area.

As soon as it clogged the tire area, everything else seemed to follow, front and back. I was literally stuck and had to push my bike. I was pulling handful after handful of mud out, only for it to be refilled again when I moved. I had to remove the mud, or else I was pushing my bike without the tires moving.

Also, by now all of the mosquitoes on the trail had found me. I am not exaggerating; it got very, very bad. Luckily there was a semi-hard mud now starting to form as I continued forward. This surface I could run on to get out of the area as quickly as I could. When I did have to stop because of mud clogs, I would immediately be swarmed by a literal army of mosquitoes. It was no joke, swatting away seven to nine off each leg with every brush of my hand. My legs were already completely covered in those mysterious red dots/blisters, and now I was being eaten alive on top of that. It got to be pretty painful being bit on top of these already painful blisters; it was an absolutely horrible experience for a few minutes, no doubt. I hope I never get caught in anything like that again.

I decided to just run, but the bugs followed still and attacked me when I stopped. I had to stop at certain points because the mud was still coming up my tires as I ran. It had turned into a repeating cycle: clear away mud, swipe bugs, run, and repeat. Finally, I made it to all solid ground and rode for a while to lose all the mosquitoes. The bugs were so bad that my mirror fell off my helmet, and I knew it but kept on running (I did a quick look and didn't see it right away).

Back on dry land, my muddy tires were now picking up every little stone on the trail. It reminded me of a doughnut rolled in toppings. The only thing I cared about at the moment was not being bitten so all was good. That really was just complete hell, and at this point, I was almost 100 percent covered in bites from a little above my knees to my ankles

I eventually finish the I&MC and have one last 18 mile road ride from La Salle to the start of the Hennepin Canal, in Bureau Junction, IL.

As luck would have it, I passed a car wash very early in that road section. I used a single bay and washed the bike and some of myself for two dollars. Perfect. We both certainly needed the wash. My bike was a lot worse than I was, mud-wise at least. The car wash was right on my route, and it was such a mental blessing to find one sooner rather than later as I didn't have to constantly search. I was staying at a lock on the trail so I didn't expect water tonight.

The road wasn't that bad but did have a few good challenging hills to climb: 600 feet gained and the same down over 19 miles. I could've shortened it, but I try to avoid the highways if I can. In the East it's easier to do; we have plenty of side roads. Later in my trip, I'd learn a lot about roads or lack thereof in less-populated states and desolate areas.

I started the Hennepin Canal Parkway Trail in Bureau Junction and didn't have very far to go to my camp. The Hennepin Canal is a 60-mile unpaved trail. It does offer plenty of free primitive camping at several of the canal locks. I'll be staying at lock 6 tonight.

The weather got better as the day went on; the sun was even out most of the day. As I got on the trail, I lost service. Last check was 10 to 15 percent chance of rain, so probably a dry night. But…

Around 9:15 p.m., I am about to go to sleep. I am really hoping the thunder and lightning I'm seeing and hearing in the distance miss me. It gets dark, and I can see the lightening flashing inside my tent; it's close. Time to put the rain fly on; no one is here, so I wasn't going use it. I hope whatever it is, it's quick. The wind is really picking up, and the storm is definitely coming my way.

There's a single vault toilet that is a little on the bigger side, and since I'm here alone, I decide to store my bike in the bathroom overnight! (It worked out great, and it stayed dry for the morning commute.)

The rain comes, and it storms eventually. I hear the thunder pounding, the rain hitting my tent, and the wind swirling around. It's a sound that should mean something bad, but I sort of like all the sounds of a storm. I also forgot my guidelines for my tent. Time to buckle up. Should be a fun one tonight…

7/14/23

DAY #17, RIDING #16

Miles—68.58 (1,193.98); Time—6:20 (104:54)
Oyo Hotel, Downtown Moline, Illinois ($77)

Well, it happened again. It's July 14—another day, and I'm another year older. It seems the past couple years I've not been home on my birthday. Since it's in the summer, I'm usually out on a trail somewhere, and on my birthday lately, I've been on bike packing trips. My birthday is just another day for me. It's a celebrated day but not particularly special anymore. It's nothing I get excited about, especially since I'm starting my forty-first year. One thing I do know is that the one or two gray beard hairs are starting to multiply. Either way, today will be a good day for a birthday.

After the storm last night, the day started with an amazingly clear blue sky, with little to no cloud cover. The day also started out on the warmer side, so my tent was mostly dry when I got up. My mornings always start the same; I've got a routine. I start by packing up things inside my tent and usually take off the rain fly to dry somewhere. I pack as much as I can, then make breakfast and coffee. Breakfast is almost always three packs of instant oatmeal and two cups of coffee. I pack up everything and get ready to go. Before I leave, I like to have my second cup of coffee and just sit back in my chair and relax one last time. Then I'm ready for the day. I might have treated myself to a third cup this morning, though.

The trail surface really surprised me here, in a good way. I had about 55 miles left to finish up this trail and thought I'd encounter lots of standing water, but the trail did an amazing job of absorbing it. There were only a few standing water areas along the Hennepin Canal, to my surprise. I was also glad I started saving water bottles. Last night, as I had thought, no water at camp, and along the trail, there were only two or three places for water.

I stopped by the visitor center and was talking to the ranger there. He was telling me how short-staffed they were, but also asking me what I thought of the trail. I thought it was in really good shape considering last night and also told him I was impressed with how the trail drained. He told me he never heard that one and that he was down to four workers to maintain the entire trail—yes, the entire 60 miles! I was even more impressed with the trail after hearing that.

Honestly the trail is in need of a little work in some spots but overall very good, all things considered. I hear about this trail getting bad reviews, but I really enjoyed it. The diversity of the trail I enjoyed. The surface is stone, but I was also riding on grass for a short period. Honestly, I don't really care what surface I ride on as long as it's tire safe. It adds to breaking up the monotony of riding a canal trail.

I also read a sign saying how important this canal was to the trade route many years ago, when the canal was still operating. This was a major intersection for the old trade routes to come together from faraway lands to get their goods to the other end of the country.

The trail did end up taking me longer to ride than I thought, and the first 15 to 20 miles were rougher than the rest. Today was going to be a good day as I would cross the Mississippi River. The Mississippi is something I've always wanted to see. Growing up, you hear about these beautiful natural American sites/wonders scattered across the country. Some of these seem to take on this almost mystical appeal, like something special or a sacred place. The Mississippi, Yellowstone, and Olympic Peninsula (Pacific Northwest) are the three natural wonders I'm most looking forward to seeing on this adventure.

In Moline I picked up another Amazon package. I got plastic utensils (I lost mine), a larger front bag, and a bear bag for out West. I'm horrible at doing this; my dry "bear" bag is way too small. I also stopped by Walmart for some food and to look for a new mirror for riding.

I came into Moline after that and came upon the mighty Mississippi River. It didn't disappoint either. It's such a magnificent river to see; I'm going to have to explore it more tomorrow.

The weather started to change when I arrived in Moline. Soon after I got to the river, the sky got dark. Looking at the weather, and given the fact it's my birthday, I decided on another hotel. I'm very glad I did because it was another ferocious rainstorm and even threw down hail too.

At the hotel my thoughts turned sort of dark. Once again the difficult part is how open I am willing to be; it's incredibly difficult and scary exposing yourself to the world. I guess there are some things that I'll either hold on to or maybe write about later. Besides my thoughts about sharing, I still have a life to live. I sort of have to be selective in my sharing. I also wonder if my thoughts might be misconstrued or if I don't properly convey my thoughts. I found out today I was denied a Pennsylvania program I applied for. Some things in life I don't understand; it seems like the state has programs to help people, but I still get turned away.

Details aren't important at this point, and I'm not sure if this will make it to print. There's a reason I have the time for this trip. Last year into this one, I sat in jail for 175 days and lost a lot, including my job. Three days before my suppression hearing, the assistant district attorney dismissed all charges and I was released. The month before that, I went somewhere to try to seek some help and clarity upstairs. Immediately after I was released from county prison, I went on those two bicycle trips, and now here I am on this trip. I haven't worked since and have been living solely off my bank account, with no income at all. That's one of the reasons why I try to avoid hotels if I can and am eating so much ramen.

Because of this, my mind fades into some dark thoughts. I hate a lot because of this. I also realize this is dragging me down and can potentially drown me if I let it. I somehow need to mentally recover and find a way to accept everything in my life and move on. I've told myself in other parts of my life that accepting something doesn't mean I agree with or even have to like it. But I do have to be able to accept the situation in order to move on.

It's hard when you don't want to go home and life seems like it's all stacked against you. Why do I feel like it's me versus the world? Why do I feel the need to defend everything I have because I think they'll just try to take it away? What is it about the nights? Why do all the bad thoughts seem to grow as the sun goes down? Why do I think and feel things that I know are not true? Why have I almost accepted this way of life? Like I said before, this trip is way more than just a bike ride; I'm also searching for something I lost.

When I left, life was at a crossroads and I kept thinking this song was the perfect one to describe me and my trip—"Don't Follow," by Alice In Chains. It sort of hits home for me. When I left I kept thinking, I might not come home, or I'll come home, pack my things, and just leave.

7/15/23

DAY #18, RIDING #17

Miles—88.13 (1,282.11); Time—7:41 (112:35)
Linder Point Campground, Iowa City, Iowa ($26, RV site, water and electricity)

One of the benefits of a hotel is I'm all packed up and ready to go after breakfast. Even though it's a comfortable bed rather than the ground, I'll still wake up early and usually set an alarm. I value the time on the trail way more than the comfort of a hotel bed. Plus, I had to cross the Mississippi River, and I wanted to spend some time there. I believe it was the Great River Trail in Moline, where I went down to the legendary Mississippi. I went all the way down to the shore, to a quiet, deserted spot. It was a busy area and rightfully so. Even with the ominous gray sky, there were a lot of people out enjoying themselves.

I just sat along the shore, thinking about how I've been hurting, letting my emotions win, and letting my darker thoughts infect my true thoughts. I need a change, and if this trip can't help me, I might just be out of options. I needed this relaxing start. I put my hands in the water and just sat there kneeling on the bank, taking in the moment. Feeling the coolness of the water on my hands, the strength of the current, just trying to indulge every sense I could. I felt like a sponge trying to soak everything in. Wow, did I absolutely need a start like this today.

I passed by this train bridge, Rock Island Lines; it just reminded me of the song by Leadbelly—I love listening to those old blues. Don't know if it's the same, but well, just a random thought I had at the time.

I ended up having to ride two different bridges to cross the Mississippi into Davenport, Iowa. I swear at some spots the river is 2 miles wide. I was very happy to see the river and can cross that off the list of things I need to see in America. Traveling abroad would be nice, but America has so much to see, I'm cool staying right here.

My riding this day was mostly roads after leaving Davenport on the Riverfront Trail. All day I thought it was close to rain, the way the sky looked. It was from the Canadian wildfires, still burning. The smoke was clearly visible, and it created a hazy fog all day. I don't think it really affected my riding or breathing. I was a smoker for years and recently quit; well, I'm trying. Its been a month since I had my last cigarette. I do good with quitting, then get on the trails for a trip, and after a few days, I'm thinking about it; I guess it's my trigger. I'm doing good and haven't bought any cigarettes or a single Black & Mild, yet. I would buy Camel pouches eventually, though; I have no desire for those at home. Yet if I bought a pack of cigarettes, I'd have to fight off that urge when I got home. Alcohol is not even a thought anymore. It's been almost seven years (January 29, 2017) since my last drink, and I've been through a hell of a lot in those years.

After a hilly road map from Davenport to Muscatine, Iowa, for 22 miles, I was deep in the corn by then. We have lots of corn at home, but once again, it's small family farms, usually less than one hundred acres. According to the Lancaster Agriculture Council, 99 percent of the farms are family-owned and mostly passed down through the generations. Out here, that would seem like a test field. It's hard to describe how huge the farming areas are out here. It's something you have to see for yourself. It's really an amazing sight—I think so, at least.

It makes me realize again how large the world is, how many people there are in the world to feed, basically how we humans are pretty much a speck of dust compared to the world we live in. My mind can drift away easily sometimes, as you can tell. Plus, I'm alone; all I can do is think. I get tired of talking to myself—joking, sort of, ha ha. It sure seems like this book is turning into one more about my mental struggles rather than my adventure…

I left Muscatine on the Running River Trail, for the short distance it covered. After 5 miles the trail ended and I was staring at a gravel road, shit! This would be something that I'd end up dealing with a lot, a lot more than I ever wanted or thought I would. I got caught up in 14 miles of good-size rocks on gravel roads. I was basically on gravel roads from Muscatine to Conesville, Iowa. It wasn't fun, and I wasn't thrilled, but ultimately I was just hoping I wouldn't blow or shred a tire on these rocks. It really made me work harder today, and of course I had stocked up at Walmart the day before. I was pretty much loaded up on weight as well. It really put a strain on my back, and I was definitely hurting that night.

There's not a lot I can do to avoid some of these roads; because I follow the GART route, I have no say in where the trails drop me off. My only "free riding" is on the missing road gaps. I must ride every trail that I'm able to with my bike and tires. If I follow that, then I must learn to accept whatever kind of road I come to. In Iowa and Nebraska, though, I would certainly be tested on the acceptance part.

Another issue arises when I need to book a campsite in advance, well in advance. I tried it, and it just created stress on me because if a place is booked and I can't cancel if needed, then I will somehow still try to make it there. Weather, bike—there are just too many issues that can happen in planning ahead five to seven days in advance for camping. Sometimes it can create a problem, like tonight. I don't know how popular some areas are, being from Pennsylvania.

Evidently the area outside of Coralville, which has lakes and the Iowa River, is extremely popular. I wanted to stay at Sugar Bottom Campground, but it was sold out; West Overlook Campground, also sold out. I finally found an open spot at Linder Point Campground. There are supposedly over five hundred camping spots combined in this lake area, and I had to try three different campgrounds, wow! I was so glad to find something, I booked it before I fully read what I had reserved. It was only twenty-six dollars, so I just wanted to reserve it ASAP. It was an RV spot, but I now had electricity and water. I had plenty of room to park my bike, though. It was nice having the driveway to dry my tent in the morning as well.

I was talking to a pretty cool guy next to me; it was nice talking with him. We both had a laugh about me booking the RV site. He did tell me about the area and how it fills up on the weekends almost all summer. While it was not as nice on the eyes as the other sites were, this turned out to be a good place for me.

7/16/23

DAY #19, RIDING #18

Miles—95.68 (1,376.79); Time—7:52 (120:27)
Deer Park Campground, Evansdale, Iowa ($15, primitive)

I had a semilate start; I was talking with my neighbor. I'm starting to actually like interacting with people. At this point I can't say whether I'm getting more comfortable or the people are nicer out here. I think it's some of both, from my perspective. He was a really good dude from Tennessee, living here in Iowa.

I finally got rolling on the road at 9:00 a.m. I wasn't too concerned about the time; I'm trying to not stress about time and distances—emphasis on the *trying*. I know I'm pushing myself a little and I don't really need to be riding as many miles as I have been daily. The miles are the part I can handle; what I don't like is starting at 7:00 a.m. to 8:00 a.m. and ending at 6:00 p.m. It makes for a very long day and starts to add up after not so long. I'm at about two and a half weeks of riding at this pace. Like I said before, I feel like a machine, or a thoroughbred raising his foot up and down in anticipation of being set free to run wild.

I had to start on a 13-mile road ride to the Hoover Nature Trail in Solon. It was a very beautiful scenic ride around the incredible Lake McBride State Park, also a very busy and fast road, with lots of travelers towing RVs and boats. I couldn't get off this road segment fast enough. Not the safest with traffic, especially since it was Sunday, but I made it. The rest of the day would consist of trafficless trails.

It was starting to get hazier with the smoke from Canada, but I was also riding north today. The riding at the start in the McBride Lake area was very populated, and it was easy to see why: lots of water activities going on, great trails to ride, and also, it looked like, separate hiking trails. It's a really cool-looking place and offers plenty for a full day outside. A few great views of the lake and a couple bridges over creeks make this a very enjoyable trail to ride.

After that was the Cedar Valley Nature Trail (CVNT) for the next 68 miles. Well, 68 miles was how far I was supposed to go, but

I would miss a couple turns today on the trail. While riding through Cedar Rapids, I lost the trail and got generally lost, but Maps got me back on track. The city seemed like it could be nice, but the trail and my detour didn't go through the nicest areas.

It was an enjoyable trail with diverse scenery. After the lake, it passed through farms and fields, and it was paved. It then changed to crushed stone with some more green and a few wooded places lined the trail landscapes. From what I remember, the CVNT was paved for a good amount of the section I was riding and was also very easy to ride. Even the unpaved surfaces are a smoother ride. I really liked this trail and would definitely recommend taking a trip on it if you can.

I would ultimately take the CVNT from Ely to near my camp in Evansdale. I like stopping to see odd-looking roadside attractions, or really any kind of roadside attraction. Today I would ride by the town of Brandon. Brandon offers us Iowa's largest frying pan. It is 9 feet, 3 inches, has a 5-foot handle, weighs 1,020 pounds, and is actually made of cast iron! It symbolizes their annual Cowboy Breakfast, held on the third Sunday in September—mark your calendars.

This trail also goes through some very remote areas, with nothing but cornfields. One thing I'd have to very quickly adjust to was riding all day in the sun. I had some shade today but not much. As I went farther west, I'd have little to none for a few days.

The trail from now on was stone, with some hard-packed dirt. I also came upon a major construction project, a total bridge replacement. Luckily it was Sunday and no one was working. There was a hard-packed mud single lane going down and back up the hill. After crossing two 2-by-4 boards, I struggled but pushed my bike back up the hill. That was a workout, but at least I wouldn't need a detour now. I also saw a bunch of people in canoes and inner tubes on the river. It was a hot day and very nice, minus the smoke.

I rode in my pants and a long-sleeve shirt today. I feel like I need to block my arms and legs from the sun for a few days. It's starting to get really bad, and if I am admitting that, it's *actually* extremely bad. My feet and 90 percent of my legs from the ankle to above the knee are covered in painful tiny bumps, with the whiteheads on them. I can feel them stretching my skin when I bend my legs; it really makes for a miserable day. It's too much, but I don't know what to do about it really. I think I'll have to do a few days of pants and long sleeves and try to completely cover my body.

On a random note, I'm at 1,350 miles, and I'm thinking I should switch my tires soon, front to back.

I'm doing good and feel good about doing this again. I get a bunch of good feelings when I think about what I'm doing. Today it makes me feel confident and, more importantly, happy. That is obviously very important: I have a need to be happy on my trip. Why shouldn't I be in a great mood? Every day is a new adventure, in a new land, on my bike—how could it get better? Despite occasional setbacks and the human nature of feelings of anger, frustration, and such, I need to be able to mentally bounce back like this. I need to be able to take how I react and think and channel that into something that comes out positive or at least neutral until I can accept it and move on.

My back is also starting to hurt more and more, but looking at my daily mileage and riding time, I can see why. I've been averaging almost 80 miles a day for 18 of 19 days. I'm also averaging end times of 5:30 to 6:00 p.m. A few of the miles are from stops, resupplying, and side trips. Who am I kidding? I'm pushing myself, but that's me. I can't explain why I feel the need to do that many miles. Inexperience on distance trips lasting over a week (I've only done two prior)? Overconfidence in my endurance? I honestly don't know. Maybe I just feel like it's something I can actually accomplish while planning. At home I was road biking almost 20 miles every other day, running 3 to 4 miles the days in between, and on the weekends, I'd usually try to get in a 50 to 75 mile ride. I knew I could handle the miles; what I didn't count on, due to having never taken a trip longer than two weeks, was burnout and fatigue over a prolonged period.

If there is an underlying reason I feel the need to follow this pace, I'd like to know and understand it. I do know now that if I have a plan, my brain won't allow me to deviate from it. I love spontaneous day trips, but on a trip like this, I 100 percent, absolutely need a structured plan. My mind—mostly my anxiety—tells me so. I need at least a basic plan; I wouldn't want to see myself out here if I hadn't done any of the planning I did.

⭐

7/17/23
DAY #20, RIDING #19

Miles—89.14 (1,465.93); Time—7:13 (127:40)
River View Campground, Mashalltown, Iowa ($26)

The start of the day was a real treat, compliments of nature. Right out of the campground, I got on the Cedar Valley Lakes Trail. I was treated to a hawk diving into the Cedar River. After the second or third time, it flew away, and of course it had breakfast to go. Very cool to see, especially literally around the corner from the campground. It was a great day weather-wise, cool in the morning and probably a high in the low eighties. This day would be more roads than trails. I would start to see that I was riding more miles than necessary because of my thoughts about sticking to the trail.

It was mostly all trail to the town of Hudson. There was a really cool bridge in Waterloo, crossing the Cedar River, with some beautiful views of the city along the water. I was also in John Deere country; I passed the tractor and engine museum and a number of statues. Given how my job ended, I was glad I was seeing more John Deere than their leading competitor, my old company. It was bittersweet: It was a really good job, but after my supervisor retired, I had zero respect for anyone in management. A change was needed, however it was going to happen. Anyways, seeing more green John Deere meant fewer bad memories and hard feelings.

I realized one of the reasons I log so many extra miles. Because I follow the trail, I'm not on the most direct route. From Hudson to

Marshalltown is 29 miles, but because of the River's Edge Trail, I had a 45-mile ride. I won't deviate from the official GART route unless absolutely necessary—construction or something that my bike can't handle. It may be strange or no big deal to some, but it's important to me. Trust me, I'll stubbornly follow the trail, even through some very interesting places for a bike. Today, for my dedication, owing to those extra 15 miles, I was also rewarded with an extra hour on my bike.

Because of the detour, I got to see something cool, and this has formed a memory from the trip. I was riding through endless acres of corn, and I saw a biplane crop-dusting. We have farms but none of this going on, so it was special for me. I'd go on to see plenty of crop-dusting along the way, but when it's not an everyday thing, it's something to enjoy even more.

The pilot must've seen me taking pictures because he made a turn and did a flyby closer to the ground above me! I thought that was the coolest thing and immediately forgot about the extra miles. Although I'm on another endless stretch of gravel roads, I'm feeling content right now. Normally I go through every road in painstaking detail while planning. I'll go over every road and zoom in to make sure I have no surprises. On this trip it would be just too much to do that; I'm not able to see every road in detail. Honestly, with my inexperience in the Midwest, I figured I'd have at least oil and chip back roads, not this many pure gravel roads. Riding through Iowa and Nebraska, man, I had way too many of those roads. The hills today, wow, there were some real tough ones to climb out there.

After that I had to go farther west, eventually to Steamboat Rock, because of the Pioneer Trail. This also added a couple miles because it went west to Grundy Center and then south to Marshalltown. The trail was a little rough and dusty but certainly rideable. This trail was deserted; most of the trails out in these isolated field and farm areas are completely empty. Once I got out of the recreational areas, the riding in Iowa really became desolate. I don't mind riding stone gravel roads, but the fact is, I probably shouldn't be riding them. I'll take them—I almost have to—but every time I'm thinking and worrying, please, please, don't slice my tires or thinking about another bike issue from the bouncing and the rough surface.

My last trail for the day was the recently opened River's Edge Trail. I was actually on the road and saw a paved trail going the way I was headed but passing through what looked like a field. I decided to try it; I figured if I ended up going the opposite way, I'd just go back. I keep a compass pinned to my front bike bag to help in cases like this. It was a relief to find this trail because it took me directly where I needed to go.

After that were more gravel roads on my way to Marshalltown. I did see a sign about the 1865 Stage Coach Road. This road I was on was traveled by stagecoaches before the railroad came around. I love seeing old American history like this. It's so different from the history where I live. We have pilgrims, settlers, Quakers, and our early settlement towns are from the late 1600s. Out here is all westward expansion, from when the pioneers came here to the Midwest to develop land and live. I also passed a cool town sign in Lipscomb: "Just a little street where friends meet." The town has only a couple streets. I love stuff like this: simple, quiet, no hustle and bustle.

Corn and soy, soy and corn—is all I've seen on my short Hawkeye State ride so far, with a few scattered Black Angus farms in between. The fields here go for miles and miles, and they're so big they're hard to comprehend. It's definitely an amazing sight to see, to get a small picture of the enormous agricultural industry.

So far my mapping is pretty good; it's getting me where I need to go. I only got off course a handful of times but was able to find my way back on track. Some just add more miles to the ride than others.

I still find myself being rushed at night. Tonight, I was still journaling at 9:30 p.m. Trying to wrap everything up at the end of the day seems to take more and more time. Trying to do Facebook posts every day can be a mental drain. I do get satisfaction from it, and I know friends and family enjoy it and follow along daily. For that I continue to post every day. Some days are pictures only for a reason. If it's just pictures and no words, I'm off balance, bothered by something, or just too tired to type.

With this, along with my daily journal and occasional self-videos, my camp nights can be a handful. Oh well, I feel I'm going to benefit from all this hard work. There would be little to no possibility of me writing this book if I hadn't done these three things.

Not a lot comes easy in life, and it'll be nice to be able to look back at all these memories later.

☆

7/18/23
DAY #21, RIDING #20

Miles—65.30 (1,531.23); Time—6:41 (133:21)
Swede Point Park Campground, Madrid, Iowa ($11, primitive)

Today was day 21, with 20 days of riding, and it's kind of hard to believe. I know I've been out that long, but it still doesn't feel like it. I suppose that's a good thing, though. It was also a shorter ride today; I think mid 60s for the mileage. I did 80 to 90-plus miles a few days in a row, and that was starting to take its toll. It's a challenging mind game for me, to try to balance covering miles and pacing myself. I still have a month and a half and over 2,000 miles to go.

This day was also a day I was looking forward to as I'd be camping 2.5 miles from Iowa's High Trestle Bridge. I only had a short 4-mile road ride, and the rest of the day would be spent on a couple different trails. First up, the Lin Creek Trail was a nice way to start the day. That led me to the IA330/US30 trail; the name is a perfect description. This 11-mile paved trail connects Marshalltown and Melbourne. This trail isn't very fun to ride; there's constant climbing up and down, and it parallels the busy highway. But it's very much appreciated and a very well-placed trail that kept me off the highway or a major detour. Even after my initial description, I still feel very grateful for the trail, for what and where it is.

It's a trail for getting around, exercise, and leisure. Also, it may be one of the few places available for a trail. Literally every open space is corn, soy, or a field. In my riding through Iowa, I was surprised to find quite a number of trails along busy roads or highways. These have been, as you can imagine, an incredible help for me, and they're paved as well.

After finishing the IA330 in Melbourne, I had my 4-mile road map to the very small town of Rhodes to pick up the Heart of Iowa Trail. This might have been the most diverse terrain, and trail, I can remember being on. The trail starts as a tree-lined all-grass path. In addition, surfaces included limestone with grass growing through, slightly larger stones, crushed limestone with some deep spots, and finally pavement. Some of the spots I had to watch; my tires were sinking in a couple parts. I really enjoyed the trail diversity, getting back into the woods, and visiting these neat little towns.

I was getting hungry, so I started looking on my phone for places. As I was coming into Maxwell, a place called Logsdon Grocery was my lunch destination. All the Maps reviews said how great the place was. It's a very cool old store with hundreds of old beer cans lining the walls. The store is run by two brothers and has some really good premade sandwiches. I grabbed one and a drink, then asked the only guy I saw if I should pay him (he was behind the deli counter).

"Oh no, don't do that; my brother will yell at me" was his reply. He then yelled for his brother, who was stocking chips on the shelves.

This brother said, "I can't hear anything stocking the chip bags; it's as loud as a rock concert." He went on, "Yeah, my brother says I don't do anything, but the shelves are always stocked."

These two guys were pretty funny, and it was just a really cool, fun experience.

He knew or at least had heard of Lancaster County. Like some people, he also knew the towns with funny and/or sexual names too. Around where I live, we have the towns of Bird In Hand, Blue Ball, Intercourse, and Paradise.

Until I get out and see this stuff and get to experience this, it's hard for me to comprehend how big each state is. I guess I'm so used to my own home area. I can go for miles out here and see nothing but corn; I'll ride close to hours not seeing anyone or anything but corn. Seeing this blows my mind, seeing how many crops we produce to feed America and allow it to function.

Another thing I'm thinking about is what I want to do. I don't really want to go back; I don't really have anything holding me back—no wife, no kids—and I feel like I have drifted away from most of my friends. I don't even have a job to go back to. I keep thinking of college; I'd like to get my bachelor's degree. I just don't know—I thought this trip would shed some light, but it hasn't yet. I guess I'm not expected to know yet; maybe that's for later on my journey west. I think I need this trip to clear some of the clutter from my head, which has been up there for a while. Some have been good, some bad, but it's been life, my life. It's how you build your life and what you do with your life currently that helps in determining what happens later in life.

I'm not disappointed in life but do wish maybe some things turned out differently. Not that I regret much, but I do feel like I'm missing out on certain parts of life. I try not to think about it much because it brings me down sometimes. But life isn't over, and I'm not dead yet. Maybe I'm thinking too much about stuff that isn't important out here or at all. I'm out here to enjoy myself, not overanalyze my life and determine my future. I think I have this idea in the back of my head that some town or person will come along and blow me away, and I'll go home, pack my things, and leave. I think that'd be amazing, but will it happen?

After a 2.5 mile ride from the High Trestle Trail, I arrived at Swede Point Park Campground. Once again, I lucked out with a paved trail following half my distance to camp. I was thinking no rain fly, but it has been getting chilly at night lately. No rain, but I've been waking up cold in the middle of the night. I wake up, slide into my sleeping bag, and am comfy through the night.

I took my first campground shower, and this one was great—clean with warm water. I'm so very glad I bought a pair of cheap rubber sandals before I left. They are for showers, of course, but I love them at camp when the shoes come off. It's such a relief taking off my shoes after riding all day and relaxing my feet, as strange as that sounds.

I'm also very happy with my new battery charger. It hasn't gone below 50 percent yet, and I recharge it whenever I can at night. Having the extra power is a huge benefit on this trip. I don't usually listen to music at night unless I know I'll have power so my phone won't run out of juice. Every night I've had service, I've been playing the SiriusXM app on my phone. I like to kick back in my chair, possibly with a cup of coffee, and listen to Grateful Dead Radio or Willie's Roadhouse (old country)—no heavy music at night. The last concert I went to before I left was Dead and Company in Philadelphia, and something changed. I'm getting to be more of a Deadhead every day, it seems…

I'm excited to see the High Trestle Bridge; I've heard a lot about it. Also, at night part of it lights up blue. I left at dusk to arrive by sunset. The bridge crosses the Des Moines River, and I got there in time to catch a beautiful sunset. This half-mile, thirteen-story-tall bridge used to be part of the Milwaukee Road Line. There were a few people out there on a Tuesday night, and from what I understand, this is a popular spot. Only about one-third of the bridge is lit up, but it's still a sight to see for sure. Along the bridge are three beams welded together, like a square missing a side. Each one is skewed slightly from the last, giving the rider the appearance of a spinning portal. There are blue LED lights running on the inside of the steel beams. A definite must-see, and if you do go, make sure you go both at night and during the day.

7/19/23

DAY #22, RIDING #21

> Miles—83.38 (1,614.61); Time—7:40 (141:01)
> Albert the Bull Campground, Audubon, Iowa ($15, primitive)

The day started out great; I was able to ride the High Trestle Bridge outside Woodbridge again. It was definitely worth going last night, and I'm very glad I did. It was a popular place too; I saw ten to fifteen people out last night, with more coming as I was leaving, and it was a Tuesday night.

It's easy to look back now and see where I could've done things differently. My inexperience on roads out west of the Mississippi, combined with the anxiety of having to redo all my maps or map as I go, prevented me from deviating from my planned route. I already had my maps made, so I told myself to just keep using them. I would struggle so much this day that I would question what I was doing out here. I really wanted to stay off the highways and busy roads as much as I could. Little did I know that so many of my maps of Iowa and Nebraska would include long miles of stone gravel roads.

Most of the time it wasn't too bad, but it was certainly hard to ride on, not to mention I probably shouldn't have been on some of those roads in first place. What I should've done was just go to the closest main road or highway, if possible, after my trail ended. Sometimes the trail ended at these desolate places where these types of roads were, and sometimes there was just no other options for roads. Or the entire area after my trail was gravel roads in every direction for miles—sometimes I just couldn't help it. I'd be in better shape physically and mentally if I had chosen easier roads. Maybe it was partly me being stubborn, but either way I powered through them.

After leaving the High Trestle Trail in Woodward, I had an easy flat 8 miles on the roads to Perry and the Raccoon River Valley Trail. Going through the town of Perry to start the 16-mile-long trail, I saw a couple of cool painted buildings along the trail welcoming me to town. I would go on to greatly enjoy this trail and its smooth paved riding. It's a well-managed trail, with some variety of terrain to ride through. I crossed a nice bridge spanning the Raccoon River; I rode through dense wooded areas and of course cornfields. I would end my trail ride in Jamaica and start my next road course.

Now here is another example of me making my ride more difficult. After Jamaica, on the GART route there is a trail gap in red on their website (red is "planned, not completed"). On Maps the trail goes south; I could've continued the trail south to Panera, gotten on Highway 44 West to Hamlin, and finally taken a short ride north to Audubon. I had a map made already, but it was mainly my need to follow the GART route.

I knew I was going to have a very hard day on the roads climbing. My final 40-plus miles from the Raccoon River trailhead in Bagley to my campground in Audubon had almost 1,400 feet of elevation gain and 1,100 feet declining. It felt like riding a roller coaster up and down, up and down, except it felt like I was pulling everyone. Of course, the worst part was the unpaved roads. I probably had about 20 to 25 miles of those today, but the hills were the problem. Very hard to climb, and literally one after another. I was certainly letting the cuss words fly today and saying things I'm glad no one was around for.

I just can't seem to escape these roads. I partly blame the trails that end and dump me in the middle of nowhere. But who am I kidding? I do nothing to better or change my situation. This goes back to a character defect I have. I like to complain about something but do nothing about it. I could've stopped and gotten on my phone for an alternate route, but I chose to suffer and ride it out. Part of the mental game I have to balance on a daily basis.

Again, I've never seen so much corn in my life. Iowa's literally corn and some soy. All day nothing but corn. It's a beautiful state, I just wish I could've avoided the roads. I've got a little over a day left and a harder map tomorrow.

A day like today will test you mentally and physically; it definitely did both to me today. I was hot, sweaty, and aggravated while walking up these huge, steep inclines. Some were so steep and rocky that I was actually losing footing because I was slipping on the gravel as I was trying to push my bike uphill. It took a lot longer than I anticipated and required a lot of energy. I tried to push and hold my bike, but when I put one foot forward, the stones below shift and I lose my footing. This happened on at least two hills, I remember. So much hard pedaling to go just 6 to 8 miles per hour on a flat surface. The road usually had two tire tracks that were slightly rideable. Some spots had deep gravel pits that enjoyed grabbing my back tire occasionally as well.

Lots of obstacles to look for today while I try to weave around the bigger rocks. I'm constantly worried a rock will rip my tire, and as long as I ride on a stone road, I'm on edge slightly. I'll climb and climb hard, but I don't want to crash and risk my trip on roads like this. Even going down these hills, I have to ride my breaks. There's so much stone, it wouldn't take much for me to crash. I already feel my back tire sliding when I get going too fast, 13 to 15 miles per hour, out here. So it's a slow and hard way to ride.

I started doing something different while riding these roads. I never play music while riding, ever. I want nature's song to play, plus being alert to my surroundings is important for me.

When I need the inner strength to push on, I turn to my heavy metal roots. I may be becoming a Deadhead, but I'll never turn in my devil horns. I play either turbo (nineties metal) or liquid metal on the SiriusXM app to give me that extra boost. I've got to say this: I'm a big Slipknot fan, but hearing them in Iowa (where they're from) gave me this instant rush of energy. I was getting pumped, a surge of adrenaline, and singing along. I get so hyped I felt unstoppable, like I was back in control of everything and ready to ride this road. I'd also get into the music, singing, head and body bobbing and bouncing to the beat, literally going nuts on my bike. Just what the doctor ordered.

I eventually made it to Audubon and my camp at Albert the Bull Campground. The statue of Albert is huge—world's largest bull statue, it claims. It looks like it's thirty to forty feet tall and slightly longer. Very cool roadside attraction to see, for sure.

After getting set up, I did laundry and got some food supplies in town. I also replaced a smaller water bottle; I now have three 1.5-liter bottles that I refill everyday. That is as much as I'd ever carry, and I never ran out during the day all trip.

Nice campground and a pavilion for me to recharge my devices. After running around town and eating dinner, I was beat and ready to crash.

✪

7/20/23

DAY #23, RIDING #22

Miles—68.31 (1,682.92); Time-5:52 (146:53)
Arrowhead Park, Neola, Iowa ($20, primitive)

Today will be my last full day of riding in Iowa, and as fun as the trails have been, I'm ready to hopefully leave the stone roads behind. It will also mostly be road riding, with 20 miles on the T-bone Trail to start.

This day would turn out to be a beautiful, sunny day. The weather has definitely turned a lot better for me. I haven't had much rain lately, and the rain I did ride through before is now hammering the area back home.

I would start off the day on the paved T-Bone Trail, right out of the campground. This trail follows an old cattle route to Omaha, but the trail ends in Atlantic after 20 miles. The trail is named after the old train that would carry cattle to Chicago and other places. It's entirely paved—at least my 20 miles are. It's a wonderful trail wandering through farms and fields. There's some shade from the tree-filled areas that gives me a break from the sun.

These trails outside of popular recreation areas are deserted. I came across very few people. Of course, I'm not sure how populated it is outside of my route, but it's sort of a shame more people don't enjoy these. Maybe it's the days and times I'm out there, or maybe these places don't have a lot of inhabitants. You'll never hear me complain about having a trail to myself, though. I would also get to see a helicopter land on a truck to resupply its liquid for crop-dusting. That was another gem to see, and those moments I happen across randomly are always the best.

After that was another brutal climbing day, with 1,350 feet up and 1,500 feet down over the next 50 miles. Iowa started out fun enough, but these last two days have been physically exhausting. Somehow, I continue to push through the pain and fatigue. The good thing about today is, all but about 3 to 4 miles are paved! I'll climb paved roads or trails—I don't mind.

Today, with the hills, I stayed in my low gears almost all day. I go around 5 or 6 miles per hour climbing hills when it gets really tough, but walking, I go only 2 to 3 miles per hour. I try to get as much out of pedaling as I can. With the hills comes the downhill riding, which can get sketchy with carrying weight. I don't like going too fast because if you start wobbling at 20-plus miles per hour, you are going down. You can't control the bike once the weight shifts around too much. I'll ride as fast as 30 miles per hour going downhill, if I can see far in front of me, there's not a lot of traffic behind me, and the road surface is in good shape. I don't want cars passing if I'm going that fast because I have zero room for error. Or else I'm crashing and crashing that fast would be very bad. I don't get nervous with traffic passing me usually but passing me when I'm going 30-plus is another story. My trip high was 34 miles per hour!

Eventually, I made it to Arrowhead Park in Neola, Iowa. This place is a must-see and an awesome place to camp. There is so much land to camp on around the beautiful lake. No chance of feeling cramped here. The views, quietness, and sunset on the water certainly make this place memorable, and it still sticks out as I look back on the 60 or so places I stayed overnight. I've ridden over 1,700 miles now and decided it's the perfect time to swap my tires from front to back. I'm surprised how well the tread has held up on the back tire carrying 55 to 70 pounds every day.

Yesterday I was angry and aggravated by my ride. Sometimes it's difficult to stay in the moment and not immediately become aggravated by my situation. This, I learned, ultimately comes down to how well balanced I am. How is the light compared to the dark? I need to maintain the balance, the yin and yang. Adversity is going to happen, this is not going to be easy, and I need to be able to react properly and precisely in these situations. I'm a full believer in the concept that you can train your brain and sometimes not do or believe what your brain is telling you. For instance, today I'm physically exhausted while riding but still have to get to a destination.

When I'm climbing up the hills in low gears, I tell myself I'll take a break at the top of the hill. For some reason I keep on going. I continue when my brain says I can't because of my legs feeling numb or any other reason. I do stop for water breaks, shake my legs out, and pace around my bike for a little. When I'm feeling like that, I can't sit; if I do, it's harder to get back up in a way. I can only describe it as akin to a runner walking in circles waiting for a traffic light to cross the street. When riding through hills, you absolutely need to pedal down them. It doesn't matter if you think you can't physically, you must. It's imperative that you take advantage of the hill also, either for the next one or just some extra speed for the ride immediately after.

Don't get me wrong here, I do stop and take breaks while riding. I'm mostly talking about fighting fatigue and pain that you can push to the side and power through. For me, it's years of reading and trying to practice some Buddhist philosophies and trying to apply them in my life. Everything I have read and tried has been very beneficial to me over time. I believe after years of getting in tune with my mind, body, and thoughts, I can push through some obstacles when my body physically says no more. Like when I pedal uphill and getting to camp when I'm exhausted and wonder how I ever managed to get there. Get in tune with your mind and body, and you'll be amazed at what you can do. Maybe I'm crazy, or maybe I'm onto something, or maybe both.

There is no stopping, and if you get tired, somehow you have to find a way to motivate yourself to keep going. I get tired, my legs hurt, but it doesn't matter—there's a destination to be reached every day. The day doesn't end until I reach camp. You have to be able to avoid the pain and push it away and not focus on it, and it eventually will subside.

I've found my comfort zone while riding, finally. I have saddle sores on my butt, but my butt's not sore. I wouldn't make it without Chamois Butt'r cream; that's a fact. Same for my neck and back. I must be keeping the same riding position and getting used to my body position. Usually, my back and neck are first to get sore.

A lot of this is training your brain and making yourself believe you can do these things when you think you can't. It's paramount you believe in yourself; if I don't believe I can do this, then I'll 100 percent fail. But I'm going to do this, and no one is going to tell me I can't or stop me. Physically I'm going to do this; mentally, if I can't, it'll be drug along for the ride at least. It's going to take something drastic to stop me. I say this about completing all of the bike packing trips I do: either my body breaks down or my bike breaks. Those are the *only* possible reasons for failure on this trip. Nothing else is acceptable; nothing will get in my way. That's my focus, my will, my mindset.

Another beautiful night under the stars with no rain fly. I love these kinds of nights, and they're hard to beat.

7/21/23
DAY #24, RIDING #23

Miles—109.43 (1,792.35); Time—9:09 (156:02)
Camp A Way, Lincoln, Nebraska ($32, electricity)

Last night, while rotating my tires, I noticed a rear broken spoke. Not sure how long I was riding with it because until now, I had no idea. Probably a good thing as it just would've added to my stress. And there wouldn't have been anything I could've done—definitely no bike shops around. Luckily for me, I will be going through two big cities today, earlier in my day. Council Bluffs is around 25 miles away, and Omaha, Nebraska, only another 5 miles farther. I'm sure I will have plenty of options to choose from.

The sunrise in Arrowhead Park was just as inspiring as the sunset, and once again I totally recommend the place. I got on the road early, around 8:00 a.m. I also had a nice downhill 16-mile road ride. Arriving in Weston, I took the Railroad Highway Trail 4 miles to Council Bluffs.

I decided on a shop in Omaha since there was one very close to my route. In Chautauqua, I had 5 miles on the road to Council Bluffs. Once I got there, I had a few short trails, so I made a map to make it easy on me. It's easier to punch a few things in Google Maps and use the bicycle transportation option, than to constantly stop and look around for the next trail, especially in cities.

These trails took me to the Bob Kerrey Pedestrian Bridge, which is also the Iowa and Nebraska border and crosses over the Missouri

River. It's a super cool S-curved, cable-stayed, 3,000-foot-long, and 15-foot-wide bridge, per the website. While on the bridge, you can feel it swaying in the wind, a kind of cool and kind of strange feeling at the same time. It was a really nice bridge, and it's a good thing they made it so wide; it has a popular park and trail on both sides. Before crossing, there was an interesting park, River's Edge. There's a really tall alien statue and one big seagull shaped piece of playground equipment. It was at least something I've never seen; it was really cool and looked like it was pretty new too.

I was now able to cross off my seventh state, in addition to DC, as I arrived in Omaha, Nebraska. Right at the end of the bridge is the Lewis and Clark Trail headquarters. They share a building with the Midwest National Park Service headquarters. Now something you must know, I'm a big Lewis and Clark fan. To do what they did, knowing nothing, exploring, trying to find a route to the Pacific Ocean, with the dangers, mountains, weather—everything about what they did and how they did it is incredible. Of course, I had to go inside and walk around. The worker at the desk offered a video on the history and trail, but I had the spoke to attend to. Plus, one downfall of bike packing is wondering, how long is it safe to leave your belongings unattended? The bike is locked up, but everything can be stolen or rooted through. So some stays at places are short, and unfortunately you have to skip some things completely; it's part of the game.

They had some of Lewis and Clark's personal belongings on display. My favorites were the sextant and compass, amazing for the times. The NPS was just offices, but I did grab a ton of park brochures. I don't know why but I like collecting state and national park maps and brochures.

Amid starting my new Nebraska adventure, I had to pick up an Amazon package in Omaha. I got a new mirror for my helmet and a Grateful Dead pin for my bag. I'm hooked after seeing their show in Philly before I left.

Then I was off to get my spoke fixed. I stopped in Endless Trail bike shop in Omaha after calling and talking to the owner. He ended up finding two broken spokes, so we just decided to just do the entire wheel. While at the shop waiting, I realized I had messed up and missed something while doing my mapping for the day. I should only have had around 30 miles left, but Maps said I had 55! I called the campground to see if I was able to cancel my reservation, but the answer was no. It was late to ride into Lincoln, and it would put me over 100 miles for the day.

But my stubbornness about not losing my reservation compelled me to get there anyway. So after forty-five minutes, a spoke tool, a fresh back wheel, and a paid bill, I was off again. Very thankful for the quick help—I'm glad I called this shop first and definitely recommend stopping there.

I either wrote down a wrong number on my camping sheet or I missed a trail while adding miles together at home while planning. Either way, I knew I'd regret it or at least regret the fact I felt like I had to do this.

Outside Papillion, Nebraska, along the Walnut Creek Trail, there is a recreation area of the same name. It's a beautiful area around the lake and the paved trail. In fact, I liked it so much I missed a turn and decided to add a few miles. Starting in Springfield, the MoPac Trail on this 17-mile segment would take me to South Bend. This part of the MoPac was all smooth riding cinders, a nice, easy, and fun trail.

Right before South Bend is the Platte River. The bridge to cross it is worth the trip alone. It's a pedestrian-only bridge; I'd say at least one-half to three-fourths of a mile long. It doesn't sit very high off the water. It has some very nice views; you can see down the river until it turns out of view.

The MoPac Trail is divided in two sections by a 10-mile road connector through some farmland. The second part of the MoPac Trail was even better than the first. This 27-mile ride into Lincoln had many shaded green spots with paralleling roads. I'd also ride through a few towns and a lot of farms along the way. It was a trail I enjoyed, but I also needed to get to camp. The last 20 or so miles were downhill, so I pushed and averaged 15 to 17 mph to finish my day.

I stopped at a Dollar General; I was in no mood to cook tonight. I bought a 9-ounce bag of honey ham, 8-ounce bag of Swiss cheese, hamburger buns, and a couple cold drinks. Easy and quick dinner.

I got to Camp A Way late; the sun was setting, and I needed to set up camp still. At some point you give up and realize it's going to be a late night. I don't like these kinds of campgrounds—four tent spots so close together I can almost hear the other camper's conversations. Water and bathrooms so far away you almost don't want to go. It was just way too crowded for me. I couldn't even find the water; I used an empty RV site.

I got to camp at 9:15 p.m.! I rode basically 110 miles, from 8:00 a.m. to 9:15 p.m. I would be up until 11:30 p.m. journaling. I wrote, "My stubbornness will eventually be my demise." Why I felt I had to make this camp is beyond me, but I know I overdid it today.

7/22/23

DAY #25, RIDING #24

Miles—73.04 (1,869.31); Time—6:57 (162:59)
Lake North Campground, Columbus, Nebraska (free, primitive)

After my late night, staying up until almost midnight, I still managed to wake up around five thirty. I usually can't sleep past six, and my body is still on Eastern time, not Central. I don't even have to set an alarm. Plus, I wanted to leave the campground before everyone got moving. There were a lot of people there, and the campground appeared nearly filled.

It's starting to become less humid; my tent has little to no dew on it in the morning. It's a big help as I don't have to spend time waiting for the tent and rain fly to dry or pack it away damp. Out here I can just pack it up right away.

On the agenda today was a ride from Lincoln to Columbus. My first full day in Nebraska, two road maps and two trails. It would be a beautiful day to ride, starting out cloudless and reaching the high eighties. Out here I would learn two things about the heat: If there's no humidity, even the high nineties aren't too bad, to me. At home there's always humidity of some level, and this time of year, it's generally high. Heat with no humidity, while I'm still careful when I'm in it, is not the energy-draining heat I'm used to. What kicks my butt out here is the sun hitting me constantly; that I'm not used to. I'd soon learn that out West, I'd have to learn to deal with the lack of shade all day. That is something new to me as back East, if you want, you can almost always find shade.

The first road map took me 18 miles into Valparaiso. It had a good mix of fields, farms, and busy residential areas. And being a Saturday, the roads seemed extra busy. In Valparaiso I picked up the 13 mile crushed limestone Oak Creek Trail. Man, was this a rough ride going north. The first 6 miles were tough riding, with deeper-than-usual stone. I could ride it but had to drop to low gears and pedal hard to maintain a constant pace of 8 to 9 miles per hour. A struggle and energy drainer for sure, but the trail offered a full rural experience. I had plenty of shade to keep me on the cool side while I pushed on. At the end of the trail in Brainard, before my final road ride to camp, I got water from a spigot at a pavilion.

There was an older guy there sitting in the pavilion. I said, "Hi. How are you?" as I was filling up my bottles. He turned around and started talking. I came over; it was hard to hear him, and he told me he was outside doing some kind of work. He had to of been in his late seventies and was waiting on his wife to pick him up. While we were talking, I was slowly trying to leave. I wanted to drop off and return some Amazon stuff at the UPS store before they closed early on account of it being Saturday. Then it hit me, an intense moment of realization. There I was trying to leave, and he just wanted someone to talk to.

The guy's wife showed up. He stood and said, "Have a good day. Thanks for talking to me." When he said that, I felt guilty and sad immediately. This guy was tired, hot, working in his eighties (he later told me his age), and just wanting conversation. I was too busy in my own world to talk. The immediate guilt was depressing, because I felt selfish acting for my own needs.

I'm always saying to myself, if a person can take just a little time to help someone, that means a lot, and or will help that person out, then what's the harm in taking some time out of your day? There I was going completely against that. It made me think, here's another example of me not slowing down. Once again, I can't help myself. Why, why, why? I honestly don't think I'll ever learn to slow down; I'll just have to learn to manage it throughout my life. I'm still trying, though, and won't give up. I'm going to try and slow down my trip. I want to learn to be able to enjoy these moments and times without the feeling of anxiety from rushing around. I want to have that conversation with that guy until his wife shows up.

The 42-mile road ride from Brainard to my camp at Lake North Campground in Columbus was mostly a rural ride through fields and farms. I got to see another crop-duster plane flying around. One of the pitfalls of this activity, though, is when the plane gets too close to the trail, you can taste a hint of the spray, yuck. Time to stop watching and start moving.

I had about 20 miles of gravel roads, but today my road riding was pretty flat. After the hills of western Iowa, I was very happy to ride these roads. The one thing that would start to get on my nerves was the trucks and cars not slowing down on the gravel roads. I would constantly encounter kicked-up dust, and only a very few would slow down and not create a mini dust storm for me. I didn't expect everyone to stop or slow for me, so it became semiexpected when I saw the dust moving in the distance. It sure would have been nice to not taste it all the time or get a gritty, dusty surprise when I took a drink.

I stocked up big time at Walmart: plenty of ramen, three boxes of Clif bars, Nutri-Grain bars, Pop-Tarts, a big oatmeal box, and my new quick-fix lunch, a jar of mixed peanut butter and jelly and tortillas. These two items take up virtually no space in the bag, and we all know how quick, easy, and delicious they are. I would be getting on the Cowboy Trail the next day and had read it was very desolate and amenities could be few and far between; I was ready, though.

I'm about a week away from one month on the road as today is my twenty-fifth day. Every day that I complete, it just blows my mind even more. And when I say what day I'm on, it almost doesn't even seem real. I know it's real because I'm going through it every day, but when I sit back at the end of the day, it doesn't seem that long at all. Every day I see my miles and times grow, I'm also gaining confidence. You can't do something like this solo and not gain confidence. I'd say it's impossible as long as you're able to give yourself enough credit. Now, applying that new confidence is another matter.

I think I've always had confidence, but applying or using it in my life was the difficult part. It may have been a difficult situation, something I just didn't want to do, but for me all boils down to fear. A fear of something is preventing me from applying that confidence. Something I don't want to face. But the real challenge is, what is that fear exactly? Is it something I know but don't want to admit? Until I can determine the root cause of this, I can't fix it, only patch it. There are a lot of things this trip will teach me, but I have to be able to apply them later in life. Trying to do something different in life if you're not satisfied is tough. Old habits…

I've not been satisfied lately with my life; I need to do something different. Hopefully this trip will kick-start the change. Because I'm now forty-one and not happy with where I am.

Lake North Campground, a really beautiful camp and park, is also located directly on Lake Babcock, in Columbus. It includes free, primitive camping, with water, vault toilets, and electricity at some spots. Given the hot day, combined with no showers for a while, I decided to go for a swim and clean up a little in the lake.

My tent opens up to the lake about fifteen feet away—a perfect view, and a perfect end to the night.

✪

7/23/23
DAY #26, RIDING #25

Miles—63.80 (1,932.11); Time—5:38 (168:37)
Tilden East Park Campground ($10, water, electricity, shower)

I have to say if you're around Eastern Nebraska, the sunrise at Lake North is a great way to start the day. You can see a pretty good distance, and the way the sun shines on the water is worth waking up early for. It's supposed to get hot today, and given the area I am in, I don't expect a lot of shade. The early starts will start to become more and more important each day with the conditions out here. Because I won't have any shade from the sun all day, I will need to take advantage of the cool morning hours.

Today will also be my last road day for a few days. I will have just over 200 miles to ride on the Cowboy Trail. That's only the first segment of the trail; there's another 32-mile western portion.

First, I had a 39-mile mostly flat ride, with a 975-foot gain and a 600-foot drop in elevation. The trail would take me straight north from my campground in Columbus to the eastern start of the Cowboy trail in Norfolk. It was a 100 percent rural, isolated farming area. I passed some huge cattle farms on the roads. This was also something new for me, seeing cattle farms; most had easily over 1,000 cows. We have mostly dairy farms back home, and they are certainly not the size of these farms. It must be a lot of work taking care of this much land and livestock. I passed areas with lots of wind turbines. As the land is relatively flat, with no trees or terrain to stop the wind, the alternative energy makes sense. There are areas with 20-plus turbines. It's a good place to put them.

Half my road ride was dirt and gravel roads, thankfully mostly hard pack, though. Some places I really had to pay attention because the road surface changes so frequently out here. There was usually a decent skinny trail of packed-down rocks to follow on these roads. But immediately on both sides is deeper stone, which tests how good your tires are. I felt my back slipping a couple times.

One good thing about the gravel roads is I'm getting a better feel for the bike and my tires. I can see and feel the gravel going through the tread and being pushed to the side. I never see stones in my front tire between the treads either. I know it's saved me a few times when I literally feel my back tire slide but I stay upright. I know if the tread had gotten loaded with stone, I would've most likely gone down at least once. I really like these tires, so far.

I made it to Ta-Ha-Zouka Park in Norfolk and the start of the famous Cowboy Trail. I've been a Rails to Trails Conservancy member for years and remember reading a few articles about this trail. I always thought it would be cool to ride if I had the chance. It's one of the trails I was looking forward to when I saw it was on my route. This will be the longest single trail I've ever ridden. I've heard mixed reviews about the surface and the actual trail. So it'll be interesting to see how the trail actually is.

Before I started the trail, I sat on a bench and took a break before starting my roughly 25-mile ride. While sitting there, out of nowhere comes this wasp dragging a cicada! It literally scared the hell out of me. It was quiet, peaceful, and then *bbbbzzzzzz*, a big wasp trying to carry something bigger than itself. Just some cool, random nature happening at my feet.

Starting off, the trail is reddish crushed stone and not a bad surface. I've never been to Nebraska before, but this area is very desolate and I see lots of open area. One great thing about the little towns out here is most allow camping at their small-town parks. A very nice and helpful thing to allow. My next three nights will be spent in these town parks. Today I'm ending in Tilden, at a paid campground, though.

Since the Cowboy Trail is my new home for the next few days, I hope the trail stays like it did today. The trail surface wasn't bad at all, but I did have my rear tire sink and seize one time. Today I wore a long-sleeve shirt and pants and may do so again tomorrow. It's the only way to protect my body from those blisters spreading—yeah, still got them. Along the trail are a lot of bridges, some over fields, valleys, and water. The Elkhorn is a beautiful river giving me a very nice and welcomed change of scenery. There were usually more trees along the water too. I would soon learn how important these patches of trees can be out here.

One thing that I can all but guarantee is my next few days will be flat. The Cowboy Trail is a rail trail that used to be part of the Chicago and Northwestern Railway, so it had to be pretty flat. That by itself is a relief to know. I've done some good climbing the past couple of days and certainly wouldn't mind staying on a flat surface for a while.

I need to be able to maintain my early starts. I'm still in areas with little to no shade, and I imagine it's not going to get better anytime soon. I get to the campground, and it's a small RV campground but still gets the occasional biker, I'm told. For, I think, fifteen dollars, I had water, electricity, and a very clean shower. It's called something else now but Tilden East Park Campground on Maps. Right off the trail and also Highway 275. It was quiet—I didn't wake up to noise as it wasn't busy at all when I was there.

There's no Wi-Fi signal here, and I'm trying to book a Yellowstone camping spot tomorrow. There are five spots that open up at 9:00 a.m., so I'm hoping to get one. Everything is sold out years in advance, but the National Park Service releases five sites two weeks in advance of a given date. There's just no way to plan that far in advance on a bike. I need to stay at Indian Creek Campground in Yellowstone to make my northern exit from the park.

I wanted to go no rain fly, but there's possible rain around 1:00 a.m. to 2:00 a.m. I get very spotty Wi-Fi, so it's hard to stay updated. I'll go to sleep without it but keep it ready to go inside my tent just in case.

Sometime right around that time, I get woken up by thunder. I sit up and fumble around for my headlamp. I get the fly, put on my sandals, and hurry outside. I'm stumbling around in a sleepy daze, not quick by any means. I'm wrestling with the rain fly and initially put it on inside out! I then get it the right way and reattach it to my tent. I crawl back inside and go back to bed. Turns out it was a false alarm—the storm just missed Tilden!

☆

7/24/23

DAY #27, RIDING #26

Miles—68.52 (2,005.63); Time—6:43 (175:20)
Mill Race Park and Campground, Atkinson, Nebraska ($10, water and electricity)

Since I had spotty Wi-Fi and really wanted the Yellowstone campsite, I asked my stepdad if he could try to book it. The five spots were gone in an instant, and I imagine it's just like trying to win the lottery, just got to be lucky. No luck—we'll just have to try again tomorrow.

I got off to a good start. I left Tilden around 8:00 a.m., and the trail started off in good shape, to my surprise, as well. After the storm passed the area overnight, the sky really cleared up. It was a really nice day—blue skies, and it did start to get hot out. It topped out today in the low nineties.

This day would at least be spent entirely on the Cowboy Trail. It would come down to the trail conditions whether I could stay on the trail all day or not. I was aware that I would have at least two detours today. The camp host was telling me that early on in the day, I'd encounter two bridges that were out. He also seemed concerned that I was going to ride about 70 miles to Atkinson in this heat. He thought I should stop around the 50-mile mark, in the town of O'Neill. I listened to his concerns; I honestly gave it consideration. He also told me about camping in O'Neill at the town park. So I figured I'd keep that as an option and just see how it goes. Of course, I eventually finished up my day in Atkinson, but you probably could've guessed that by now.

When the locals tell you about the weather patterns, roads, anything when you're in an unfamiliar territory, you'll be way better off listening and remembering their words. Whether you decide to take it or not, it's always valuable. Locals would continue to help me more than I could have ever imagined on this trip across the country.

The trail is all crushed limestone, with varying levels of depth. Also, watch out for the tire-grabbing quickstone, as I call it. The stone only froze my tire a couple of times, but it's certainly something to pay attention to. For me it was a slow or leisurely pace all day because of the surface. But overall, I probably averaged 10 miles per hour, which is a little slower for me than my speed on hard-packed limestone. I did notice the trails become nicer coming and going into the trail towns. After struggling through some of the deeper parts, I really appreciated this.

My first detour was within the first hour, I believe: there was a bridge completely missing over the Elkhorn River, outside of Neligh. Too wide and probably too deep to walk back and forth a few times with the bike and gear through the water. It wouldn't matter if it took a few trips—I love getting in the water—but it just wasn't safely possible. I turned around and wound up on Highway 275 about 6 miles into the town of Neligh.

One very nice thing about the trail is every town has a sign announcing itself on the trail. It includes the town name, miles to next town, the trail map, and amenities in town—very helpful out here. These are also important signs to pay attention to, particularly the miles to the next town. You do *not* want to get stranded out here, especially alone; it potentially could get very serious as there isn't anyone out here.

The biggest thing was the constant beating down of the sun. There is no escape from its reach or wrath. There is no shade on the trail besides the occasional tree. Every once in a while, I'd find relief and have a quarter-to-half-mile stretch of shady trees. It got up to ninety-one degrees today, with only a little reprieve from the occasional helpful and sympathetic clouds.

I know toward the end, I was feeling dehydrated and a little out of it. It's 100 percent a different animal biking out here in the heat all day. I've never experienced anything like the physical toll it takes on my body. I've done weeklong trips in the middle of July, gone through heat waves back home, but I eventually or regularly had shade. I can't think of a trail back home that has zero shade at all, much less multiple days in a row.

Today I only drank two of the three water bottles, but I could've easily drunk the third. I just wasn't 100 percent sure about water at the campsite, so I had to keep some for then. I probably suffered some form of heat exhaustion. One of my problems, I know, is I don't stop enough and that also means fewer water fill-ups. I only have one water bottle on my bike frame. It's something I take notice of more as I go along. I also have more blisters on my legs in spots; if it's like usual, it'll multiply by the morning. I was wearing shorts for a few days, so now I need to start wearing pants again tomorrow.

As for the trail, I enjoyed it, even though the conditions vary and there are other obstacles as well.

I just missed the Antelope County Fair by a week I see while riding through one of the towns on the trail. I would've really liked to of been able to see that, a Midwest county fair. As I live in a farming area, I like these types of settings, the country, and the different versions of a "country setting" I get to experience on this trip. Although the trail follows Highway 275 for a while, it certainly has lots of solitude.

There was another detour, most likely another bridge out over the Elkhorn. Thankfully a sign before told me the trail was closed up ahead. I had another short 6-to-7-mile detour into Clearwater to rejoin the Cowboy Trail again.

I must've passed a monarch butterfly habitat because in this one spot especially, there seemed to be a lot of them around. I just don't remember seeing them a lot at home, so seeing them was a nice surprise.

There were a lot of bridges to go across along the trail. Most are wooden ones spanning the rolling fields and little valleys. There are fields with high grass along the trail and a lot of desolate area to be alone in. The stone seemed to be getting deeper as the day went on. Although, at least I'd knock out a 70-mile ride today and complete just over one-third of the Cowboy Trail.

Two trip firsts also happened to me today, and I can't say either of them was a good thing. I was not paying full attention while riding on a bridge and ran into the side with my bag. Something grabbed, and I went down. I was coasting around 5 miles per hour, luckily, and had no cuts, just some scratches. I must've banged my knee because that was hurting some. Secondly, I got my first flat tire. I picked up one of those infamous damn goatheads along the trail. The good thing was it happened to be a very slow leak. I was able to pump the tire 6 to 7 times and made it the 7 miles to camp. I'm down to one more spare tube, and I decided if I use it, I'll have to exit the trail and ride the roads.

I hopped on Highway 20 because I could make it to camp a lot quicker. I didn't want to change a rear tire in this low-nineties heat on either the trail or the highway. I eventually made it safely to the campsite. Even with the issues, I was still at camp by 5:00 p.m.

The campground has at least twenty spots, and I have it all to myself. Literally no one here and I love it. Changed my tube, got a shower, and then relaxed for the day. If there are repairs to be made or any kind of work that needs to be done, I like to do it before I sit down. When I sit and relax, I'm done for the night, game over. I'll listen to either the usual, or a Baltimore Orioles game on my phone, and sitting in my chair, legs kicked up, of course with a cup of coffee. I'm enjoying that after today. I also hit the 2K mile mark.

Overnight, though, I'd be suddenly woken up by a surprise storm again. This one was no drill—I didn't miss the storm this time. Oh well, back to bed.

7/25/23

DAY #28, RIDING #27

Miles—68.52 (2,074.15); Time—6:09 (181:29)
Wood Lake Park and Campground, Wood Lake, Nebraska
(donation, water and electricity)

My third day on the trail would be another spent entirely traversing the Cowboy Trail. The stone was definitely better today, and I could at least maintain a 10-mile-per-hour speed. But once again, my main adversary to contend with was the sun and the heat. It was hot the prior two days, and this day, it would continue to climb. Today would top out at ninety-four degrees for a few hours. There was definitely a heat wave rolling through, but the kicker was this heat had humidity included with it.

There wasn't much to see along the trail from Atkinson to Wood Lake. A lot of open land, cattle, and prairie fields. This was pretty much another desolate stretch of Nebraska and the trail. The occasional towns were scattered along the route, spaced just enough to break up the monotony of the riding through the same scenery. Mind you, I'm just describing what I'm seeing. Don't get me wrong, I still like the landscape out here; it's so different and a new experience for me, and it just continues for miles. I am still glad I'm getting a chance to ride the Cowboy Trail for sure. I think canal trails can be the same way: just because a trail has the same landscape for many miles doesn't mean that I don't still enjoy riding them.

There literally just isn't much out here. I like riding through and seeing these new landscapes and terrains, though. I enjoy the ride but definitely also know I couldn't live out here. I still manage to make the most of my time out here, even with the obstacles.

I did finally try out these metal rest spots along the trail. They consist of an all-metal covered park-style bench with a piece of metal bent overhead. It's bent at the top to give cover from the sun, and as an added feature, it curls down, giving some protection for the eyes as well. There are holes punched throughout the whole thing for airflow. I'm also guessing this is how the metal doesn't get warm to the touch in this heat; it was surprisingly still a little cool as I sat. The shade it provided was essential. I hung out here for a while to recuperate a little and try to lower my body temperature.

Today I was feeling the beginnings of heat exhaustion while riding into Ainsworth, where I came into the Sand Hills region. I just hope that isn't a sign of things to come, a description of the trail, sand and hills.

I stopped at the Red and White grocery store for some lunch and a cold drink and of course to cool down. Before arriving, I started having these very strange thoughts and feeling sweaty with goose bumps. I have no memory of my thoughts, but I did note it in my journal. I can only attribute this to the heat. I was feeling lightheaded but kept on telling myself to keep going. You've got to make it to the next town, I said to myself. I can't explain my reasoning, but I can say heat was only partly to blame here. This problem, I believe is more deeply rooted somewhere else in my mind.

I was going to stop earlier but I came to a sign that stated "Trail closed to public." I had to exit the trail; I didn't want to pass the town and then backtrack on the trail into town. So I decided to take Highway 20 for a short distance until I could regain the trail. I had no idea why the trail had been closed or how long it would remain so. I got on Highway 20 until I figured the trail was open again. And by then I was closer to the next town over from the one I had planned to camp at.

I made it to camp at the town park in Wood Lake. I was the only one at first, but after a couple hours, another biker showed up. He was riding eastward, and we shared some good trail tips and camping spots. Tomorrow I'll wrap up the eastern section of the Cowboy Trail in Valentine. I've got about 25 to 30 miles to go on the trail. Wood

Lake is a very small town. The town park offers an electrical outlet, water, and a bathroom. Make sure the sprinklers are turned off before going to sleep, though.

Today I randomly checked the Indian Creek Campground at Yellowstone and happened to see an A (available) in the sea of Rs (reserved) on the site list. I needed a spot on August 28 as this is the northernmost campground closest to the north exit. I saw that A and immediately booked it. I can only assume someone canceled and it opened up. It wasn't open before; I just got extremely lucky.

About the extra 20 miles I decided to do: That's not something I can continue to do. I got here, obviously, but I don't think it was the smart thing to do. I can't keep pushing myself as often as I do. Now it gets more into isolated, empty places, and I just can't do it. It's not smart, it's not good, and it will eventually lead me to making a mistake or doing something I normally wouldn't because I'm not thinking clearly.

The bugs at camp are attacking me nonstop, it feels like. Between the bug bites and the blisters, I don't know how long it'll take to clear up. These blisters are getting out of control again, and the only help, it seems, is covering up all day.

I just want to escape from the sun, to hide for a while. Now I understand why the guy at camp was the first person I have seen in two days. I have literally seen nobody riding the Cowboy Trail since I started. I get it: the heat lately has been almost unbearable, and I can see why some people would avoid the trail. Even with the heat, I'm still glad to be out here riding it.

Tomorrow I really want to start before 8:00 a.m.; it seems to be more important lately to start as soon as possible. I don't know if I can take another day in the heat. It's still seventy degrees at 9:30

p.m., and I know I'll be turning and sleeping on the ground tonight. I have a hard time falling asleep when I'm sweating lying down.

After I wrap up the trail tomorrow, I have a long road ride. I'm assuming or hoping to have a little more shade on the roads. I would find out tomorrow that was just me hoping.

★

7/26/23

DAY #29, RIDING #28

> Miles—61.91 (2,136.06); Time—4:42 (186:11)
> Cody Park, Cody, Nebraska ($10, water and electricity)

I did wake up and pack early for the ride today. I was ready to head out by seven thirty. As I was walking to the road, I noticed my front tire was flat. I was all packed up, so for some reason I just tried pumping it up. I waited for about five minutes, and no air left the tire. I decided to try it out; somehow that single inflation lasted all day—very odd. I decided since I got a flat at camp, that between the goatheads on the trail and only having one more spare tube, I'd try to get the most out of this current tube. I'd replace it if it went flat again or when I could buy more tubes.

It appears my first round of the Cowboy Trail is over after the 24 miles to Valentine. The trail continues for another 20-plus miles, but the conditions aren't suitable for my bike. I tried for about a quarter mile, but it was obvious I couldn't continue.

This brought me to a bigger town, Valentine. No bike shops, not a lot of places to find bicycle parts, but there were a few places to check out. I eventually went to the True Value, and they had some bike supplies. They had three tubes my size, so I just bought them all. Knowing I already had one to replace, I would now be safer with two extras. Now I'm in good shape, and the chain I'll replace next chance I get; it's just starting to wear and stretch according to my chain tool.

Back on the trail, it would get even hotter today, reaching 97 degrees. I would luck out by starting early and by having 40 to 45 miles of much easier and faster riding roads. I figured I would be able to really move if needed.

I also hadn't seen anyone still on the trail, and I wouldn't that day. Every smart person was standing over their AC units at home, not out riding bikes. Right after the Valentine town sign—"Small Town, Big Adventure"—is one of the trail's surprise gifts.

Sometimes I get these surprises while riding that completely blow me away. If I had just been planning a trip on the Cowboy Trail, I would have seen it prior, but as I was planning a much longer trip, I didn't. I skim over my entire route to make sure all roads and trails connect. If I'm not zoomed in close enough, I miss these on Maps or don't realize how big something is. Or I just completely forgot about something—believe it or not, that happens.

The Niobrara River Bridge was such a beautiful sight to see. It was probably even more special to see as the last 200 miles had been almost all the same. It's an original (looks like it at least) steel railroad bridge, with new wooden decking over the frame. Amazingly it's only a quarter-mile long and 150 feet high; it stretches and seems much longer both ways. The bridge is high above the trees, and the clear sky offered me a view as far as I could see. The Niobrara River was big and wound through the beautiful, green, rolling hills that also swallowed it up. I took a couple minutes here as this was such a wonderful surprise after an exhausting trail ride. A reward for the hard work, all thanks to the Cowboy Trail and the town of Valentine.

Next up was the 20 miles on Highway 20 to Cody. The Nebraska byway is called Bridges to Buttes. Given where it's heading and all the bridges I've crossed, its name is an obvious choice. The scenery hasn't changed much, though; it's still a lot of vast, beautifully unused open space of field and prairie.

Right before the town of Kilgore, I entered the mountain time zone. I gained an hour in the day. But, more up my alley, I also gained earlier mornings and nights. I honestly actually enjoy getting up early and starting my daily adventure before eight. And now I can start an hour earlier, no rest for the wicked.

I did see some more of these newly discovered (for me) monarch butterflies along the way. One insect stood out, though, and I kept seeing it all over the road. It looked like a supersize grasshopper. But when I stopped and took a look at one, it also almost looked like it was suited in armor. The one I took pictures of was also missing one back leg. Strange and cool-looking at the same time.

Along the slight incline to Cody, I was so far north in Nebraska, I was 20 miles south of the South Dakota border. Also, I started seeing more signs for some Indian reservations (Rosebud and Pine Ridge) in South Dakota. The riding wasn't bad at all, and I was able to fly on the roads. It was a much easier ride immediately, and I didn't have to pedal as hard but could almost double my speed on the road.

If I'm on a road ride, I will push slightly depending on traffic and road conditions. I may want off the roads because of traffic, and on these long trips, it's also very nice getting to camp early. There are a few reasons to try to take advantage of a smooth paved road surface. The rolling hills along the way are certainly a welcomed sight. It also really spreads seamlessly across the landscape of the land as a whole. Not a lot of flat land out here, nothing huge here, just little hills.

Arriving in the small town of Cody, I was told about the student-run Circle K market. It's a short walk, only a minute or two from camp, too. Students from the high school run it, and they have a good selection for being such a small-town store. I bought a couple of cold drinks, a single mac and cheese cup, and a can of chicken breast. I would also return before they closed for my customary ice cream since it was available within walking distance.

With the time change, the early start, the road, et cetera, I was at camp by 1:00 p.m.! I decided to make ramen burritos the other night, so today would just be something simple and I'd split the chicken between lunch and dinner. For both meals, I had two packages of ramen, made the mac and cheese, mixed that with the chicken, and added some crushed Fritos. I mixed it all together and given that hot water was the only thing cooking it, it was a good meal. After the riding, this was needed, and it's always nice to have something close to camp like this was. If you know about this ramen cooking and the burritos, well, then hopefully you have made changes in your life as well and moved on. I hope those days are behind us both.

Tomorrow will be another scorcher, pushing the thermostat possibly up to triple digits, with the rare humidity out here amid the heat wave. I already booked myself a hotel because of the recent heat. Another early start is important as ever as I want as many miles done before noon—ideally before eleven. I have a slightly longer ride tomorrow, but a lot of that is traversing the shoulders of these Nebraska roads. I'll be dreaming of the AC tomorrow, tonight.

7/27/23

DAY #30, RIDING #29

Miles—69.72 (2,205.78); Time—6:05 (192:16)
Nebraskaland Motel, Rushville, Nebraska ($50)

I did manage to get an early start, even though I had to change the front tube. Why I decided to wait and see if the tire would go flat again I can't say. I guess I was filled with hope rather than what would really happen. The tire went flat before, it needed replaced. Nothing good could've happened trying to chance it and ride with that tube. Point is, I should've changed it last night. I must've been ready to go at sunrise because I still managed to start pedaling by 7:00 a.m.

That was great because today would be the final day in this sweltering heat wave. With three-fourths of my riding today on the road, I figured I could control my speed easier if it really got hot. I would have about 50 to 55 miles to go to reach Gordon. After that would be another round of the Cowboy Trail, but only for another 30 miles. I would only ride 20 of those miles today. I would take Highway 20 the entire way. I would basically throw out the Wyoming Maps I made, and little did I know, Highway 20 would be my new home for a while, a long while.

The sun is so relentless and unforgiving that while riding I get this feeling like I'm beat and I don't know how I'm going to do this today. Being out here in this heat wave, the riding is very hard and just drains the energy out of me. I'm only 25 miles into my ride at this point, but I feel like I have completed 90 percent of my ride already. This can create a couple of different feelings and emotions. At first it causes me concern because it makes me question if I can get to camp today or how I'll ever get through the West. At this point a person will either give in to the struggle or keep pedaling. There are no options here—I must keep on going. I'm not in any trouble or pushing myself too much; it's just the initial wall I hit and need to break through. I think about just slowly pedaling until I can stop for a break. I'll get off the bike and pace around kicking my legs out. Sometimes I need to pound my fist on my thighs and rub them back and forth to get some feeling back.

The road today was basically a flat route, a very gradual incline of 300 to 400 feet over 50 miles, basically nothing—perfect.

At times like this, I'll turn on some music on my phone. I almost never listen to music when I bike or hike. But when I need to dig deep down and find something extra, music always fills that need. It's amazing what your body can do when your mood and outlook change for the better.

I put on some heavy metal because I need to get the adrenaline pumping. I feel exhausted but also defeated in a way. The mental part of my ride is fading way faster than the physical side. Music brings me back to life. I don't have anything downloaded on my phone; all my music is from the SiriusXM app or YouTube, on which I search for individual songs. I really start getting into the music I listen to. I guess it puts me in a good mood, and I start to feel it inside as well. I nod my head and move my body to the rhythm; I might sing and sometimes just scream out something because I can, now flowing with energy. Music is the drug that keeps me going.

Halfway through, I realized I was hearing an odd noise coming from the rear, like sort of a rattling. I stopped and inspected my tire and rear area. I noticed a spoke looked odd to me. I touched it, and the part that the spoke threads into fell into the rim. Looking over my tire, I noticed two spokes loose. Luckily for me, they weren't broken and had just wiggled loose. I know I looked at it before I left, but either they loosened up or I just missed them. Heck, at this point, maybe I didn't check before I left.

Lucky for me, the parts were trapped in the rim. They couldn't fall out because the rim tape prevented them from doing that. So I had no worries about their falling out on the road and being lost, but I absolutely couldn't lose this piece. Finally, I also knew I could fix this at the hotel. I was just stressed out because I had never done this, and I had to ride most of the day hoping the spoke wouldn't actually break off. I wouldn't even know how long I'd have to wait to fix that; I wasn't exactly in a big biking area, and there were no bike shops around. At least I knew exactly what to do and it was a relatively easy process.

I did speed up my day a little because of this, though. I was disappointed and missed some things because of the spoke issue. The biggest one was the Sheridan County Fair and Rodeo in Gordon. I really wanted to go to this, but my bike was a concern. It could possibly be days before I could get the spoke fixed, and in that time, the potential for more spokes to break… (Looking back, it's easy to see how I could've done things differently, that I could've stopped for things like this. But decisions are very easy when you're looking from the outside and not in the heat of the moment.)

I finish up on the Cowboy Trail and make it to my motel, Nebraskaland Motel in Rushville. It's a very nice motel run by a nice, easygoing local owner who lives right in town. It's a great location for me, and you can't beat the price. Definitely recommend this place, 100 percent. The guy knew I was riding and had the AC already cranked up for me when I got in the room, coldest setting too! That initial rush of cold air embracing my body as I opened the door—that in itself was worth the price.

I unload my bike and get ready for the process of fixing the spoke. I take the tire and tube off the rim and place that stuff to the side. Next, I slowly peel off the tape from the rim until I come to the hole where the loose spokes are. I'm careful to keep the holes up so the part doesn't fall out while I'm not looking. I have a long stretch of rim tape across the bed. I stop peeling and shake out the part I need. It's just a little tiny piece, but I need to protect this with my life.

I walk down to the Dollar General and buy a worthless tool that doesn't help me. But the ladies working there tell me about a hardware store down the road. I walk the third of a mile to the motel and then another half mile to the store. There is an elderly lady working there; I'm guessing she's also the owner. I tell her my problem, and we go searching and brainstorming ideas.

The piece has a through hole that is partially threaded for the spoke. She came up with using a small drill to stick in the hole just enough to hold it. I need to guide this piece through two small holes in the rim and then thread it on to the spoke. The part that came loose is maybe a quarter-inch in diameter. This lady had the absolutely best idea, and it worked perfectly.

I get back to the motel with my two-pack of drills and go to work. With the part wedged on the tip of the drill, I am able to guide it through the two holes in the rim. With the piece sticking out, I attach the spoke in place and start turning the drill, slowly guiding the threads together. I then use the spoke tool to tighten it up, roll the tape back on, and reattach the wheel. I go for a quick test ride to the grocery store to find my dinner as it is now starting to get late and of course also to check the tire.

Today was the thirtieth day of my trip, and it's hard to believe. Well, it is and it isn't. I've only had one off day so far. I'm at 2,200 miles, in 29 days; that equals an average of 76 miles per day. That's a hell of a pace for the month, I think, and I'm feeling it. I only took that day off because of the rain. The past two days have been so incredibly tough with the heat, not having any escape from the sun, starting on the Cowboy Trail and now continuing on Highway 20. There is nothing out here besides these small towns, and you're lucky if they have a gas station or a grocery store or any place really to stop for a break. I haven't ever had conditions like this before.

Today, the first 25 miles wasn't too bad, just a little climbing close to Merriman. I wasn't making great time because of the heavier winds blowing today, which helped with the early morning heat but made the pedaling harder.

The second part was about 35 miles from Merriman to Gordon. That was where I was pedaling and wondering how I was going to make these little hills. I felt like I had used all my energy in the first 2 to 3 hours but just kept pedaling. As long as I'm pedaling, it's progress; progress will get me to the end.

Sitting here in my hotel, I start to think, how can I do this? I'm not doubting myself but wonder how I'll continue in days like this. Even the local people out here are suffering with the heat. There is a lot of humidity in the air, and out here there usually isn't much or any. I'm getting more into a dry, arid climate now.

Oh well, at least I'm in a motel sitting in the air-conditioning. The whole day I was stressing out about my tire and the loose spoke. It seems like it's been getting tougher the farther west I go, and I just wonder about Wyoming. How am I going to make it through the Cowboy State?

I'm up at 7:00 a.m. and on the road, an hour after sunrise; it's hot by nine or ten. You can't really do much about this heat wave. Just try to get as early a start as possible. I guess I got a reality check on the West, and yeah, it's freaking tough (I'll keep it clean). If you bike out here regularly, more power to you. Maybe it's just the humidity. The wind could be a problem, I can see; there's nothing out here to block it. Welcome to the West!

★

7/28/23
DAY #31, RIDING #30

Miles—61.21 (2,266.99); Time—4:36 (196:52)
Fort Robinson Park and Campground ($15, primitive)

I guess with the past few days being a heat wave, something was bound to break up the heat in a big way. I was caught in a rainstorm for the first time in almost two weeks. The weather went from soaking rain to a higher temperature, drying out the storm's attempt to saturate the ground and plants. I managed to get all my bags packed the night before. A coffee maker in my room and some microwaved breakfast Hot Pockets from the grocery store made up my breakfast. I try to eat stuff I can't cook with the Jetboil; getting variety and mixing things up is key to avoiding feeling stale in the long run.

After eating I loaded up my bike and still got off to a 7:00 a.m. start again. It was a cool, cloudy start in the morning. It was a beautiful view: there were dark skies above me, but I could also see the sun behind that, shining through ahead. I knew whatever would come my way I could pedal out of at least.

The local news in my hotel covered Colorado, so that didn't help me too much. I was at least 100 miles from the Colorado border. The rain wasn't on the weather when I checked my phone prior to heading out. From the time I left though, it was only a matter of time until the rain came. The first two rains were only a drizzle and were over fairly quickly. Then, while riding Highway 20, I got caught in a good ten-minute soaking shower. As I was on the highway, I had nowhere to go, and before I could stop and put on a poncho, it was already too late. The important thing, though, was I had the covers on my pannier bags; I had put them on earlier. I just decided to enjoy it, to embrace the rain. Nothing I can do, so I might as well enjoy it, I thought. I was just hoping it wouldn't last long; I would not want to get caught out there in a long storm. Luckily after a good ten minutes, it stopped. Looking at my pictures, as I entered into Dawes County, the stormy sky switched to a sunny blue one.

I was going to ride the Cowboy Trail for a few miles, but the trail condition was not close to rideable. So I just ended up riding Highway 20 instead. I would end up on Highway 20 almost the whole way to Fort Robinson, in Crawford. Talking with people at campgrounds, I've gained some good knowledge about the roads out here. They provided a lot of help, which I was very grateful for. In most of my mapping, I tried avoiding busy highways. We don't have many, if any, stone roads off of main roads back home, but out here it's common. Being inexperienced, I didn't expect so many unpaved roads out here. Some in Nebraska. But in Wyoming I would basically throw out all my maps and ride a revised route—you guessed it, Highway 20.

The ride from Rushville to Crawford was very nice and easygoing with good shoulders, which I was happy to see. I passed a lot of historical signs along the way. I was getting into some more historical Indian territory, American settlements, and because of that eventual war sites. It was a lot of vast, open space. It would be a short, easy day riding, with only 60 miles on the road. It started out with a decline and eventually climbed back up, sort of like a bowl. About 600 feet up and down, well, more like down and then back up.

The reason I didn't mind the rain was I knew it would keep the temperature down and, hopefully, drive away the humidity. My bike also seemed like it was running so smoothly that day. I just rolled through my climbs and the rest of the day. I guess maybe I was in a better mood, less stressed, so that impacted the rest of my day. Good head space equals a good ride. No stress equals fun, pleasure.

I had plenty of time, so I stopped in Chadron at the post office. I've been accumulating more brochures and pamphlets. I mailed these home, along with some other papers I was done with and a couple of random things. I probably shipped out five pounds and freed up more space.

One of the greatest parts of riding so far has been seeing the transformation of America and its many landscapes. Today I'm in the butte part of the Bridges to Buttes byway. Highway 20 is now called the Chief Crazy Horse Memorial Highway. I'd say now I'm officially in the West. The prairies and small hills are now small mountains, plateaus, and buttes. It's an incredible thing to see, especially from the slow pace of a bicycle. It's all exciting for me; I feel like I'm entering a new ecosystem. Everything is now looking different, and it's an exciting change. I'm also fearing the West in a way, well, not fearing, but I know I'm going to probably be climbing huge mountains, and that goes through my mind. In my mind, I assume the West is all big mountains, that nothing is flat there. I try not to think about the past few days and not really climbing too much. I need to shut these thoughts out and concentrate on today.

I liked the new scenery today, but most of all I enjoyed the high of only eighty-eight degrees. So much better overall today as far as riding conditions. I decided to stay at Fort Robinson State Park Campground. It was right off the highway and had fifteen-dollar primitive sites. The amount of history that happened here is mind-blowing. The fort was relocated here in 1874 and was at the center of the Indian Wars. Crazy Horse, the Oglala chief, surrendered here May 6, 1877, and sadly was also killed while in custody on these grounds only a few months later. A major battle was fought here against the Cheyenne in 1879. Later it was the world's largest remount depot and even later a German POW camp.

There are plenty of historical markers and plaques to read while walking around this huge property. I also took a nice bike trail into the campground. Some camping spots need to be watched out for here. I always choose a spot far away or by itself; I like the privacy and quietness. When I got set up in my small, separate three-site area, there were so many mosquitoes I had to retreat inside my tent. I was the only one in this area, so I switched sites, which did help a little bit.

While walking to get water, I passed an area that was crowded but didn't notice any bugs. But a couple of the campers had fires going already, so I'm sure that all combined to help. I got back and of course forgot about the OFF! bug spray I bought! It got better as the night went on.

I stopped at a grocery store in Crawford and bought some quick dinner supplies. My limited choice came down to ham, pepperoni, Colby jack cheese, tortillas, and some knockoff Oreos. Quick and easy, and a good change from the Ramen.

Tomorrow I will enter Wyoming and, I'm guessing, the hardest part of my trip. I'll say I'm a little nervous and worried about riding, but I'm so excited for Yellowstone National Park. Right now I'm planning on being there three days.

My mental state bounces up and down with my confidence in completing my trip. Today with my bike rolling along, and the more manageable heat and humidity, I feel great compared to yesterday. I know I can do this, but when times are tough, it's easy to come down hard on myself. I almost demand perfection and optimal performance while riding. I think that comes from me being a machinist and needing to produce perfect, in tolerance, parts every time, in everything that I make.

The zipper on one of my pannier bags broke off today, resulting in losing a little space. Tomorrow, Wyoming, and knocking off Nebraska brings me to eight states and DC.

7/29/23
DAY #32, RIDING #31

Miles—59.88 (2326.89); Time—4:42 (201:34)
Prairie View RV and Campground, Lusk, Wyoming
($20, water and electricity)

Very early this morning, I had a midnight rainstorm drill. This was a complete surprise to me as I had my rain fly off. I also didn't have it ready to go either. So being woken up by thunder and a very slight drizzle was a good thing. Fumbling around, I found my way out of my sleeping bag and located my headlamp in my overhead storage space. Then I dug out my rain fly and a tent stake. I got out of the tent and attached the rain fly. It ended up raining for almost thirty minutes. This was the third time I encountered an overnight rain and needed to put on some cover.

I started off with a good high climb for 6 to 7 miles to get out of the long, deep valley I was in. My 60 mile day to Lusk, Wyoming, would be almost split evenly between the two states, with a slight edge to Nebraska. I was starting to see more large mountain ranges in the far distance as the landscape was still transitioning. The ride itself was a breeze, with only a few smaller hills to climb and then fly down. With the road surface, the tires, and everything else, I could really get some high speeds going downhill. Coming down one hill, I got up to 28 miles per hour—that was really, really fast with the weight I was carrying. It would only take one thing, and I'd be potentially done, trip over, at that speed. But I do enjoy riding at the low, controlled 20 to 23 miles per hour range. The more I was on the roads, the more my confidence and ability on them increased.

I also noticed now the road surface seems to make a difference and affect my riding. Coming out of Fort Robinson, the road was blacktop. I think my tires stick more to this surface, creating more resistance in pedaling at 12 miles per hour. Then the road changed to a hard pebbled stone surface. I felt I was pedaling with roughly the same effort but could go 14 to 15 miles per hour. Whether I'm right, just crazy or there's another explanation, I had my preferred pebbled surface for the rest of the day.

I entered Sioux County, still in Nebraska, and was loving the new views. I came across a marker for the Cheyenne Outbreak and was just trying to imagine what this was like back then. I can't imagine coming out here in the beginning, trying to establish a presence. All the unknowns and dangers—it blows my mind how incredibly tough, and brave these people were.

There are farms, or I should say ranches, now out here. I see a lot of grazing livestock in the fields. Other than that, it's still those endless fields, which are now prairies that extend as far as the eye can see.

I entered Wyoming to a very blue, warm, nice, relaxing scene, as if from a postcard. Little did I know this would become my favorite state to ride through and visit (maybe a close tie with Washington).

I cross the state line on good old Highway 20 and enter into the sprawling metropolis of Van Tassell, Wyoming. The sign for the town lets me know that 22 people call this place home and it has an elevation of 4,736 feet. The elevation makes sense as I've had more climbing lately overall. I assume it all comes down to the Continental Divide, but that's just an assumption. The land in Wyoming today was surprisingly very, very flat. An ever-so-gradual climb the whole day—I would hardly feel myself topping out at 5,015 feet in Lusk, my camping spot. I have to mention how nice, clean, and good-riding the shoulders were out here. Thanks, Wyoming.

I followed a train track most of the day. I see a good amount of trains out here in the Midwest and West. After passing into Node, which doesn't even bother to list a population, I dropped down to 4,935 feet. I came across what must've been a catastrophic train crash. A bunch of train cars twisted up, some peeled open like a sardine can, completely mangled up. There was a pile of wheels and axles—must've been thirty-plus lying there. It's amazing seeing steel that thick twisted and wrecked like a piece of flimsy, lightweight aluminum.

Starting in Wyoming today brought me some excitement and nerves. All I knew was my assumptions, and that was huge mountains and hard riding; boy, was I ever wrong. I've had to basically reroute my trip to stay on Highway 20. I've learned so much from talking to the people out here about the roads and getting around. That part has been amazing and so helpful. I can't put words to how valuable that information was to me. Now I should not have any more unpaved roads to deal with.

I remember talking to a guy at a campground and just realizing for the first time how wrong I was about the West. He was from Wyoming, and I showed him a few of my maps. He knew the towns I was naming and was exactly the person I was hoping to happen upon. Basically, in my maps through Wyoming, by avoiding Highway 20, I was on "roads" that were mostly dirt ranch roads. He told me that there really aren't many secondary roads like I was used to in Pennsylvania. Some roads just lead to people's property or are used by ranchers to access various areas of their property. He told me just stay on Highway 20, that "We're used to watching for animals anyways." That just made everything so much easier. Just stay on

Highway 20 West—I can handle that. I would take it the whole way into Yellowstone. And for the record, I wouldn't have tried those "roads" after arriving at them, I hope.

After an extremely fast and early day, I was at camp by 1:00 p.m. I went 61 miles today, and my readout said my tires were spinning for only 4 and 3/4 hours. I definitely crushed it today. One thing I realize is I don't like stopping on the road out here, literally on the road, because there's nothing around.

I stayed at Prairie View Campground in Lusk, and if I'm mentioning it, you know by now, I recommended it. Great price—even gave me a deal for biking—and the facilities are very nice and super clean. You can do laundry, of course take a shower, and there is water and electricity at each site. The bathrooms were pristine, very clean, which delivered a great experience. The couple that runs it are also first-class. I had a good conversation with the guy while checking in. His wife took the time to look into something for me that I wanted to know about in town also.

Coming through Lusk, I passed the Niobrara County Fairgrounds, home to the legend of Rawhide, and noticed they were setting up for something later on. The Legend of Rawhide is actually a sort of grisly tale I never imagined; I just knew the theme song. A pioneer was determined to kill the first Indian he ran across. The victim turned out to be a princess from the local tribe. He was turned over to the tribe in exchange for the wagon train being allowed to continue unharmed and was later skinned alive.

I later found out the event was a stray gathering and started at 6:00 p.m. It was only a 2 mile or so ride from my camp. Of course, I was planning on going out to see this. The stray gathering was local cowboys and ranchers competing against each other in two-person teams. They were timed in cattle roping. First there was an auction for picking teams, and it was big money. It sounded like they auctioned picks for the cowboy teams on who would win, take second, and third, in order of time. The first auction was the most expensive, because they had first pick of the teams. I'm guessing a sort of 50/50 auction to help with costs of maintenance. I remember hearing the person who picked the third place winner got $1,800, I think. It was a lot of fun going and seeing this. Part of the trip is experiencing new things, doing and seeing things that aren't available back home. Back home there's no need to rope dairy cows, so this was a totally new experience for me. I'm glad I went, and I had a good time.

7/30/23

DAY #33, RIDING #32

Miles—52.35 (2,379.24); Time—3:57 (205:31)
Riverside Park, Douglas, Wyoming (free, water and shower)

This was a simply beautiful and perfect day to go for a bike ride. Same early start, same highway, and same weather. When I started my morning at six thirty, it was cool, in the low sixties. It would only climb to a high in the mid-eighties. Today was all clear blue skies, with no hiding from the sun. Although I'd start getting the Western heat, I'd lose the humidity. I'll ride through one hundred degrees if I have to; I've done it before, with humidity, back home. But where I find myself struggling is not being able to escape from the sun and its radiating heat.

On Highway 20, I passed some very, very long trains, multiple times. These trains were miles and miles long. One train must've been 120 to 140 cars. I have a video of myself riding in the opposite direction of a train, and the train passes for two and a half minutes while I'm riding. I didn't start at the front of that train either, I have no clue how long that one was. This was right before Keeline, elevation 5,377 feet. Not sure why or where they're all going, but it sure is a very busy train area.

My route today on Highway 20 takes me to Orin, and then I need to make a decision: I can either ride the interstate or an old highway that parallels the freeway. Out West, in some states, bicycles are allowed to ride on the interstates. I would later find out sometimes I won't have a choice in the matter.

I decided to skip US 25 and ride Old Yellowstone Highway into Douglas. I enjoyed the side road here, mostly because I hardly saw any traffic. If I did, it was locals, I'm guessing, which was good because the cars were flying out here. Don't get me wrong, 95 percent of my trip the drivers were very good to me. Out here, it's so flat and straight; I can see why this road has a 70-mile-per-hour speed limit, but that makes it sound worse than it was out there.

To do this, you need to be OK with cars going past you very fast and possibly very close; there has been a speed limit of 70 almost the entirety of Wyoming so far. You can't be scared of it; be mindful and aware, but also ultimately realize you can only do so much. I have accepted what may come from me road riding out here or anywhere, really. If I go down for the long count while riding, well, it's something I love at least. Basically, you can't let it take up too much thought, but you must still be aware all the time. Most of the time cars are at least halfway over the yellow line, giving me space. If you're new to these speeds, like me, after a few passes and "holy shit" comments, you get used to them and it becomes normal. But that first time a car passed me on the interstate with a speed limit of 80, it was a very, very surreal experience, and I first questioned what the hell I was doing.

The land out here is incredible. It amazes me how different it is, the openness of it all. I pretty much passed large-acre ranches all day, with livestock and horses grazing throughout the plains. I'm starting to see more sand and what I'm guessing is sagebrush dotting the landscape. It's odd to me to go past so much land and not see any trees. They're few and far between out here, but that all just adds to the mystique of the area. The land is so vastly open that along the road and highways, they have places with a barricade arm so long it can block the entire road in case the weather gets so bad you can't continue on, I guess. Maybe the winds pick up into something fierce and dangerous. There's nothing out here to stop the wind or anything, for that matter. One of my fears in Wyoming is getting caught in an area like that in a storm. I have absolutely zero options out here if I get caught in anything. If you're on a trip out here, this is something to think about; at least it should make you pay attention to the weather.

Right outside of camp in Douglas, I passed the Wyoming State Fair. I would've loved to visit if it had been going on when I came through. Arriving at the free, primitive campground, Riverside City Park, in Douglas, I read the sign I remember from the Google reviews. Every other day the sprinklers come on, and Sunday is a sprinkler night. The sign asks you not to camp on the grass, but I have no choice. I can't camp on the dirt/gravel RV spots; I'd rip the bottom of my tent. So I'll inspect the ground and take my chances. I got to camp around 1:00 p.m. again, got set up, took a shower, then relaxed by the North Platte River.

Tomorrow I've got hotels back-to-back, getting ready for the 100-mile day coming up. Before that, though, I have a hard climbing day tomorrow, then 4 to 5 days until Yellowstone National Park (YNP)! The only real date I have set is my August 10 campsite at Indian Creek Campground. A hotel will do me good; I'm starting to feel drowsy and slow, and my head is in the clouds. There are a few days of rain coming, but the weather changes by the hour out here in Wyoming. It reminds me of the people in Ohio who would tell me, "You can never trust the weather in Ohio, changes by the hour."

I think I'm going to look for a belt buckle here in Wyoming. I want a keepsake from my trip, and I think a buckle would be cool.

I also need another long-sleeve quick-dry shirt to wear. I left one in a hotel somewhere in Ohio or Illinois. I want to find a brown one with a mustard colored Steamboat Wyoming logo. I'm in Casper tomorrow, so I'll be in a big city and should have time to look around. I think I'll go out for food; I miss not going to eat at new, interesting places I see and pass.

It's amazing to think I've been out on the road and riding 32 of 33 days. I'm almost at 2,400 miles, and my bike computer told me I've had the tires rolling for over 200 hours now. One thing I'm realizing is how wrong I was about Wyoming. A lot of the roads are flat, and I remember people telling me that prior. So far, I'm happily amazed by how flat it has been, but I do realize I'm also only two days in. There are mountains out there if you want them, but Highway 20 has proven a pleasant surprise in that regard. It's my perception of the West versus reality.

It's really rewarding being out here and riding on days like today. The day's that get hard and on which I get down on myself—that's when it starts going to my head. Thoughts of how am I going to do this? Why am I doing this? What am I doing out here? It's not all the time, but those thoughts do occur to me. I feel it's a natural human experience when facing hardship. A good friend of mine once told me "Hardship is the pathway to peace," which I believe to be very true.

The rewards are fantastic; I'm being blown away every day by what I'm seeing. The friendliness of people, their willingness to help and answer my questions, is a welcome surprise. I've gotten help from people at campgrounds, on the phone calling campgrounds, Facebook, from almost everyone I've run into, actually. Trail magic is real, and some people actually care.

Rain is coming in the forecast, so I'll have to plan by the day. I absolutely can't try to push myself out here; I need to be able to stop if needed. There is no help or shelter if I get in a bad situation out here on the road, and that's a chance I can't take.

★

7/31/23
DAY #34, RIDING #33

Miles—70.47 (2,446.71); Time—5:48 (211:19)
Super 8 Casper West, Casper, Wyoming ($122)

About the sprinklers last night—they did go off and get me. If I had an option that wouldn't have torn my tent, I would've stayed off the grass. I didn't, but I camped right on the edge of the grass and stone drive. I got woken up at 11:30 p.m. by the powerful shots of water from the sprinklers. The sprinklers went on until midnight, I know—it was loud inside the tent, and the sprinklers soaked the rain fly as expected. I figured, what's the difference between sprinklers and a rainstorm? Nothing, as long as a sprinkler doesn't shoot up through your tent! My tent and rain fly were completely dry by the time I woke up around 6:00 a.m. This was just as I expected as well.

Today gave me a riding option to get to Glenrock and Al's Way Trail. I could go 26 miles on the Interstate 25 or head north on 93, then west on 95 into Glenrock. I opted to take the highway and avoid the interstate unless necessary. I would have some big hills to climb this day. Four big hills stood out to me, and I also remember having to walk twice. One of them was a really tough one; I probably walked a mile on that one alone.

Out here it seems like I'll do a gradual climb over a few miles, then encounter the peak. This is where it can get steep and hard to ride, and eventually I need to walk if I can't continue riding. I'll ride until I go below 5 miles per hour or it's too hard physically or it doesn't make sense to continue expending the energy to pedal.

It was a perfectly clear day riding today, probably warm or hot—I can't remember exactly, but I do remember the sun shining during most of my time in Wyoming, early in my travel across the state at least. I did start to see some new wildlife along the road. My first was this silhouette of some animal with what looked like horns, but it was sort of small. It was on a high hill in the distance, and as I got closer, it came more clearly into view. It was some animal sitting upright with a rack of horns. Something started to seem odd the closer I got. I started to realize it wasn't real, and then I passed it by. It was a metal silhouette of the infamous Wyoming jackalope. It had me fooled from a far distance; I figured it was a pronghorn.

I did get to see my first pronghorns along the road. They were off in the fields, not too far away, maybe a couple hundred feet. It was really cool seeing them; it's always cool seeing wild animals I haven't seen before in my life. They could really move, jump, and get away fast; when I stopped to take a picture, they'd always take off. Guess they're maybe used to being hunted, just skittish, or just don't like being photographed.

I passed an area of wind turbines, and there must've been fifty or more of them scattered around. There's, from what I can see, mainly just ranch land out here. A lot of livestock on these endlessly stretching acres of dry-looking prairie. There is some green around still, but the landscape is starting to turn to the classic Western brownish color. It's a beautiful land, though, and I'm really enjoying my ride.

I couldn't wait to get off 93 North. I was on it for about 19 miles, and there were a lot of big trucks hauling heavy weight. Almost all the time they were able to get over to pass me, and if traffic was coming, they gave me what they could. Only one person, I'll say, was an asshole. No one was coming, and he didn't move over; it was close, and it was a big dump truck! He either wasn't paying attention (I'm always wearing my reflective vest) or just didn't care. No way someone just misses seeing a biker when there's nothing for miles and the road is as straight as this one was. It was a heavily trafficked road for sure.

I'm finding out I love when big trucks pass me. The wind is so strong that I literally feel it pulling me forward and I'm usually able to shift into the next highest gear with no extra effort. But when a truck comes the other way—you better hold on. When I see a truck coming the other way, I scrunch down as far as I can on my bike. I try to make myself tight and compact. The blowback wind from a semi can be something fierce. It can blow you around and possibly even suck you off the bike at these speeds. I haven't felt like that, but I did experience some frightening times when I maybe wasn't gripping the handlebars tight enough and felt like I was being physically pulled away from the bike.

The speed limits are between 60 and 70, so I figure, add another 5 to 10 miles per hour to that—there are no cops on the side roads worrying about speeding. A truck passed me a few days ago, and I guess I didn't have my head tucked down far enough. The wind caught the visor on my helmet or something, and it jerked my helmet up with some force. I could feel the strap under my chin get pretty tight around my jaw. I'm surprised my mirror held on. But I must say thanks to all the truckers out there who gave me some space on my trip.

Today overall I had around 1,900 feet of elevation gain combined. I will say that I'm very glad I was going the way I was, east to west. The hill going into Glenrock was a literal monster; it was one of my walks. Going down into town, I had to constantly ride my breaks to stay around 25 miles per hour, the speed I wanted to go. I don't want to imagine having to ride up that hill, and these aren't short length distances either. After Glenrock I would take Highway 87 West into Casper.

Another thing I contend with almost every day is the numbness in my left hand. I lean and think I put more pressure on that side while riding. I know my body alignment is off, starting down at my hips. It causes problems in my back, and when I'm stretching, it's very obvious I have more movement on one side compared to the other. I think because of that, I shift my weight around and try to compensate, which causes more weight to press down through my left arm down to the handlebars, which I think causes some of the numbness. I also notice the numbness when I'm climbing for a while. All I can do after that is sit up on my bike to relieve the pressure on my arms and shake my hands to regain the blood flow. It can get difficult to shift, and holding onto the handlebars also gets tougher.

I'm worried about all the marks on my arms and legs. My concern is I'm going to have these scars all over from whatever the hell these are. I just wish I knew what caused these painful blisters that won't heal or go away.

I got into Casper and got a hotel in the western part of the city. It's a big, popular city, and hotels were cheaper west of town. I also rode two trails today, the only two trails on my Wyoming route. Al's Way was a short trail of 3 miles in Glenrock; I also rode the Casper Rail Trail for about 6 miles. That's it for the trails in Wyoming! Everything else is roads, basically Highway 20. Riding the rail trail took me away from the hustle and bustle of Main Street. It was nice, but I also missed seeing the town. Living in Amish country back home, I understand the tourist traps. Now that I'm the tourist, I want to see the touristy things out here I'm missing. Well, some of them at least.

There's so much history out here with Indians, mostly bad—fighting and war—but good too. I see a lot of very cool statues and monuments out here. The first was an incredible Wyoming Fallen Veterans Memorial. The other one outside Morad Park was a large piece, an Indian on his horse getting ready to put his spear through a running buffalo. It's so cool, to me, riding past and through this American history. The Wild West story is different from the founding Quakers' story in Pennsylvania and what I have been used to seeing my whole life. That's why it's so interesting to me out here; it's 100 percent different, and it's like a whole new world has opened up to me. It blows my mind thinking about how incredibly diverse and different our country is. It's an incredible sight to behold. Get out and explore; don't take me at my word.

I finish up early again because I was on the roads basically all day. That's something I'd get used to out here, finishing my ride around 12:00 p.m. to 2:00 p.m. And of course, I absolutely love it.

I take some trails around Morad Park to get to the hotel and check into the Super 8. I see Wally World and decide to get some supplies. At Walmart I hear a loud thundering boom and think, uh-oh! It was a surprise heavy rainstorm, and I got stuck inside the store for an extra thirty minutes. With the rain still coming down softly, I decided I had had more than enough of the excitement of Walmart and just left for the hotel. It was only about a one-fourth-mile ride. Tomorrow is a long day, 100 miles from Casper to Shoshoni with absolutely nothing but asphalt and one rest area halfway. Nothing else—no gas stations, towns, shade (probably). Nothing!

8/1/23

DAY #35, RIDING #34

Miles—94.41 (2,541.12); Time—7:46 (219:05)
Love Hotels Desert Inn and RV, Shoshoni, Wyoming ($125)

Today was one of those days when it was just so freaking tough, both mentally and physically. It was definitely a test for me. Going from Casper to Shoshoni is a part of the trip that's tough but must be done, and there are no detours. It's 100 miles, climbing constantly 1,550 feet to about the 55 to 60 mile mark. From the high point, it then declines 1,900 feet for the remainder of the ride into Shoshoni. As I've mentioned, there is a single rest stop halfway. One must definitely be well prepared to tackle this segment. My customary early start is more crucial today than it has been on any other day so far as I need all the help I can get today. I got my start while the sun was still coming up this morning.

It was a beautiful morning as I looked over the North Platte River into the mountains in the distance. I started on the Platte River Trail to get back on my route and Highway 20. It was a terrific paved trail with lots of cool statues along the way. I got on Highway 20/26 and started my day. Getting prepared mentally to ride 55 miles uphill is difficult, but the thoughts can be much worse than the action. You just got to get out and do it. Don't think; just do what you do and react accordingly.

The first two hours uphill weren't that bad, and at least I was moving. Then a few things happened, I think. One, the wind picked up, and that did make it tougher. I was going uphill constantly and feeling fatigued, but I had to keep going. For about 2 hours, I struggled to go 8 to 10 miles per hour.

That brought on the intense mental fight of knowing I had 100 miles to ride and I was not even halfway. I was pedaling with some good effort to go just 9 miles per hour. That's defeating when I think about it while riding. It makes me think I can't do it. It makes me want to give up. It's hard to push through that way of thinking when it happens. But it does happen, and if it does, I have to deal with it.

I know deep down these thoughts aren't true and it's just my mind telling me this. It's me being put through an extreme physical test, truly being challenged. I must not listen to my brain here and just keep on pedaling, knowing I'll arrive eventually.

About 8 miles before the rest stop was Hell's Half Acre, an area of deep canyon where the Indians used to round up herds of bison for slaughter. It was completely fenced off, which was a bit of a disappointment. The steep walls of this canyon are certainly a beautiful sight. It was incredible seeing this in the middle of nowhere and provided me a visually inspiring resting place. The multicolored rock layers and formations reminded me a little of the Grand Canyon. I absolutely enjoyed this natural wonder, right along the highway.

I'd eventually arrive at the rest stop, and let me tell you, it was an absolute thrill to see! I felt dead physically and definitely on the last of my reserves. I found a shaded bench with a table and sat there almost forty-five minutes. I absolutely needed to stay at least that long to recover enough to get back on the saddle again. Although there were no vending machines, I ended up filling up my water bottle with cold water. Anything cold at this point would be as valuable as gold to me.

The place had a moderate amount of traffic coming in and out. A woman came over and gave me a cold water bottle as well, which I thanked her for. Two white, skinny dogs showed up and walked through the parking lot. Kind of strange, and they looked odd too. Not sure if they were part wolf or coyote, but they left and then so did I. I think they were ranch dogs; I saw them while riding away. They then also saw me and evidently were interested because they followed me for about a fourth of a mile. I had a constant eye on them because they were trotting, not walking behind me. Always be aware of any animal's predatory instinct to give chase, *always*. An animal of any size can pose a threat, or at least bite you.

After the rest stop, I had one last big hill to climb before my descent. I reached a high elevation today of 5,998 feet in the town of Hiland, population 10. Going downhill, my low average speed was about 13 miles per hour, but overall, I probably averaged 16 to 20. It was such a relief when I got to the high point knowing that the hard part was done. I can't fully describe how good it feels amid a century ride to know you're halfway done and more importantly, it's all downhill from now on. It's a great feeling, a confident feeling, a feeling of relief, but ultimately a feeling of accomplishment. When I do century rides, I break it down into digestible segments, and my hardest segment was over.

I rode the entire 50 miles without taking a break. I hate saying it was easy because it wasn't, but it was easier riding; I was pedaling with little effort and still getting those high speeds. Exactly what I needed after the first half of my day. I did stop to fill up my water bottle and to pee on the roadside. I'm doing that more than I'm drinking, somehow, which probably contributes to the dehydration that I don't feel.

I got to see some more interesting things too. I saw a lot of metal 307 signs along the road, and I saw more pronghorns, some marmots, and to my surprise, some oil wells pumping away. The marmots always made my presence known by chirping and alerting the others. They always ran into their holes, so I couldn't get a good picture. I would also come to a single lane construction area with a stop light. There was a pilot car that escorted the cars each way. I rode in construction until I got to where they were stopped. I rode to the front to make sure the pilot car saw me; everyone definitely knew I was there. When traffic started moving I let all the cars pass me so I could get over in the only traffic lane, knowing traffic was stopped behind me. I was really hustling because I wasn't sure if the pilot car would wait for me to exit. Of course he didn't; he brought traffic down the single lane toward me! I had to find a spot to get over in the blocked-off lane. I was extremely pissed off about this; I feel this guy really put me in a dangerous spot. I looked at him and gave him a single finger, guess which, for watching out for my safety and holding traffic until I was safely through.

I rode the last 50ish downhill miles in about three and a half hours, I think. It was crazy how my mind, thoughts, and attitude completely changed just like that. All because I stopped to recover, and now was on an easier downhill ride. The wind also slowed down a little bit. I could see the sagebrush on the roadside moving when it was windy earlier, and it was blowing pretty good on the first half. I think it died down; I didn't feel my bike being pulled or see the brush blowing around anymore. A few contributing factors aided me on the second half.

I see lots of big mountains in the background now. It's a beautiful sight to see, and I know it's only going to get better. It's supposed to rain the next couple days. I got a hotel and am planning to do a half-day ride tomorrow to Thermopolis. It's supposed to rain all day from midafternoon and through the night.

It was an extremely tough day, but I made it into Shoshoni. I got checked into my hotel and settled in to begin to relax. Thinking about my day, I'd rather bust my butt climbing in the morning, screaming and definitely cursing, than to have that to end my day. The ride to start was incredibly difficult, and all I could think was, How can I ever finish this? It's a tough mental roadblock that one must be able to overcome. The mental side of a day like today will test your mind, its abilities, and whether you can handle intense pressures. When I have 100 miles to ride and I'm only going 9 miles per hour, in the beginning, it doesn't go over well upstairs; honestly, it's very defeating. As physical as the trip is, it's mentally just as tough.

I thought I knew what I was getting into, but I had no idea until I was out here experiencing it all. Doing a rough day ride, a century ride, is not too big of a deal; I'll just do it. Out here it's different: there's nowhere to go, and the sun finds you no matter what, all day. But there is no humidity. Today it was in the high eighties, and to me, that's almost nothing. I hardly even broke a sweat today. I do get hot from the sun all day, and I'm sure my body temperature rises, but I don't feel that hot. I do pay attention to my body, though, as I know these thoughts can turn into potential danger out here. For as much as I push myself, I do also pay attention to what my body is telling me. It's just a matter of whether I choose to listen to my body or not.

I don't take a lot for granted out here in the West because of my inexperience. This is based on the stories I read about people underestimating the heat out here and the fact I refuse to be one whose ignorance, pride, ego, or anything else, gets them into serious trouble out here. I take the West and its inherent dangers perhaps too seriously. I respect the West for all that it is. I also have much respect for regions I don't know about and try to just be as smart as I can out here. Bottom line, I'll never have to make an SOS call because of something easily avoidable, or at least I very much hope that's the case. SOS calls are for life-threatening circumstances and are not to be abused from inexperience. I would hate to potentially put someone else's life in danger because I wasn't taking proper precautions. Remember, inexperience is not an excuse for stupidity.

Pulling into that rest area today, all I was thinking is, How can I go another 50 miles? When you're only halfway, whether the rest is downhill or not, keeping my composure and persevering is a major mental boost. Well, for one, what else are you going to do? Call someone? Nope. An ambulance, maybe. My point is, you're all on your own out here in that regard. If you get to a certain point riding and can't continue, then you've just made a huge critical mistake. Out here, for example, there is no one to turn to, no one else to finish the ride. Everything on this trip comes down to me. No tagging in a partner to take over, no backup, no support trailer following me in case I run into bike trouble; basically I have little room for major errors.

With the heat, I sat at the rest stop; I didn't eat—no stomach for it—just rested my legs and got rehydrated. Going downhill completely changed everything around, all the cursing of my long ride dissipated. It's OK to have these hard, aggravating, frustrating feelings and thoughts; it's human nature. But what do I do about it? Will I let it drag me down, or am I going to work with it? Will I sink or swim? Out here you're doing one or the other. You're not coming up for air every now and then; you'll eventually drown out here. Pass or fail. I got to keep control of my mind, know when to listen and when not to. I got to train myself to sometimes shut my brain off and not do what I'm thinking.

A good example today was my brain telling me I can't make it. I continued to pedal anyway. Sometimes my mind tells me something is too physically tough or I can't do something. It's time to push those thoughts aside and keep going. Don't run to harmful levels, but the body is certainly capable of going past the levels the mind tells you it can't exceed. Sometimes it's as simple as that phrase "Just Do It."

8/2/23

DAY #36, RIDING #35

Miles—69.34 (2,610.46); Time—4:33 (223:38)
Econo Inn, Worland, Wyoming ($122)

A morning like the one that greeted me today is very hard to beat. Getting another early start gave me a picture-perfect view along the Boysen Reservoir—the sun still rising, shining its bright rays through the scattered clouds, just over the mountain range in the distance, and a winding waterway. Just like that sign told me a few days ago: Remember these days; they're the good old ones. Or something close to that. That was exactly how this day was, at least the riding part. This would turn into one of the most scenic riding days, maybe ever, for me. I have to now say it's hard to beat a Wyoming sunrise. Honestly, it's hard to beat any day in Wyoming, I would later find out.

Today originally I was planning on staying put here in Shoshoni because of the rain. Luckily, the rain got pushed back to 1:00 p.m. I figured now I'd have time to get to Thermopolis, about 35 miles north on, you guessed it, Highway 20, which was good because it meant I could keep moving. It was the only hotel in town here, and there was not much to do either.

On the way to Thermopolis, the rain got pushed back again to four or five in the afternoon. By 9:00 a.m. I was at my hotel in Thermopolis already. I'm telling you, I can really cruise on the roads, even just riding with a casual effort. With the rain delayed a few hours and with it being so early, I figured I'd ride another 40 miles north and stay in Worland. I eventually got ahold of the hotel and asked for a cancellation. They gave it to me thankfully, and I was on my way to see what was going on in Worland.

I don't feel like I'm rushing here. My thinking right now is focused on getting to Yellowstone and spending as much time there as possible. Since I have no real timetable, I'd like as many days in the park as I can get. I have a camp booked on August 10, so I potentially have more days than I planned. Great! As of now, if I am able to ride through, I can be there in four days, including today. But there is rain coming, so I'll just have to let the weather decide when I can arrive.

It was a good day for riding, a very good day, actually. There was partial cloud cover, but it was still warm out. Enough clouds to block the sun on and off, which I also appreciated. The temperature was perfect; it didn't really get hot but was very comfortable. Earlier in the day, outside Shoshoni, heading north, I passed a sign telling me I was now entering the Wind River Indian Reservation. Little did I know that very soon I would get to enjoy probably the best and most scenic bike road ride I've *ever* done!

Today I would ride through the Wind River Canyon. It had these really high canyon walls on both sides. Once I got into the canyon ride, the left side of the canyon was across the clear water of the Bighorn River. Also, across the river was a set of train tracks. The route was amazing, with the train going into a tunnel in the mountain. I'm thinking it's still in use and this would be an absolutely breathtaking train ride. The colored layers of rock wall were hundreds of millions to billions of years old. I even got to ride through three short tunnels cut right into the mountain! I can't speak highly enough about this ride through the Wind River Canyon. It's a very sacred area for the Native Americans. It's also the "Marriage of the Waters" where the Boysen Reservoir dams up and starts the Bighorn River. A place I hope I get to ride again and will never forget.

After riding through the canyon, I came into Thermopolis. Right before town I stopped at a store looking for a belt buckle. I noticed the bear spray on the shelf and started talking to the guy working there. I knew I was buying the spray—I needed it—but I asked him some questions. Obviously the first was, Where are the high-concentration grizzly bear areas, and where do their territories start?

At that point I was not in their area, but I was heading in that direction. They were around there, but like in most places, they were in the high back country, I'm told. I did buy the bear spray. I asked the guy what he was concerned about or watched out for. He said cougars for sure; they're silent and stealthy, and in his words, "You won't see them until they want you to."

Moving on through Thermopolis, I passed a dinosaur museum and would soon find out I was in the middle of a huge dinosaur fossil area. Just north of town is Hot Springs Park. The world's largest mineral hot springs was bought from the Indians in 1869 and made into Wyoming's first state park the following year. It's also home to the central Wyoming bison herd. I went to the entrance road, but the rain prevented me from taking a short out-and-back ride into the pasture. After that I found the sulfur springs, which the Indians believed had magical healing powers. The Shoshoni and Crow Indians both believed in these "medicine waters."

I knelt down and stuck the palms of my hands in the water. I then wiped two fingers on each hand over my forehead and down the side of my face. I certainly could use some healing medicine water. Maybe wiping these sacred waters on me will help me somehow. Before I left, I passed the Tepee Fountain. As water escapes the top, it cools and deposits layers over the existing ones—very cool to see.

Checking my directions, I see, yup, still the same old same old; I get on Highway 20. Outside of town I stopped to see the park from a higher elevation. On the mountains, spelled out in rocks, is "World's Largest Mineral Hot Springs," with a big arrow pointing to the site. Must be big as it's clearly visible far away. There is also a large T in rocks on the mountain. The towns out here usually have the first letter of the town name in stones on the mountainside.

I was moving pretty good today; it was slightly downhill and an easy ride. I was riding in the low to midtwenties all day; I even hit a trip high of 34 miles per hour for a very short time! It was a short day as I rode about 70 miles in about 4.5 hours (riding only). Entering Washakie County, I arrived in Worland.

While riding to Worland, I heard a clicking sound coming from the rear. I turned to look at the tire and noticed it was wobbling. After checking into my hotel, I inspected my rear wheel in greater depth. The bead was beginning to tear away from the tire. I'm not sure what to think about the lifespan of these tires. The bead looks bad, the tread is good still, but I got 2,600 miles on them too. I guess with the miles, they did a good job. I thought since they were new to start, I wouldn't need to replace them; maybe I was being naive there.

Luckily there happened to be a bike shop in town. I headed there after checking in and bought some tires very similar to the ones I was riding on prior. I got Specialized gravel tires, with a size of 700 by 42, just one size larger than my old 40mm. I was very glad to have found a shop right away. I didn't want to be on these tires anymore after I saw what was going on. I never want to be stranded in the middle of nowhere. I would end up glad to have a hotel because it rained a lot.

I was starting to get very frustrated now with my gear breaking down. On Facebook I wrote, "One of these days on my trip, can I just have a single day of nothing?" Nothing breaking, nothing to buy, no weather to rush through. The past few days, a zipper head fell off a pannier bag flap, the new front phone bag lost its handle on the zipper, the inside frame bag zipper broke on me, then the mirror, and now the tires. Its not that it's major stuff, it's more a frustrating snowball effect.

I would end up having so many bike issues that would ultimately test me like I've never been tested before in life. At one point, I wanted nothing to do with riding again. Sometimes I was incredibly lucky with bike issues on prior trips, but it's all coming back to me on this trip.

✪

8/3/23
DAY #37, RIDING #36

Miles—4.83 (2,615.28); Time—0:27 (224:05)
Econo Inn, Worland, Wyoming ($122)

Today I decided to stay put because the rain was coming all day. I will ride in light rain but not heavy rain, especially if it lasts for a majority of the day. There's no way to tell how hard the rain will get. If the storms get too bad, I have no shelter from the storm on the road. Out here it is so vast and open, with long stretches of desolation, that if a bad storm happens, there's just no escape from it on a bicycle. With the potential for a very bad storm with wind, rain, or hail, it's just not a chance I'm willing to take. I don't know if it's fear or respect, but I'm overly cautious about bad weather riding in the West. Or maybe the fear causes the respect.

I have to say how hard it was to stay put. I woke up at 5:30 a.m. and was weather watching every quarter hour, it seemed. I watch outside, like I expect it might change and I can keep going. I wanted to keep going and make it to the next stop for a couple reasons, I think.

First, it's so very hard for me to stay still on this trip. Who am I kidding? It's not just the trip. It seems like I can't slow down and make a final decision on somethings. I have a tendency to try to shuffle things around to make the best possible outcome for myself. It's like I'm trying to make everything accommodate me instead of adjusting and rolling with what comes my way. It's something

I think I've done most of my life, trying to make the best possible outcome for myself. I do think some of that is necessary to maintain a good life. Nothing comes easy or without action, so you have to actually make changes to experience change. I should only try to control what makes sense, though, not everything. But you do need to advocate for yourself a lot of the time as well.

Second is the money. The next hotel on my route is forty to fifty dollars cheaper. Having no income for a whole year has started to weigh heavily on me during this trip. I don't know why I don't try using a warmshowers.com-type of overnight stay; I'm sure it has a lot to do with why I tend to avoid people. I'm not sure if it's agoraphobia or stems from another reason. Maybe it comes down to not feeling like I fit in with most people, or maybe it's acceptance? And maybe my saying "maybe" represents a gradual acceptance of the issue or realization without me actually admitting to it.

I wish I could learn not to worry about trying to optimize everything according to the way I think it should be. Maybe it comes down to a few different things: pride, selfishness, ego, greed, and others may or may not be underlying issues here. I'd have to really think deeply about it, and now's just not the time to try and dissect my thoughts.

Today I took it easy, rode around town, and eventually found my way to the Washakie County Museum. It was a really neat place to visit. They had a bunch of dinosaur bones, including a bunch belonging to a woolly mammoth—a skull and some teeth. The Old West wing had exhibits about the early settlers' life and some Indian artifacts and tools. The other exhibit was "Wyoming Wildlife," showcasing some of the animals found throughout Wyoming. Some I'd like to see are the bison, rattlesnake, bighorn sheep, elk, and a faraway grizzly or cougar, basically everything there. They also had some animals I wouldn't care to see on my bike, like an up-close grizzly or cougar and this angry-looking badger. It's interesting seeing the history of the areas I'm riding through. The museum includes a lot of cool local history, and it was a good way to spend part of my day.

I'm two to three days outside of YNP! I saw something else along the way I'd like to take time to look further into. I want to stay in Cody; they have what looks like a big rodeo arena. They advertise daily shows and claim the place is the rodeo capital of the world. I definitely want to go see a show there. Maybe if the rain holds off, I can be there by Saturday.

The rain was off-and-on all day; I was glad I got out and did something today while I could. As much as I want to keep moving, this is my first off day since the Ohio and Indiana border, which I passed on July 8. It's been almost a calendar month! Altogether I've had 2 days off in a total of 37 days of riding. Adding up my miles, I'm still averaging around 75 miles a day. I'm going to assume I'm covering more daily than most might do.

★

8/4/23

DAY #38, RIDING #37

Miles—38.17 (2,653.45); Time—2:41 (226:46)
Historic Greybull Hotel, Greybull, Wyoming ($72)

Today would be a short day, sort of like a half day, only 40 miles to Greybull, and nothing after that until Cody, which was another 55 miles west. I had to stop just a little north of Worland. I only had an early 3-to-4-hour window this morning and decided I needed to leave immediately if I wanted to avoid getting wet on the way to the next town. The riding today would be cloudy and a cooler temperature; a decent couple hours I'd have starting off.

I'm used to riding on the shoulders of my new friend Highway 20 by now. How quickly I'm eating up the miles, combined with my early end times lately, has me overflowing with confidence.

The landscape is slowly getting a little greener; I see a lot of irrigation out here. I imagine no farming would get done without these pipes carrying water. Coming into Big Horn County, I continue to see farms, cattle ranches, and beautifully decorated prairies leading to the mountains in the distance. I'm also on a downhill slope to Greybull from Worland.

As I ride past a couple of towns, I see the elevation dropping on the signs posted. Coming into one of the more populated cities today, Basin, population 1,288, the sign tells me I'm 3,870 feet above the sea. I'll continue down a little farther to 3,800 feet in Greybull.

It's a nice change going downhill all day, but that also means I'll be making it up later.

I was on the bike less than three hours today and got into Greybull around 10:00 a.m.! I had a few options in town, from a $40 KOA tent site to the hotels which ranged from $60 to $75. With the rain coming eventually, for $25 more, I decided I'd take a hotel if I could check in right away.

First up was the Historic Greybull Hotel, right in the center of downtown. I stopped, parked my bike outside, and went inside to ask about the rooms available. The lady who owned and ran the place with her husband looked at the day's bookings and then took me upstairs to look at a couple rooms. I had done my research the night before and already knew what the rooms looked like and was OK with the place. I took a room upstairs and was checked in and in my room unpacking around 10:45 a.m.!

The rooms were all upstairs and shared a common bathroom, which wasn't a problem at all. There was a shower in all rooms, though, and that was perfect for me. I just had to bring my gear and bike upstairs; I unhooked my gear and took my stuff up in a couple trips. Great place, amazing owners, and of course stay here if you're in town.

I did some exploring around town after getting situated and ended up at two different museums. The town museum had a wide variety of local pieces and donations from the townspeople. They of course had dinosaur bones, local fossils, and some military artifacts. While there, I was talking with the museum curator, and she told me that there are so many dinosaur bones out here, it's no big deal to them anymore. This blows my mind; having not been around this part of this country, I assumed a dinosaur bone was something special and most had already been dug up.

I left and continued my walk downtown. I stopped at the Geological Society Museum, which was just a small room but had some really cool fossilized rocks, turtle shells, and of course dinosaur bones. I was talking with the two people working there, once again I was told dinosaur bones are everywhere and an almost daily thing. One talked about often finding them on her grandparents farm, often just tossing them aside to farm the land. While I was in the Geological Museum, they get a phone call from a town resident. This person had come upon a place littered with fossilized turtle shells, lots of them. Apparently, there's a ton of fossils out there waiting to be discovered.

I'm trying to not think about it but wondering about the weather tomorrow. I have to plan and check the weather, but I also want to try to limit the time I take looking into this. I think I try to maximize a lot of things, stretch something out so thin it has no chance of lasting long. Maybe that's just me?

I'm trying to get to Cody tomorrow, which would put me one day away from Yellowstone. I'm hoping to be there in two days, but the weather will determine that. I'm planning on a hotel across from the famous Cody Rodeo; it's also on the outside of town and the cheapest option in an expensive-hotel town. They have a nightly show at 8:00 p.m., and I'm definitely going. It has a variety of events and is something I really want to experience. I want to leave early because Cody is also a big tourist town and I'm a tourist now.

There are some things I want to see and shop for: a trip souvenir and a long-sleeve quick-dry shirt with a Wyoming bronco logo. I also need to stock up for Yellowstone. I bought my YNP pass today; it's good from August 6 to August 12. I also got a discount for being on a bike, $20 instead of $35!

8/5/23

DAY #39, RIDING #37

Miles—56.32 (2,709.76); Time—5:15 (232:01)
Holiday Lodge, Cody, Wyoming ($116)

I got off to sort of a late start; I didn't really get going until seven thirty. It didn't look like that hard a day, though. But then again, until I'd get out there in the elements, of course a 56-mile road ride doesn't seem bad.

It started out cloudy, with a dull gray sky. Eventually it would turn into a nice day, with the clouds to help me hide from the sun. After finishing breakfast downstairs, in the restaurant part of the hotel, I went back up to get ready. I brought my gear and bike downstairs, loaded up, and headed out.

I knew I had some climbing to do today, and actually it was a constant climb to get to Cody. I gained 1,760 feet steadily all day, and I didn't mind the hills. I actually like riding up hills and the climbs like this; well, I guess it's more like I don't mind it. As long as it's not crazy steep, I'm fine with something like this all day. The highway, for the most part, has been like a rail trail as far as the grade; you can hardly tell sometimes. What I don't like is wind, and it certainly got me today. I like the challenge of this ride but don't like riding with the wind resistance. Who does? I will say, though, today I'm very glad the wind was blowing north to south and not directly at me. I guess with the storms coming, the wind is following along. I could feel the wind pushing my bike to the left (south), toward the road. I had to sort of ride at an angle, slightly leaning to the right. Not that it was pushing me into traffic, but I had to be mindful of the fact this wind was blowing me toward 70-plus-mile-per-hour traffic on the highway.

The winds slowed me down, and of course I had to pedal harder. I had to put out some good effort to go 10 miles per hour, and that lasted for the first 2 1/2 hours of my day. Definitely a tough start, but the wind would eventually die down. It was a little slower-moving today. I got to see a lot of beautiful scenery. It was a very desolate ride again, with absolutely nothing in between my starting point and destination but one town. If you ride this route, I can tell you that there are no stops in the town of Emblem, population 10, elevation 4,438 feet. I encountered this place about one-third into my ride; I would not see anything else until Cody. The highway also changed its name to Wild Horse Highway.

I came upon an interpretative trail sign for wild stallion horses outside of the McCullough Peaks. It's a vast, wide open prairie landscape that goes as far as you can see. It's very flat out here, with a big plateau in the background. There is a trail here, but I'm taking this time for a break. There are a couple signs and a bench to sit on, with a short awning that gives enough shade for me and my bike. I walk out a short distance, carefully scanning the ground for rattlesnakes. This looks like a perfect area for them to live in. I'm also convinced that I can see a horse in the distance but am not really sure.

I did see my first and only cactus on my trip. It was a small one that grew close to the ground, possibly a prickly pear.

After resting up I was off again, entering Park County. I'm also learning about how all this land is owned by BLM, the Bureau of Land Management (or Mismanagement, depending on who you ask). I was curious about this fact because I haven't even seen any ranches lately. It's all just open land, government property, I suppose. There are still ranches and some farms around; I have even seen some Amish families out here, which surprised me. The closer I got to Cody, the bigger the mountains were. I wonder if some are part of Yellowstone since the East Entrance is only about 50 miles west! I also see these big, beautiful mountains all around me now.

Arriving in the city of Cody, I realize this is definitely the largest city I have encountered so far in the Cowboy State. The town sign said 10,028 people live here, 5,000 feet above the sea. Now I can say I'm a tourist in a faraway town instead of being the local in the tourist area I live in.

I finally got my trip memento; I bought a belt buckle at a store in town here. It features the Steamboat Wyoming logo; I like it. I also bought a few shirts downtown, doing the tourist thing. I was hoping to save a few dollars before likely going crazy in YNP buying gifts to send home.

It was an interesting ride through town in Cody. It was definitely busy, and in the heavy shopping area on Main Street, I just walked the bike. The Buffalo Bill Museum is here, and it's huge. I saw at least three museums and other elements on the property. There were some cool statues out front, but I was ready for the hotel.

Rain, rain, go away; Yellowstone can't wait for another day. I'm sooo close, but there's rain for the next 3 days. I'm 80 miles from my first YNP camp, so 1 more day of riding! Now it's all a matter of when the rain will let me move on. Normally with something like this, I'd say "The hell with it" and go. Here in the isolated West, feeling like I'm a complete amateur out here, I'm more cautious. I feel there are too many different factors telling me there's no need to ride the 80 miles in this weather. Plus, if I ride through it, then what? I just sit in my tent wet all day and night? Can't forget that's a long ride with rain most of the day as well.

I booked this hotel for two specific reasons. First, I did it so I could go to the Cody Rodeo; it's right across the street. The second reason is every hotel in Cody is around two hundred dollars or more. This hotel was a little over half that and is just on the edge of town. Great hotel, though, very clean, and I recommend it.

The rodeo starts at 8:00 p.m. and goes for a couple hours. They say Cody is the rodeo capital of the world. World-class bull riders come here, and the rodeo has been in operation since 1938. The Cody Stampede Park is a very big arena with an amazing backdrop. To the west are some very big mountains, with a valley cutting its way down the center, which will be my route to YNP, eventually.

Most of the cowboys and cowgirls were local people on this night. They have a show seven days a week. The rodeo was a lot of fun and very entertaining. Before the event, they say a prayer, same as in Lusk. God is a very important part of life out here in cowboy country. Whether you're a Christian or not, I love the fact they do what they want to. They don't succumb to changing their ways, like praying, because of the ways of America now. I think America is getting soft at its core.

The events tonight include bareback riding (ouch), bronco riding, steer roping, trick riding, barrel racing, bull riding, and more. The bronco riding was crazy; those horses go wild and literally seem to kick their legs up to the sky. Seeing bull riding in person was absolutely insane. The bulls were enormous, mean-looking, and still had horns, shaved down no sharp points. No one rode a bronco or bull to the time limit of eight seconds.

The bronco riding looked harder than the bull riding. Not as intimidating, though. I saw one cowboy on a bronco get thrown down face-first in the hard dirt. He went down hard and fast; he was also wobbling standing up but had a shoulder to lean on leaving the arena. That had to hurt, no doubt. These people are tough, very tough, and they put on a terrific show. It was a blast to see, and I am very glad I went. Those cowboys get on these big-ass bulls with just their cowboy hat, crazy! Much respect to all of them tonight, for sure. If you're in Cody, then you have to see the show.

★

8/6/23

DAY #40, RIDING #37

Holiday Lodge, Cody, Wyoming ($116)

With the rain and storms coming today, I decided to stay in Cody at the same hotel. Today would be my third zero day. It was calling for rain starting early in the afternoon and continuing all night.

The Buffalo Bill Center, as I've mentioned, is huge, with five museums, but with rain at 1:00 p.m. and the museum being 2 miles away, that was crossed off the list. Across from my hotel was Old Trail Town, so I decided to go there when it opened up for the day.

The weather here in Cody was clear until later than expected, but the weather in Yellowstone was my concern. It was all-but-guaranteed rain from now until tomorrow. My thoughts were, If I'm going to be stuck in my tent and have everything become damp all day and night, then I might as well stay in Cody. It's so hard for me to accept this and not being able to move on. I actually get irritated and restless, and then the gears begin to grind in my head about how I could've done something different. It's like I go into this mode where I don't consider all the circumstances. Or maybe I don't want to consider them all because then I'll plainly see that my thoughts are irrational.

I do realize how I'm acting in the moment, but it's easy for me to have a lazy mind and seek the easy way out, which is sometimes negative and usually leaves me complaining about things I can't control anyways. I guess I'll have my moments, realize it, then try to find a solution. I think it's a normal reaction to get nervous, maybe even upset with things, just as any other emotion is normal. But that's exactly it: they're just feelings, normal human reactions we can't really help. People also have different feelings about the same exact event, issue, et cetera. I personally think we have very little, if any, control over how we feel; it just happens naturally in response to interaction, within you.

What we can control is how we respond and react to these feelings. Some are easy, some are hard, and some seem impossible to control. But in fact, we are in control of our actions no matter the feeling. I feel as long as I can see and understand my actions, I'm already halfway to solving and fixing them. I certainly don't need to get off track in my head anymore.

So today I hung around the hotel area and didn't go far. There was a Walmart three-fourths of a mile away, and the only time I'd get on the bike this day was to go there. I wanted to really stock up for YNP since I wasn't exactly sure what the stores there had.

After returning, I walked across the street, and went to Old Trail Town. It was only a ten-minute walk, same distance as the rodeo, just the opposite way. The site consists of a bunch of early 1800s cabins from surrounding areas that were relocated here. All the wood was original in all cabins, and that was really neat. Even back then they made some very solidly built cabins. The cabins were lined up along a boardwalk that guided the visitor around the town. A lot of cool cabins and a lot of history: General Custer's Crow Indian scout Curly's cabin, an old general store, River's Saloon with bullet holes, an original National cash register, and the most interesting for me, the hole-in-the-wall gang cabin. This was the hideout of Butch Cassidy, the Sundance Kid, and other gang members, relocated from west of Kaycee, Wyoming. I also visited the Mudspring Cabin, which Kid Curry and the Sundance Kid used as a hideout prior to the attempted holdup of Red Lodge Bank in Montana.

There are also a few people buried here: John Colter, a hunter from the Lewis and Clark expedition, remained out here to trap and explore. John Johnston has an absolutely wild revenge vendetta story. First of all, this guy was 6-foot-6 and 250 pounds, in the 1800s. He was a trapper out here who had a Flathead Indian wife. One day when he came home, his pregnant wife was murdered by Crow Indians. This started his revenge quest, which lasted 12 years. Supposedly, he would occasionally cut out the liver of his enemy and take a bite out of it.

After leaving, I walked a very short loop trail that went around the original site on which the town of Cody was built. It was Colter's Hell Trail, named after the man buried at Old Trail Town.

It's now 2:00 p.m., and of course it was still a beautiful day. It was going to rain, but I couldn't help but think again about how I could've moved on. Once again irrational thinking and not considering everything. It's like I'm thinking with my eyes and not my brain. So far, the Wyoming storms have mostly been all the same. Hard and heavy for the first ten to fifteen minutes, then the rain either stops or drastically slows down. It just happened again now, and I'm hoping this storm moves through so I can move through too.

I'm a little concerned about a tunnel at the very beginning of my ride. I could see the yellow flashing lights from the rodeo last night. Watching the rain from my hotel door, I'm thinking about Yellowstone tomorrow, maybe. My seven-day pass is valid starting today, and I have until the twelfth.

8/7/23

DAY #41, RIDING #38

Miles—50.36 (2,760.12); Time—4:20 (236:21)
Pahaska Tepee Resort, Cody, Wyoming ($215)

CRAIG MARTIN • 201

Today would be another day that tested me both physically and mentally. I'd like to say the physical element was worse, but that would be me avoiding the truth. From my hotel in Cody to Bridge Bay Campground in YNP was 80 miles—normally very doable and not to much of a problem. But out here it's so different. Most of my breaks out here involve me standing, leaning over my seat, and pacing around the bike; sometimes I'll just sit my butt down off the shoulder of Highway 20. In some instances, I'd get my chair out and sit off the road in the prairie. What else is there? Nothing. That's mostly how I took breaks on the road in Wyoming. While it's a break for the legs, I'm still baking under the sun, and being in the sun's direct heat is no break.

Because of this, I don't stop as much as I probably should and end up struggling later on in the day. Or rather, I don't stop long enough to rest up enough to take on the miles ahead. That leads to me struggling to maintain a pace of 8 to 10 miles per hour.

I left this morning knowing the weather in YNP wasn't good after 1:00 p.m. and through most of the night. But I left anyway and couldn't get a signal the rest of the day. Normally on my rides, I could care less about this, but I wanted to get weather updates. I had my route memorized: stay straight, don't get off Highway 20. The riding would involve a full day of climbing. The 50 miles to the East Entrance of Yellowstone gained nineteen hundred feet of elevation alone. Little did I know how much hard climbing I'd do on the way to Yellowstone today.

The day started out beautifully sunny, with blue skies. It did stay on the cooler side most of the day, and the closer to YNP I got, the more steadily it stayed in the midfifties. I started on the road just before 7:00 a.m., and for a good reason: the tunnel. The tunnel wasn't terribly long; I was told about it and its lack of any shoulder.

It probably took less than four minutes, and thankfully only two cars came up to me, at the very end. Only one had time to pass me before I exited the tunnel. I was very glad they gave me space, and of course I had my lights and vest on.

The views and mountains surrounding me—wow, I can't describe them. This is some incredible road riding. I couldn't care less about the fact my panniers are bursting at the seams and hauling at least seventy pounds uphill all day. Although my back wants to speak up to that remark.

Riding past the Buffalo Bill Reservoir and its beautiful blue water, I exit the first canyon. Yes, the first canyon. Now I'm 100 percent on alert, constantly searching the landscape for wildlife. I'm now specifically in a heavily populated grizzly bear territory. I'm also in the Shoshoni National Forest, and it's incredible. High mountains with steep rocky terrain littered with pine trees randomly placed. The highway mostly follows the north fork of the Shoshoni River, so I'm always scanning along the river. I always have my bear spray on my hip, from the time I step out of the tent, or hotel in this case, in the morning.

As I will be in a tent, I'm not even allowed at any campgrounds 40 miles outside of YNP. Too much grizzly bear activity, so they only allow hard-sided RVs. I'll soon learn more, but as much as I want to see one, I think I'm actually terrified of them too.

I take a break at a really nice stop on the road. The Wapiti Wayside provides me with both shade and plenty of seating. Back on the road, I'm cycling through these high, steep walls and am just amazed. There are good shoulders to ride on along the way too, and I don't have much traffic. I also constantly check my mirror because I ride partially in the road too. As long as I can see a good distance behind me, these cars are going at least the posted speed limit of 70.

That doesn't give much time to get back on the shoulder if I'm not paying full attention.

It was somewhere out on the road this day that I had my absolute scariest road incident. I have just been passed by a car, and there is no one else behind me. I am getting over a little into the road since I hardly have a shoulder. There is a line of cars going the opposite way, with a passing lane. This lady pulls out to pass a car and gets into my lane of travel, and I can only wonder if I'm going to go through the windshield or, hopefully, roll over the hood. The speed limit was 60 or 70 miles per hour, and wow was that close. She must've been so stuck in her own world of being late to go somewhere that she didn't see me until we were playing a game of chicken I never signed up for.

I had to stop and pull over after that one. I'm glad she didn't.

I got to see some big mule deer along the way. The more I ride, the more I think I don't really want to see a grizzly out while riding solo, with no one around. I don't ride any differently and just try to keep looking around to just be aware of my surroundings. As of now, there's a beautiful blue sky, but I can see dark clouds up ahead. It's amazing the difference a mountain can make in the weather. Yellowstone would show me that very soon.

Two miles ahead of the YNP East Entrance, I stopped at the last resort before the park. The clouds made it look like there was a guaranteed storm over the mountain. I wanted to keep going, but I decided to stop in and ask about the weather and rooms. There wasn't any weather info available really, and the cheapest rooms were $215. I walked outside, thought about it, and decided to try my luck by moving on; it was only around noon.

Outside there was a decent hill to climb; I got to the top and looked on ahead. I decided it just wasn't smart to continue, turned around, and took my financial hit. I found out the room was basic, with only a bathroom and shower. I had to use my Jetboil as there was no microwave. I didn't care about the Wi-Fi, or tv but could have used some tunes and weather updates. I could get Wi-Fi; I just needed to walk down to the store or restaurant, but even that was pretty spotty, with one bar.

I settle in my room and make lunch, peanut butter and jelly on tortillas with coffee. Now that I have an extra fuel canister (I'm still on my first), there will be absolutely no rationing of the coffee. Even this bad instant coffee still tastes good when it's the only option, especially when it stays in the fifties all day. I think I'm getting dehydrated again; I haven't felt right lately. I don't think I'm drinking enough water, but I don't feel thirsty. There's a lot, I think, going on, and it's wearing me down. I do feel tired a lot more, and I think I struggle biking out here. There is usually a good wind blowing out here too. And then there's something I wouldn't think about for a while yet—the higher elevation.

This all comes together, and I get a wide range of feelings and emotions. Everything from "I can't do this" to "I got this." So many ups and downs—it's a mentally draining roller coaster. I'm waiting for the end so I can get off. I just wasn't happy with myself, the planning, and choices I made today. I don't like looking or feeling inexperienced, and I feel I made those mistakes today planning. I also know I'm certainly being too hard on myself, again. After all, what do you call a person with no experience, and have I ever been here in the West before? No, so even by my own definition, I am an amateur out here. And that's OK. I need to accept it and understand I'm doing a good job out here, but good luck with that one. I also know how fast the weather can and does change. But once again, I won't give myself any of that credit.

After lunch and a good rain, I headed out for a hike. I had heard about a trail just up the road. The resort also had Buffalo Bill Cody's original hunting lodge, which he later turned into a bed and breakfast. Outside the general store / gift shop, I was talking to a couple on a motorcycle. They were soaked, and they told me they had come through a rain and hailstorm in Yellowstone just then! Guess I did make a smart choice by staying here. After that I left for the trail.

I guess I'm not happy about how I ended up here at this place, just 2 miles from the park entrance. I decided to press my luck and said I'm going to Yellowstone come hell or high water. I kept going knowing the weather was terrible. Then I get to the last possible campground and get mad at myself, why? I looked prior to leaving, I knew where the campgrounds were, and I still think or feel like I messed up. The ride out here was unreal, with blue skies and good weather, then I got here and, bam, a 100 percent change for the worse. So how can I blame myself for being here? I made the right choice; I would've had to ride through hail! The weather will be the weather, no matter what my phone tells me.

For some reason I'm mad at myself out here; I think I'm pressing my luck. For whatever reason I keep thinking I'm making bad decisions out here, and I'm not happy about it. I don't think it's acceptable for me.

My lips feel pruny—I'm dehydrated still. I don't know what's going on sometimes; like, I lose track of things temporarily, or get slightly confused. I don't know if this is too much. It's getting real tough all of a sudden. I wonder if I've been out too long (no way!)—it's just been the last few days to a week that I haven't been right. It's hard to explain. I feel like I'm rushing and making bad decisions, probably from feeling the effects of dehydration. I stop and pee six to seven times over a daily ride, and I know I'm not drinking that much water. If I know my body, and I think I do, I'm dehydrated, and it's completely affecting most of my thoughts. But I'm still able to function. I think I'm also feeling fatigue starting to set in—mostly physical but also a mental fatigue, I feel. I just feel off. Stress, anxiety—they're starting to weigh me down.

While out on my hike, I was making a video diary entry on my personal thoughts. When I was almost done, I saw something in the brush with a tail. I literally just turned around, and ten seconds later, I saw something was following/watching me from the cover of the brush. I wasn't that far from the road, and it looked like some kind of small cat. I turned and walked backward slowly away, toward the road. Then I saw it: a fox was poking its head out of the brush, eyes fixed on me. It was probably only fifteen feet away, and it was strange having a fox track me. I'm sure it was watching me way before I got a glimpse of it. I got back to the road and took a walk along the river. I cut that short: one worker at camp told me about a grizzly that likes to hang out under the bridge. Being now in their territory, I would soon find out that I couldn't hike to far into the back country here. The fear of having animals out here that can do some damage or kill makes me very timid, I'm quickly learning.

Back in my room, I'm waiting for tomorrow; tomorrow is the big day.

8/8/23

DAY #42, RIDING #39

Miles—46.09 (2,806.21); Time—4:06 (240:27)
Lake Lodge Cabins, Yellowstone National Park ($400)

I was up early, hanging outside the store, trying to get some kind of weather update. Although, it ultimately wouldn't matter—I was going. No luck on an update. I got packed up, had my breakfast and coffee, and headed out. Before I left, I stopped one last time to try for a weather update on my phone. Success—it was supposed to rain from 7:00 a.m. to 9:00 a.m. in Yellowstone. Around seven thirty I hit the road and was on my way! The East Entrance was only 2.2 miles away but was 289 feet higher than my current elevation! But that wasn't what made those 2 miles memorable.

As I'm riding, a car came into view pulled over on my side and then leave. I'm thinking either bathroom break or animal. I get there and on my side of the road, no more than ten feet in the brush, is a bear sticking his head out! The bear's head is smaller than mine, or maybe the same size, and has this grayish/cinnamon color. The ears are rounded, and the face slopes down to the nose. It looks like a stuffed teddy bear. I'm certain it was a juvenile grizzly.

Holy shit. I'm looking around, hoping Mama isn't around. I have my bear spray on my hip, but on a bike, if I'm charged, I stand no chance. I pedal to the other side of the road immediately and continue keeping a very close eye on my mirror. Luckily, it doesn't chase me or anything else.

No time for a picture, of course; I just wanted out of there. Looking back now, I get angry with that car for leaving me in that potentially very bad situation. I'd assume they saw see me in the rear-view mirror before pulling out, but they may not have either.

Yellowstone National Park—I made it! After getting through the ranger gate, I got off my bike, threw my arms in the air, and yelled as loud as I could. This was a major milestone for the trip, and of course one of the places on my route I looked forward to the most. It was this amazing feeling inside knowing where I was and how I got there. Now I just had to ride up some mountains. The 30 miles from the East Entrance to Bridge Bay Campground gained 2,175 feet and dropped 1,365 feet. The worst part was, I had to climb 2,100 feet in the first 16 miles of the ride! It was a hell of a climb, for sure, even if I had nice weather.

Getting into YNP, I could see it was only a matter of time until the rain came. Thirty minutes into the park, it started coming down as a heavy mist. The temperature, though, was only in the high forties to low fifties; it felt incredibly cold in the mist! That heavy mist lasted almost one and a half hours, until I found my first shelter. The first shelter from the cold dampness I was feeling was a vault toilet. It had a covering I could park my bike in and also get my chair out. I was all right at that point, except I was blocking the bathroom door—it was a single toilet hut. A few people came, and I just moved. Everyone was cool; they understood and most had a laugh about it, but what else could I do? I had my cover, so I was content. Cold but content.

I waited a little over an hour, hoping the rain would stop. It didn't; it only lightened up a little bit. I was wet and cold, and I was bundled up for the high forties, wearing two long-sleeve shirts, pants, gloves, a beanie under my helmet. Of course everything on me was wet. I was bundled up with the clothes I had with me, which obviously wasn't near enough for the cold, wet weather here.

Eventually it dropped down to a light mist, and I just took off. It was cold and cloudy all day. It would also rain on and off all day. I quickly learned that YNP has its own ecosystem. The views and scenery were breathtaking, and I was trying to enjoy it as much as I could under the circumstances. It seemed like I was going to climb past the clouds. One of the highest elevations I encountered was on

Sylvan Pass; the sign indicated the elevation was 8,530 feet! I was so incredibly happy to see this sign as I hoped that this was the high point of my day. As I remember it was or very close to it.

After being out there in the cold, being wet, and having no change in the weather or temperature, I was slowly losing the feeling in my fingers and toes. It was starting to become a challenge to move my fingers. Pulling my brakes became difficult, and to change my Shimano GRX gears, I had to use two or three fingers to push the lever hard enough. Of course, having wet gloves didn't help, but it was still better than nothing. I didn't have much choice but to continue on in this already-tough, incredible park.

I rode by an old wildfire burned area that was really neat to see. The huge Yellowstone Lake, even with the gray cloudy skies, looked like it went on forever. I also started seeing my first wildlife in the park, a bunch of elk with big racks on top. They were just hanging out in the tall grass by the road. This would also be my first sight of the tourists piling up, clogging the road to take pictures and crowd the animals. Charge, my friends, charge the overcrowding few!

It was starting to clear up a little, but it would rain off and on a couple more times throughout the day. I eventually made it to Fishing Bridge RV Park and stopped in. I knew I would be better off in a room, but I also knew from my past research I would be spending a minimum of three hundred dollars. I also knew my "warm" clothes, which I was wearing, were wet. If I camped, it would almost be guaranteed that everything would become wet, and the temperature was still maybe in the low fifties.

I went inside and talked with a lady behind the desk. This woman was amazing. First she offered me a hot shower (free of charge). I said thanks but no thanks, only because I knew I had to get back out there and ride more to wherever I would camp. Then she went in the back and microwaved a small piece of chocolate cake for me! It was warm, and I really needed that—incredible!

Then we got down to business, and I asked, "What's the cheapest room available?" There was a big lodge, a hotel, and cabins in this lake area. The cheapest option, in the $300 range, was sold out, so my next option was a $350 cabin that basically came to a total of $400! Also, there were no amenities really, only a full bathroom, microwave, coffee maker, and—what I was most looking forward to—heat. I was already dreaming of maxing it out!

I caved in and got the cabin. I knew if I camped in this weather, already very cold and wet, it was essentially a sure thing I would get sick. The weather wasn't getting any better, the sun wouldn't come out, and more rain was on the way. I didn't want to get sick so close to the end, and I didn't want to be wet and miserable. This was my Yellowstone trip, after all! After breaking my previous record for most expensive hotel last night (by myself), I also broke that new mark and set the bar incredibly high when I handed over my credit card.

OK, time for my rant. It's ridiculous but mostly sad to see stuff this expensive. The average family will be priced out at these rates; I can't really afford it either. Why, why so much corporate greed? Not everyone can camp; not everyone can rent an RV, only to pay RV rates or even get lucky enough to find available sites. Bottom line, there's just no reason to charge that much for enjoying a national park. It's a damn shame that not everyone who wants to stay here can. The greed to increase profits fuels the divide between rich and poor, able-tos and not-able-tos. In the end, nature should be affordable or free for everyone.

The camping rates here are great—$20 usually and $10 for hikers/bikers—but how can the average family afford to visit YNP for a few days? You expect them to shell out a grand for a night or two? For some families, that's either just not possible or will take a long time to pay off. I feel this is all just a bunch of you know what. There's absolutely no reason to stick it to the people. There should be high-end luxury housing for those who want and can afford it but also plenty of affordable lodging to satisfy both sides. OK, now my ranting is over, for now.

I can't believe I actually paid this much for a cabin; part of me is disgusted, and part of me is relieved. Relieved since it did rain on and off the rest of the day. When I got to the room, I immediately maxed out the heat at eighty degrees, made a cup of coffee, spread everything out in the room, and left to go see some things. It was a two-bed room, and there was another cabin at the opposite end of my entrance.

The lake area was beautiful, and at least I could walk down there from my room. I wanted to go see the Mud Volcano and go into the Hayden Valley and hopefully see some bison. I started that way, but it began to go downhill, and I just didn't want to do anymore climbing. I turned around and rode to Bridge Bay Campground, the spot where I had originally planned to camp, and intended to hike to see the Natural Bridge.

I started on the trail and came across a huge animal right off the trail. All I could see was a tan rear end and a short tail. It must've been an elk that was turned away from me. I decided to turn back, and then I realized I had a mile and half hike to the bridge. I was kind of angry with myself; the bridge was a lot further than I realized, and I had biked 2 miles to get here. I wish I had seen the distance to the bridge before I went because I wouldn't have time to get back before dark anyway. I don't know how I would've known; I wouldn't get any signal until I was almost out of the park. I was still glad I was in YNP and went back to the heat of my cabin.

I stopped at one of the gift shops and bought a few things as gifts. Yellowstone also has a US Post Office, so I was able to mail everything home in a flat-rate box.

I'm trying not to think about all the money I spent today. With the hotel and gifts and everything else, I'm in for five hundred dollars today. Here I am eating ramen noodles and peanut butter and jelly on tortilla shells for dinner and managing that so I don't run out, but if I do, I can buy more at the stores here. But of course, with the way my twisted mind works, given the money I've spent in the past two days alone, I need to start to tighten up on the credit card. This has been an issue for me recently because of my current financial situation. When I spend more than I feel is necessary, I make up for it in other unhealthy ways, like not filling up at dinner to make the food last longer. I hate when I do this because it reflects self-destructive behaviors and habits that are just so totally unnecessary.

The roads through YNP are pretty much what I was told, not very good for bicycles. Most shoulders so far are three feet wide or less. Most drivers at least slow down and get over if they can. Tomorrow, I want to start early, get to Old Faithful ASAP, and try to beat the crowds. It doesn't appear overly busy here, but I'm not at one of the popular spots yet. I can tell the roads will be tough riding when I got to climb. I'm also figuring at some points I might not even have a shoulder to ride on. But I'll take everything as it comes.

I went down to the lake, elevation 7,750 feet, at sunset, but it started misting again. I didn't hang out long but did enjoy it for a little. At least all my clothes would be dry; even my shoes were relatively dry in the morning. I basically hung out in shorts and used the heater as my dryer. I'd get as much out of my four-hundred-dollar room as I could.

YNP has already started the fight, and it put up a hell of a first round. I'm exhausted and ready for bed. My bags will also be lighter as I did free up a bunch of space from shipping things home.

8/9/23

DAY #43, RIDING #40

Miles—57.45 (2,863.66); Time—4:35 (245:02)
Madison Campground, Yellowstone National Park
($10, primitive)

Today I know I won the second round against YNP; it was a much better day all around. First, the weather was so much better. It started cold and chilly, but the sun came out with only a few clouds. Eventually it warmed up enough that I could even shed some clothes. I started out riding wearing my two long-sleeve shirts, pants, gloves, and my beanie under the helmet. I eventually got down to just riding in normal clothes again, a long-sleeve shirt and pants.

My camp was at Madison Campground and only 50 miles away. However, I'd have a lot of mountains to climb today. I would ride uphill a total of 2,257 feet and cruise down 3,215 feet of elevation over those 55 inspiring miles. Almost all the climbing was before or around Old Faithful, which was about halfway.

I started the 18-mile ride to the West Thumb area. It was an incredible way to start my day, blue sky ahead and a ride along the lake edge mostly. I saw a huge elk on this strip of land going out into the water, an incredible scene. I saw my first of many thermal areas, with the sulfur-smelling steam coming off the water. These would be scattered throughout the entire park. It was so inspiring I almost didn't mind the up-and-down climbing of 1,000 feet to get there.

At the West Thumb Geyser Basin, I was greeted by this bubbling, gray-dirt-colored pool of water, maybe five feet in diameter. I figured the bubbling was from the water temperature but was later informed it was gases coming to the top to escape. My first sightseeing stop, my first geyser basin area, first hike of the day, and finally my first introduction to the many YNP boardwalks. Pretty much anywhere around thermal areas, the park has boardwalks that also go past many of the trail attractions. There are a couple reasons for the boardwalks: (1) to provide a safe trail to see everything and (2) to protect the natural wonders from (sadly inevitable) eventual destruction by humans. At that point the worst atrocity will occur: no one from then on will ever get to enjoy it ever again. Please, if you go, follow the rules; they're very easy, and the animals will thank you too. I didn't see too much bad behavior; my issue was people crowding personal space, seeking out every available inch between others at the natural wonders. I expected any and everything from the wildest of all animals, humans, so I was fine the whole time with the people, at least.

I probably took a good 1.5-mile walk around the loop trail. It was so cool seeing all these steaming, very nice blue pools of water. There was water flowing out of places, with goldish, green and other colors under the water flows. It was amazing out there, and I was just starting out.

From there, it was an 18-mile ride to the famous Old Faithful geyser. Wow, did I do a lot of climbing on this segment. I would actually pass over the Continental Divide, twice. I would gain 1,100 feet and drop down 1,900 feet over this part alone. The high point, based on the signs, was at the Continental Divide, the highest elevation so far, at 8,391 feet. The elevation in Lancaster County, where I live, is 495 feet.

The uphill riding would've been hard enough alone, but add the weight, then it gets fun. The thing I couldn't ever prepare for, though, was the elevation. Wow, was that something fierce to deal with. I would soon find out even a small hill that would ordinarily never cause a problem would take a good amount of energy in these conditions.

The hardest part, though, is when I'm breathing heavily, I feel like someone is choking me out. I can't breathe enough, fast enough; I feel like someone stole all the oxygen—it's wild. I've never had to deal with lack of oxygen like this. It just doubles my effort, and sometimes it literally feels like I can't breathe. These are some seriously big mountains, and try climbing them while gasping for oxygen;

it's a hell of a challenge, especially since I'm experiencing all of this for the first time.

From there I hit some *huge* downhill speeds. I was going up to 32 miles per hour, usually I stayed around twenty-five, though. There were a lot of mountains in this part of the park. One thing that helped was the road construction. I would wait for traffic to pass me because cars had to wait for the flagger, then start to ride. I had a lot of time to gain ground until the next round of cars would come. In the 5-to-7-minute intervals between cars, going 25 miles per hour downhill, I could gain some ground without having to worry about traffic behind me. I loved that for sure. At one of these stops, waiting to go at the front of the line was a group of bikers (motorcyclists). The guy in front with his big ape hanger handlebar bike gives me this little clap and nod in respect; not knowing what to do and full of energy I just looked at him and screamed as loud as I could "*Yyyeeaaahhhh.*"

I made a stop at Kepler Cascades and definitely was glad I did. All the water coming down over the boulders, surrounded by very tall ponderosa pines. I can't go into much detail about a lot of these natural wonders. Looking at my pictures, while writing, how do I even begin or do any of this any justice? Everything out here is a sensational treat for all my senses.

I take off again and ride to see Old Faithful. One great thing about riding a bike in YNP is there is no stopping for traffic jams or waiting in line for a parking spot. I go where I want and just leave my bike. I'll take valuables with me for longer walks but generally just leave the bike at the trailhead or an out-of-the-way spot.

I got pretty lucky at Old Faithful and only had to wait ten minutes for the show. It's a cool experience seeing it start to bubble, push out some steam, a few warning sprays, and then finally erupt. It lasts about seven minutes and goes off a little more frequently than every hour, I think.

After, I walked around the rest of the Upper Geyser Basin. There was a lot to see on the boardwalk trail and stone path. I probably got about a 3-mile loop in. It's so cool just seeing these pools boiling and shooting up water, not far off the trail in some cases. I guess it comes down to lucky timing in terms of whether you see this. There are a lot of geysers along the trail; the formations are incredible. All the colors from the algae and minerals staining the ground were something new to me. Some of these were really vibrantly colorful.

After climbing all day, I'd be rewarded with a mostly downhill ride the last 18 miles to Madison Campground. I stopped in at Biscuit Basin and did some hiking around. Two geysers went off right off the boardwalk. Great timing. One was a smaller geyser that was only five to seven feet away. It was not that far away, and the steam felt like a sauna. I can't imagine how painful that water would be on the skin. Before leaving, I'd see Mustard Spring erupt as well.

My favorite site of the day would be my next and final stop before camp: the Grand Prismatic Spring. The outer rings, coming off the pristine blue water, wow, they are a sight to see. All these colors are so vibrant and lively; they just all go together so perfectly. The best way to see the Grand Prismatic Spring is the bird's eye view from the hiking trail viewpoint. I won't lie, it's challenging, a steep hike of 0.8 miles one way. But you 100 percent won't be disappointed once you make it to the top.

I then rode into Madison Campground to find my camping spot. I was originally told of the four sites run by Yellowstone Park Lodges that have a no-RSVP, walk-in hiker/biker ten-dollar sites. All other sites are run by the National Park Service and require reservations a very long time in advance. Bridge Bay, Grant Village, Madison, and

Canyon Village are the four. I would later find out that Indian Creek Campground also has two walk-in sites that were not listed or noted anywhere online.

The road riding is crazy out here at times. On average I have a 2-to-3-foot shoulder to ride, but I've also gone more than a few miles with no shoulder. I just ride the white line and hope I don't need to bail and roll down the hill to avoid anyone not paying attention. Luckily, I didn't have many issues, maybe 2 to 3, and they were rented RVs that didn't give me any room. I've also had freshly paved road with 4-foot shoulders. It just randomly seems to change.

I met some cool people at the walk-in area. One guy from LA started from home, went north to Canada, and is just going on a huge loop back home, he tells me. Another rider here is just planning on living in YNP for the month of August. We all hung around the campfire for a little bit and talked until I went to bed around ten thirty. This was the only campfire I had on the entire trip; when I'm alone by the time it's getting dark, I'm usually beat and in my sleeping bag reading. When I bike pack, the sun going down signals my bedtime.

Today was way better mentally. I know I crushed it today, and I also saw a *lot* of truly inspiring natural beauty in America's first national park. I also hiked probably close to 8 miles. Today was definitely one to remember; that's for sure. Tomorrow, I'm going to try to find the bison before I head north to Indian Creek Campground. I'm only 26 miles from Indian Creek, so I want to go east toward Canyon Village, then back west, and finally north to camp. Hopefully I'll see a bison in that area, but I need to be cautious. It's their rutting season, and since I'm hunched over on a bike, to them I look like them. I certainly don't need to be charged by a two-thousand-pound beast, our nation's largest land animal.

One more full day after today in YNP, maybe—it's been an inspirational ride so far. It takes a certain type of individual to actually enter YNP and go through the park on a bike. I give lots of credit and much respect to anyone in Yellowstone not in a motorized vehicle. And those people backpacking through the back country—wow-they're fearless. I couldn't do it, at least alone. Well, it's hard to say, because alone I can't even hike out here. I'm always looking around, and half the time my heart's pumping faster for no real reason. I would need to get used to it; well, I'd need to get accustomed to grizzlies, somehow. There's something about them; I love them—they're so cool looking—but wow, do they terrify me too.

I sat around thinking, YNP is wild and its elevation is really kicking my butt. It's unreal out here on a bicycle. If you try it, you'll probably at some point question yourself. But hang in there: the rewards from riding are sweet and can't be beat. It's been really tough out here; it was so hard riding up those hills while I was being strangled by some invisible set of hands. At least I mailed out close to six pounds of brochures, shirts, and gifts I bought. I have pannier room again.

Riding is more enjoyable now; I think I was getting burned out. I think I was just getting sick of riding, maybe, at some points but just kept going and going. What else are you going to do? With that I was probably burning myself out. I needed this injection of YNP to revive me, to bring the fun and excitement back. Get myself motivated again. I don't know if it's the highway riding, but I want trails again, or maybe I've been out too long. I don't know.

When I had reception, I was checking my phone more often to see how many miles I had to go. Normally I don't pay too close attention to my distance to go, at least not all day. That's not me enjoying the riding; that's me just wanting to be done for the day.

I think I got lazy having those hotels and got a little used to having it easier that way. Yellowstone is putting up a fight for sure, and by my scorecard, we're tied at a round a piece. I've been feeling like I'm on a roller coaster lately, good highs and some low lows. Hopefully this trip clears some things up and kick-starts some change. I don't know what I'm looking for, but I think I need to find something new. Maybe I'll find it out here, or maybe doing this will give me the strength to go find it.

This is more than a bicycle ride; this is a journey, an adventure, this is to save me, this is my at the moment life story. I'm being honest and open, frightening as it is to me. How can I do this for the rest of my life? How can I make money off of this and maybe do this for a living? How can I just ride my bike and not go back into the workforce? How can I just ride? I'd love to be a tour guide; it'd be a dream to start my own touring company. But past lifestyles and choices would probably prevent that from happening.

Can I get paid to take people out on tours? Would anyone want me to be their guide? Would anyone even want to ride with me? I'm already touring on my own, always fully self-supported, and doing all my own planning and mapping. I don't really want to go back to work. Who does? Who knows what the future holds?

Maybe this book will take off, and I can ride and write. Tour around the country or the world and write about my travels. The way the world is today, you just never know. All you need is an idea to take off, and the sky is the limit. There are things a lot worse than my boring writings out there making money.

Now that the weather is nice, I don't want to leave Yellowstone, perhaps ever. I might just have to stay an extra day…

8/10/23
DAY #44, RIDING #41

Miles—30.75 (2,894.41); Time—2:27 (247:29)
Indian Creek Campground, Yellowstone National Park
($20, primitive)

Today was my last full day at YNP, and I had a very good day all planned out. I was going to ride 14 miles north to Norris and see the Norris Geyser Basin and head east from there to the Canyon Village area to try and find the bison, then back to Norris. From there it's 13 miles north and downhill to my campground. I would have about 900 feet to climb right out of the gate, but then my ride would peak and level out before my downhill cruise to home base.

It was a great start to the day—beautiful day, actually, with sun and a mildly warm temperature. I ate my three packs of oatmeal and drank my two cups of coffee, then started my day. I usually buy the oatmeal variety packs; I worry about big containers or bags coming loose in my bag, so I just eat a few packs a day. Plus, I like to grab multiple flavors and make my own creations. Got to do what I got to do to keep things fresh on the trip. Variety in life prevents the daily routine from becoming stale.

I started out on the road to some spectacular views, the Gibbon River set against some high peaks and cool-looking mountains. The surprise of a gray cloudy mess swept over and, thankfully as quickly it blew away. Then it was back to the perfect near cloudless day. Then it happened.

About 5 miles into my ride, I'm climbing this mountain, then all of a sudden, my rear tire completely seizes up. Oh shit! I'm at a very bad spot for this too. To my right is Gibbon Falls, this huge, beautiful cascade attraction. I have no shoulder, maybe a foot, with a four-foot-high stone and cement wall. On the other side is a paved walkway to view the cascade, which is the only good thing going for me right now. I hop off, lean my bike against the wall, and inspect the rear end. Oh no, now the opposite screw snaps off and does the exact same thing as the other side did: become recessed inside the frame.

Shit, shit, shit is all I can think as I rush to get off the road. I am sort of on a curve as the road wraps around the mountain to the left, a semiblind spot with no shoulder. I unhook my bungee cords and toss my sleeping bag over. Cars are passing me by this time, and like I said, I might have a foot, but really probably less. It doesn't matter; I just need to get off the road *now*. I unhook my bags and toss those over as well. Now I pick up my bike, put it on the wall, and while balancing that, climb up too. I hop off onto the quiet safety of the walkway trail.

I'm close to half losing my mind because this is what I fear probably the most: breaking down with no one along to help if something happens. I know I'm in a packed national park with lots of people, so it's not as bad as my mind tells me. I think I'm amped up from it happening in such a potentially dangerous location. Not to mention I had no warning; imagine if I had been flying downhill at 25 miles per hour. I am rushing; I have to, so I won't get hit by a car or RV.

At least I got a good idea as to how I react in that moment to a randomly dangerous situation. I took care of what needed to be done, no hesitation, but after I was safe, it turned into a mental minefield of thoughts.

Oh by the way, it's a beautiful sight to see Gibbon Falls. I get a couple chances to see them while carrying my gear and then walking the bike up the trail to the parking lot. All throughout this ordeal, I was wondering why there weren't any people around. Luckily for me, there was a crew painting lines in the parking lot; the lot was closed for this reason. I asked one guy if he had any zip ties. He asked what happened, and eventually we were both looking at the damage. At first, he did a little hand drilling to get some of the screw out.

I was hoping, watching nervously, that he wouldn't hit the thread with the drill. Same as last time, drilling out a small broken screw without damage, nearly impossible by hand. I was not naive enough to know it wouldn't happen, but I had no other option. What could I say? "Please stop; don't drill"? He'd say, "OK" and leave, as I would expect, if I said that. I had nothing to fix this, and he possibly did; of course I let him do it. It would be nearly impossible not to hit the thread doing this on the side of the road; they're M5x.8 threads, a small size, same as your water bottle screw threads. Doing this would also cause an issue between me and Diamondback later on with the warranty. Well, it was my problem, not theirs, obviously.

The worker had heavy-duty zip ties and pulled one side tight with pliers. This was done with two of the ties, bike rack bottom leg directly to frame. For the other side he had, I'm guessing, 1/16-inch thick steel wire, and he wrapped the wire with pliers around the bike, like he did the other side. I thanked him and tried to offer some money (about the only thing I could offer), but he said he wouldn't take it. I was so thankful; I would've really struggled to find something to hold the weight of my bags. As I left the parking lot, they opened it up, and in flooded the masses.

I wasn't sure what to do now. His work looked very solid, and it appeared I could go on. But safety and camp was a short coast downhill, and Indian Creek was only 25 miles from my camp straight north. My worrying mind won the battle, and I started my descent back to Madison campground. I quickly thought, What will they be able to do that is any better? as I was riding. It was not a parts problem; it was now a problem requiring minor surgery. I hit my brakes, took a deep breath, and started my climb back up that damn mountain. I turned around and had faith the fix would hold. I made it the remaining 20-something miles to Indian Creek Campground.

It was such an amazingly beautiful, picture-perfect day. The trees, the mountains, the colors blending and contrasting—it was just spectacular. Unfortunately, I only stopped for roadside attractions; I just wanted to make it to camp and not press my luck touring the park today. Once again, I would be on grizzly alert; I was passing signs for trails closed due to bear danger. I also passed a sign for a moose habitat area. That's an animal I'd love to see—a big moose. I arrived at the campground early since I went directly there. It was a perfect place and had the Obsidian Creek going past it. I saw a ton of fly-fishing out there, by the way.

I only have maybe 13 miles to the North Entrance, the camp hosts also tell me. I'll get cell service around the Mammoth Springs area, only 5 miles north. I haven't had a signal since the day I was at Pahaske Resort. Three glorious days without a phone, total disconnection from everything except Mother Nature at some of her best in America. It's been better than you can imagine, escaping everything, and not being able to be contacted.

Gardiner, Montana, is the town on the north border of YNP. I was planning on riding into Livingston, Montana, which was also a 70ish mile ride. There is camping but no real town in between, so it's Gardiner or Livingston. Not sure if I could make it, but Gardiner has bike outfitters and hopefully a mechanic or possible ride if things go south.

I'd find no help in Gardiner, though I stopped at a business and talked with someone.

I felt like I was in a three-round fight with YNP. Day one was close, but Yellowstone won. I took the second with a fabulous, jam-packed day, and today was a draw, I'd say. YNP knocked me down early, but with some much appreciated and needed help, I got up and finished strong. I'm still enjoying myself, my time here, but wish I had more time and was able to see some bison. But overall, this was a completely amazing experience—to go through a national park, Yellowstone, no less, on a bicycle takes a certain type of individual; it's certainly not for everyone, but I do recommend it. The roads are a little scary, though, no doubt.

I actually give a ton of credit to the hikers in the back country. I tried to hike a few times, but I got overly cautious and went too slow. I guess I have a fear of coming face-to-face with a grizzly on the trail. The fact is, there are a handful of animals out here that could do some serious damage if they wanted to.

I tried hiking again at the campground. I got there very early since I hadn't really stopped anywhere too long. I had my lunch and after headed out on the Bighorn Trail. I probably made it 1 mile in, which was pretty good for me. It was a really cool trail; I enjoyed being out there and walking along the creek too. Back on the road I did see some mule deer again. I tried getting a picture, but they started jumping away. It was cool to see; they're a lot bigger than our deer back home but seemed just as agile.

I did hear that there's a lot of wildlife around the Mammoth Hot Springs area, which I'll pass on my exit. I'm hoping to check off a couple more animals before I leave. I really wish I could stay another day, but even if I did, I wouldn't want to take my bike out unless I was leaving. I can't afford to take any chances with this. I knew it would be very tough out here, but honestly nothing could have prepared me for the pure beauty, horrifying climbs, incredible ecosystems, and environments that make up this magnificent place called Yellowstone National Park. America's first national park was signed into protection by Ulysses S. Grant, on March 1, 1872.

The best advice is to be as much a part of YNP as you can. Just immerse yourself in it and try to soak up as much of the vast wilderness as you can. I know I did or at least tried my best. There is so much to see out here, and not being in a car, I have to choose more selectively what I want to see.

I'm happy and grateful for what I did see and most of all what I got to experience. That's the real treasure I'm taking from Yellowstone. YNP was tough and a challenge, but I didn't give up. Sometimes I felt like it but only for a fleeting moment.

It gets really cold here; it's probably in the low fifties. I'm fully loaded with my usual campsite attire here: two long-sleeve shirts, pants, and a beanie. It rained a little less than an hour last night, not sure what time—I fell back asleep right away. Tomorrow another state down and another up, Big Sky Country!

8/11/23

DAY #45, RIDING #42

Mile—67.16 (2,961.57); Time—4:43 (252:12)
Yellowstone Park Inn and Suites, Livingston, Montana ($127)

One thing about my time in YNP was the mornings were cold! It must have been in the midforties when I first woke up at 6:00 a.m. I was also in a tree-filled, shaded area. It would warm up very quickly today, though. But in the back of my mind was the fact I had bike issues that needed to be fixed ASAP.

The first attraction on my map was Mammoth Hot Springs. It was only 8 miles north but also required a massive descent of 1,100 feet. More on that later. There were a lot of beautiful views along the way, and after my descent, it became flat for a little bit. Some of the riding out here had no shoulders; I did some white line riding today. The elevation would still affect me. I was riding a flat surface while making a video, and I could barely speak. I was huffing and puffing riding at a normal pace. There were some people out on bikes riding around this area as well; I wouldn't see too many people on bikes in the park overall.

While riding before Mammoth, I was going down this beautiful canyon with the Gardiner River on my right. All of a sudden, there was a pull off, and I stopped. I was treated with an incredible surprise cascade waterfall. It might have been Sheep Eater Cliff, but that's only a guess.

That started a completely inspiring descent into Mammoth Hot Springs. Riding down the Golden Gate Canyon was an unbelievable experience. It was incredible and semidangerous. There's no shoulder, and it twists and turns. The worst is it's just a sheer drop, hundreds of feet into the river below, on my right! That only lasts a short distance, on this road that hugs the canyon wall. I would have almost no shoulder from here on out, with steep drop-offs.

The descent into Mammoth just got more scenic as I went on. One thing I would do as a biker I want to describe as I think more should do this, if they don't already. I have no shoulder. I'm braking to maintain 25 miles per hour, and a line of cars is forming behind me. When it gets to be three or more, I start to look for a place to pull over. I don't want those people trying to pass me on a narrow road, with a metal guard rail preventing me from bailing off the bike if necessary. Someone eventually will try to pass you, all but guaranteed. It takes no effort to pull over, let them pass, and then continue. If I want cars to watch out for me, then I've got to do my part too. Plus, it's so much safer for both of us.

Just after the Mammoth sign, elevation 6,239 feet, I saw a herd of elk on the left, in a field. There must've been 15 to 20 of them, just hanging out. There were a lot of people there too. I stopped for a little and then parked my bike for a hike. I walked up the boardwalk, and there were a few more elk, just hanging out. One thing I've never seen in the wild in Pennsylvania is an elk. So seeing these huge animals up close was a special treat. They must've been only 15 to 20 feet off the boardwalk, sitting in the shade of the trees. They have a beautiful tan body, with darker-colored necks; this was another gift from YNP to me. They don't seem to mind the people, although I'm always on guard around these, or any wild animals.

Given my bike problems, this would be the last hiking I would do and attraction I would see in YNP. I did a good bit of walking around the hot springs. It was a really well laid out trail network, with different routes to take. All walking is done on a boardwalk; the ground is too fragile to handle all the foot traffic. The boardwalk walking trails are an incredible sight alone.

Then came the infamous last 5 miles to the North Entrance. I've been told about this section and have seen it on the map. It's a drop of 1,000 feet in 5 miles! There is a sign warning of the 10 percent grade and the 15-mile-per-hour speed limit. It's a series of switchbacks, with no shoulder. I pulled over multiple times, and thankfully no one tried to pass me. Once again, let traffic by if it backs up behind you. A driver only has so much patience before they might try something that puts you in danger.

I was again riding the brakes almost the whole way and still maintaining a speed in the midtwenties. Yes, I was officially speeding on my bicycle, ha ha!

Once again I'm hoping my bike holds up. I don't want to think about what will happen if it fails going this fast with cars behind me.

I make it to the bottom finally, and I exit Yellowstone. It's only noon, but I still have business to take care of.

In the town of Gardiner, Montana, I got some pictures of the big YNP sign and the Roosevelt Arch. Also, now I was in Montana and out of the Cowboy State. Outside the entrance there was another herd of elk grazing in the yards of the ranger/maintenance buildings. The group was around fifteen strong, and there were some very big males in the group.

I got on my phone and saw a bike shop in Livingston, Montana. I called, talked to the mechanic, and found out I had time to make it in by the 6:00 p.m. closing time.

I would have to move, though; it was 58 miles away. It was mostly downhill, so I could fly if I needed. My concern was of course breaking down and being stranded, but I had no other options. I would end up riding Highway 89 North, so I'd have some traffic if I needed help.

Wow, this first glimpse of Montana was love at first sight. The route to Livingston was one of the most scenic road rides I've done. One of the main features was Yankee Jim Canyon. That was the highlight, but the huge mountains along the way in the distance were very inspiring and memorable. The road followed the crystal-clear Yellowstone River. I would also need to stay on high alert; I was still in a heavily saturated grizzly territory. I also saw my bison along the way. I forget the location, but they had five of these massive creatures in a pen. The head alone is enormous; I was told so they can see more from their sides as they look out for predators or any other trouble.

I made it into Livingston and went to Dan Bailey's Outdoor Co. It has a lot of fly-fishing gear and some bike stuff as well. I was talking with Jordan, their mechanic, about my issues, and we took a look. I already had a plan but wanted his input as well. First, he got the screw out and informed me, as I had figured, I now had two trashed sides where my rack attached. My thinking was, since it was a blind hole and thread, meaning it had a bottom/end, we should just drill the hole out—drill through the frame to the other side, and then thread the entire hole, making more and new threads, hopefully.

So that's what we did on both sides of the bike. Jordan threaded a nut on a longer bolt; now I had bolt through the frame with a nut tightly screwed on the opposite end, holding it very tightly together. Now because of the nut being close to the gearing, I lost my highest gear—no room for the chain. Something drastic would need to occur for this to break again.

I was very happy with his work, and he even stayed fifteen minutes late. He was just a real cool dude whom I very much enjoyed talking to. He gave me some good road tips, too, for riding out here.

I also got a hotel room while I was there waiting. I needed to relax.

Back to YNP. Like I said, it certainly felt like I was in a three-round bout, and I'm not sure who exactly won. I had a blast there, though, and thoroughly enjoyed it. I really wanted to stay, especially since the weather cleared up. But with everything going on with the bike, I had to leave.

The bike is fixed but as of now retired from backpacking trips. This was a major reason I bought the bike. I wanted to step up to a higher quality component bike and really liked this one. I was OK with the $3,000 price I paid only a little over a year ago; the bike performed superbly. But in this moment, stewing in my hotel, I'm mad about even buying it. I've taken this bike out before for up to a week and half, no issues, but now I'm questioning why the screws are so small. I'm wondering why it failed now under the weight and did not perform up to the standards expected of it.

I feel like my brain is overloaded. I feel like I'm in such a scattered head space right now. Part of me feels like saying "The hell with everything." I want to ride tomorrow and feel the physical pain of pushing myself. But I know how bad doing that back in Pennsylvania was for me and see it for what it is now. I know I absolutely can't do that out here. That could possibly be deadly if done alone. And no matter my thoughts or words, I still have some small sense of logic I try not to ignore. If I knew my definite route tomorrow, I'd continue on. I've gained so much knowledge that my maps are mostly worthless now. My head's going to explode; I need to calm down, relax, and just go to bed. This is the start of the condition of my bike really starting to mess me up; I can't really describe how let down I feel by the bike.

Tomorrow would be a zero day, the first of my choosing. I'm suffering from burnout, big-time. I think I just need to stop and chill out for a day.

8/12/23

DAY #46, RIDING #42

Miles—10.62 (2,972.19); Time—1:08 (253:20)

Yellowstone Park Inn & Suites ($127)

As I previewed, today was the first zero day of my choosing. I needed time to decompress from Yellowstone and recover from feeling burned out. I also wanted to go over all of my Montana routes. Since I'm now so much more informed about the roads, what to ride and not ride out here in the Wild West.

Even on a day when I know I'm not moving, I wake up around 6:00 a.m., usually a little earlier. It's that internal clock; I can't sleep in. My sleeping in means waking up at seven to seven thirty. I'm fine with it. I like the mornings—the cool air, the sun coming up, and no matter what happened last night, it's a new day.

First, I walked five minutes down the road to start my laundry. I decided to go back to the motel for breakfast and then go switch the clothes to the dryer. While waiting on the dryer, I made a game plan for the day. I'd get groceries, mail a package, and hang out at the park in town.

After doing laundry, I took the bike to the grocery store and stocked up again with the usual. Everything was less than a mile away, so that made the location all the better.

After getting back from the grocery store, it dawned on me: it's Saturday, and I want to mail stuff out! I had exactly zero minutes to spare before USPS closed at noon. I had to swing by the bike shop first; I had left my YNP park guidebook there. Rushing around, I made it literally just in time. The postal worker actually closed the metal gate behind me; I was her last customer! I thanked her, then went back to hang out and talk with Jordan a little bit. He was really helpful with roads, places ahead, and just good conversation.

I guess I don't meet many people I feel I connect with. It seems to me the people I meet and talk with here as I get farther into the West don't seem to care as much about other people's business. It's a freer, looser, open feeling and attitude out here, for sure, compared to the more uptight, close-minded, and rigid ways I'm used to. Well, at least my area is that way; I shouldn't speak for areas I don't know. I love Pennsylvania and the East, but feeling the free, more liberated feeling that I get out here is refreshing, something I sometimes lack at home. The breathing is good out here, in more ways than one.

A very special thanks to Jordan and Dan Bailey's Outdoor Co., Livingston, Montana.

After saying our goodbyes, I headed out for Sacajawea Park. There was a bike/walking path through the park along the Yellowstone River. It was the perfect day: few clouds, pretty blue sky, in the mideighties. I went as far down, maybe a mile, as I could and then walked down to the river. There was this perfect rock to lie on. It had three perfectly shaped curves at just the right spots. This perfectly crafted rock had spots for my head, butt, and feet! It was also smoothed over and in the river. I didn't want to move, so I didn't. I literally lay there for an hour, just listening to the water rushing over the rocks. I may have dozed off; I'm not sure. The wind was blowing just enough for it to be cool without being uncomfortable.

It was a perfect, serene place to just be. I really enjoyed it, but most of all, I needed it. I saw a bunch of rafts and canoes going past. It was a very beautiful park and had extremely clear waters. I continue to see lots of fly-fishing and see parking areas for fishing along the road. It's supposed to be some of the country's best out here, I hear.

Today was a good day. I got some necessary things done and had some fun. For real, I honestly enjoyed every second of this wonderful day. It's not very often I can honestly make that statement. Best of all, I could actually relax for as long as I wanted—well, all day. I certainly took that opportunity. Tomorrow will be my first full day in Montana, and I'm excited.

It's hard to believe that just today, three-fourths of the way across America, I decided to take a break from the action. All other zero days were attributable to rain. Although, those were rest days as well, just under different circumstances.

Oh yeah, Jordan also gave me this baked stuffed croissant. A local shop owner drops off these delicious items, different meats and cheeses stuffed inside this flaky-style baked bread. Michael (Eastside Coffee, Livingston)—his stuff is top-notch. Jordan gave me a bacon and cheddar one for my lunch tomorrow. Go to Dan Bailey's and shop there; get your bike fixed there; go there for anything you may need or think you need. Great guys and great shop. Before and or after that, make sure to stop by Eastside Coffee as well.

Tomorrow I'm staying at the confluence of the Jefferson, Madison, and Gallatin rivers. Those combine into the headwaters of the Missouri River. Lewis and Clark also stayed here a few days on their journey west.

8/13/23

DAY #47, RIDING #43

Miles—57.88 (3,030.07); Time—4:22 (257:42)
Missouri Headwaters Campground, Three Forks, Montana
($38, primitive)

Waking up in a comfortable bed and being able to just walk down to the lobby to eat breakfast is always nice on the road. Knowing I have a good 60-mile ride, it's nice to relax in the morning, not having to pack and make breakfast.

Today would be my first full day in Big Sky Country, and I was looking forward to it. I would also have perfect riding weather—beautiful, clear skies. It started out great. I rode Highway 10 West because it paralleled US 90 West.

It wasn't a very busy road at all, so I didn't mind not having much of a shoulder to ride along. The landscape and scenery, to start, would continue being first class. Some scattered housing, with the Montana mountains in the background. Such beautiful land out here. I passed a sign that I loved: "No county zoning, instead zone county authorities." This, to me, is more evidence of the independent feelings and thinking of the West, which I feel I belong to. It seems like in America more people are standing up and speaking their minds to the state and government. Good—question things, and don't eat everything they feed you. Be wary of authority, state, and Big Brother government. I feel like too many look out for and cover for their own. The middle and lower classes are usually the target, it seems.

I did see something on my route yesterday that I wanted to be sure to see. After 14 miles and a steady ascent of 1,200 feet, I wound up at the Montana Grizzly Encounter, outside Bozeman, in West End. I knew I was going to stop but still got there early and waited 30 minutes for them to open at 10. It's a smaller sanctuary habitat with a few rescue bears. The only bear I got to see was Max, an orphaned 1,100-pound cub from Alaska. He was absolutely monstrous, so big and thick. I couldn't imagine him fully grown and encountering one of these if I were in Alaska. He was cool to see, but I was hoping to see more bears and bears from this area. Still, it was a fun experience, and I'm glad I waited.

After leaving, I had a choice: continue on a side road or hop onto US 90 here. I would have to ride the interstate anyways as there was no side road for the 3.5-mile ride into Bozeman from Chestnut. I just decided I might as well get on now and ride the 8 miles into Bozeman. I had no idea how I'd feel, but after a few cars went by at blazing speeds, I settled in for the ride. Let me tell you, the first time a car flies by at 80-plus miles per hour a few feet away, wow, that's a hair-raising feeling, and I was wondering what the hell I was doing riding this road.

I had a good wide and clean shoulder of 4 to 5 feet, but sometimes it shrunk to 3 feet. The posted speed limit was 80 miles per hour, so as you can imagine, most were going 85-plus. There was also a constant stream of cars and traffic, but I was really able to fly with the road conditions averaging around 20 miles per hour. One thing I wouldn't have thought about until I started riding. The wind generated by the traffic in the lane closest to me helped me so much, and traffic the other way was too far away to have any resistance from wind blowback.

I got off the freeway after my 8-mile ride, then continued on Frontage Road for the last 35 miles with a 1,000-foot descent. It was good riding, but the Frontage Road shoulder was narrow. Sometimes, I had to do some white-line riding because there was no shoulder. The speed limits on these side roads vary from 60 to 70 miles per hour, so you can make your own decision on what's safer to ride out here. I'd say the interstate is safer, but I want to stick to as many side roads as possible.

I would also pass by a few Lewis and Clark historical markers. I was coming to a very important place for them, the start of the Missouri River. In Fort Ellis, on the Bozeman Trail, I got to see some cool Western history for sure.

I entered Bozeman and rode the Gallagater Trail into the Bozeman Sculpture Park, looking for a place to rest and eat my lunch. I found a nice, shaded place and ate my bacon-cheddar croissant with a lime Gatorade. If I can't find my cucumber flavor, I always go for the lime, but really, it's whatever is on sale. I always look for the two-for-one deals, so later when I'm in the middle of nowhere, I have something besides water.

I passed some neat towns—Belgrade, Manhattan—and the Bozeman Yellowstone Airport. I unfortunately just missed the Manhattan Potato Festival by one Saturday.

I continue to see a few trains along the way. I see a lot of brownish color in the fields. I see the hills in the distance, with trees scattered along the landscape like polka dots. Everything out here appears dry and somewhat close to death. But I'm sure my perceptions are way off from reality. This can be a harsh, unforgiving environment, but the flora and animals are survivors, able to adapt to the climate. It must be such an incredibly delicate ecosystem out here. Or maybe not—maybe everything is actually well equipped to handle Mother Nature's weather, wrath, and fury.

Along the ride I get some awesome views of the Gallatin River. I turned onto Trident Road to go to my campsite in Three Forks. Actually, I was surprised to see a trail following the road to the Missouri Headwaters Campground. There was a house on the trail that had decorated and themed birdhouses. My two favorites were the cabin with bears and the Sasquatch. This is an important historical place for a few reasons, namely Lewis and Clark and the start of the Missouri. Lewis and Clark stayed here for three days in July 1805.

I arrived early, as usual out here in the West. I would take a hike after setting up and eating my lunch. I hiked up to a lookout where Lewis and Clark saw the three rivers converging into one for the first time. Clark would stay here again on his return. He would do some mapping for their trip atop some of these lookouts.

It's really cool to be able to stand at the exact place where so much history happened and to put my feet exactly where Lewis and Clark did. It was good hiking out to the High Rock lookout. It took me a little time to find it; my first trail ended, but I eventually found my way to the trident of the waters. A good 2-mile hike after my 60-mile ride. It's relaxing to me; I don't mind walking. What I see is well worth it, and what would I think if I didn't explore these new areas I'm in? I feel almost compelled to do it in a way but also want to see the most of America I can.

At this camp I would luck out and meet a really cool dude camping right next to me. Bob was traveling back home to the Northeast and was hauling one of those campers you crawl into and sleep in. He had a Grateful Dead sticker on the camper; at first I didn't get the joke. But seeing the Working Man's Dead sticker was a hint. Bob from Connecticut was a friendly person, and we had some good conversation. I think it started when I was in my chair listening to Grateful Dead, actually, and he came up and started talking. We talked until we turned in and later would get to share one of the most amazing sights I saw on my trip.

I knew this could be a perfect night for star watching as the sky was cloudless and there were no lights anywhere around. We planned on coming back out to see but didn't have a time set. I heard Bob outside later at night, so I crawled out. It was completely dark, and in front of me one of the most incredible things I've ever seen in my life. There were so many stars out, hundreds, maybe even thousands. Without any light around, we had a spectacular 360-degree view of the stars. I got to see 3 shooting stars! Best sight so far, and it was definitely a magical night.

8/14/23

DAY #48, RIDING #44

Miles—65.42 (3,095.49); Time—5:44 (263.26)
Motel 6, Butte, Montana ($98)

Last night was epic, such a memorable night. I wish I could've gotten some pictures; my phone is bad with night pictures, or I just don't know how to use it—both are possible. Either way, it was a special sight to see.

This morning would start with me on a couple trails and ending up on Highway 2. The waters of the Jefferson were like all the waterways out here, pristine. I can't believe how clear these rivers are. I would have about 35 miles of highway and 25 of these had no shoulder at all. I had fewer than 8 cars pass me, but I'm still not a fan of white-line riding.

Once again, my jaw dropped looking over this landscape and the views from my bike seat. I rode past the Lewis and Clark Caverns State Park. It would've been cool to take a tour of the caverns. The canyon, or mountain walls, whatever they technically are, surround me. I'm down in the valley with the Jefferson and a train track that wanders through the rock. How is it possible that every single view, every second, is a picture-perfect postcard sight? It's completely cloudless, in the high seventies to low eighties, with the bluest sky, and if I asked for more now, I'd be getting greedy. This is already a gift for the eyes. Big Sky Country—I'm loving it.

I stopped in the town of Whitehall to take advantage of a shaded picnic table off Main Street. While I was eating lunch, a lady passed me, and we started talking. I knew I had a huge mountain to climb and asked her about it. Turns out I'd be riding up the Continental Divide again in a very short time. I decided to do my ascent on I90 West because of the huge shoulders, as I knew walking would be involved at some point. Also, I assumed the interstate was newer and generally had lower elevations than the old highway. I started the day at around 4,100 feet, I think—the elevation of Whitehall is 4,360 feet—as I headed for Butte. I had a 14.5 mile ride from Whitehall to the Continental Divide with a cresting elevation of 6,393 feet! Yes, roughly 2,000 feet in 14 miles.

Most of that climbing was in a 5-to-7-mile stretch; that was a challenging mountain. While riding the interstate, I always play music, since all I hear is cars. Might as well hear some music, but it's mostly drowned out. On this climb I'd need my heavy metal to get the adrenaline pumping. It was a tough climb for sure. I did a good job riding, though; I only stopped 4 times. I only had to walk twice, once to catch my breath, and the other a 10-minute walk because I was spent. It was a lot to climb, and there's absolutely no shade on the interstate. I eventually made my final ascent and got on top of the divide.

I'm really hoping to have some long downhill days from this high point in America.

Entering into Silver Bow County, I started my descent; there would be 5 more miles until I'd exit the American autobahn that is I-90. Going down that mountain was a wild ride, a 6 percent grade for 3 glorious downhill miles. I was holding the brakes so I wouldn't move at the same speed as traffic. It wasn't that fast, but braking to maintain 25 miles per hour indicates a serious decline. Flying down this hill, I thought I was going pretty fast; I looked down to see my readout: I was going 32 miles per hour! Way too fast, especially with the interstate traffic, any crash greatly increases a fatality risk.

When I'm going this fast on the interstate, I don't look in my mirror. I need total concentration in front of me; I need to constantly scan the road in front of me for debris. Whatever happens behind me is going to happen. If I turn for even a second, that's all it takes to hit an object going this fast and crash. At 25 miles per hour on the interstate, that can never be remotely close to good; no crash is, but on I-90, the stakes are greatly increased. I exit 90 before Butte; I don't want the extra off-ramp traffic of a big city.

I got on the Ulrich-Schotte Nature Trail for a little while and enjoyed its beauty as it dropped me off in the town of Butte. I decided on a hotel; it was only thirty dollars more than the KOA tent site. The KOA wanted fifty dollars for a tent site—no way. I've never stayed at a KOA and hope I never will. They're usually expensive and are packed too closely together, it's like you're sharing a spot. This is true from my experience with KOA; maybe one day I'll find the exception.

I ended up riding right by it and am very glad I didn't stay there. But I also didn't know Butte was built on a monster-size mountain. Of course, amid my hotel budget shopping, I unknowingly booked the one highest up on the hill! At one point I gained 270 feet in a half-mile distance; it was steep. I walked the last 5 to 7 blocks to my Motel 6 room for the night.

It actually turned out to be a good thing I chose this hotel. There are a couple of old mines and lookouts onto the city higher up the hill. At least I'm most of the way up already starting from the hotel. I plan on riding up there tomorrow with no gear; I'm exhausted and did my share of climbing today. Although, I do end up going for a walk later to find my treat and satisfy my ice cream needs.

Butte was an interesting old town, but because of that, there were a lot of old unused buildings. It's sad to see more homeless here and more open issues with drug use, or the effects from it, I should say.

Tomorrow is downhill, so it'll be a shorter ride. It feels like something is building up inside me, in a good way. For some reason I get emotional lately. I hear a certain song, complete something difficult, et cetera, and I feel it, something deep inside, and I start to get a little teary-eyed. It's strange because I can get that way without really caring too much about what is causing it. I can't explain it, but I'm hoping it'll be something that will open up the floodgates. Maybe I will relieve myself of some of these burdens I feel like I've been carrying for way too long. I've been through a lot again in the past few years, and I don't think I've ever gotten over or really dealt with, nor do I feel like I have closure on some of it.

I know either I haven't or I struggle to deal with acceptance of some of these issues. Some of them seem like a lifelong journey—one of accepting something you don't know whether you ever can. I know from my past I don't have to like something, but in order to move on (to really move on, not just invoke meaningless words), I *must* accept it. It happened, and nothing can change the past. We need to accept this in order to start healing, and move on with our lives. Just try to work on it in a healthy way. Maybe this trip will provide the tools to help with that.

8/15/23
DAY #49, RIDING #45

Miles—56.13 (3,151.62); Time—4:48 (268:14)
Bernie and Sharon's Riverfront RV Park ($34, cabin, AC)

I started my day by waking up early once again to leave by 6:30 a.m. I wanted to go see the old mines, monument, and overlook in Butte. I did this with only a small repair kit along because it was higher up still on the mountain. I certainly didn't need the weight as I still had to do some walking. Wow, does it make a difference to ride with no weight. It's a strange feeling, and of course I'm enjoying it.

It's like this town was built on a forty-five degree angle. I had two guys yesterday tell me it's just like San Francisco. Butte is an old mining town, mostly abandoned mines. On the massive mountain the town's built on, up closer to the top, where I stayed, half the old buildings were vacant. Some still had the old advertising, which was pretty neat to see, and scattered among them were newer remodeled buildings and businesses. Hopefully the businesses are able to sustain themselves because it seemed like a struggling area.

I pedaled as much as I could on the paved trail, but it had a serious incline that would give anyone a workout. There was a trail that took me past some old mines, benches, and fantastic sunrise views over Butte. I passed a few old mines that were interesting to see. The Con was the world's largest copper producer, in operation from 1886 to 1974; it was 5,291 feet deep! Also, it tragically took

172 lives over the course of its existence, which is one of the reasons for the Granite Mountain Speculator Mine Memorial on the top of the mountain.

It was a very well done memorial and had a great view of one mine with its multicolored sides. Twenty-five hundred people lost their lives between 1870 and 1983. The deadliest event happened right at this spot, on June 8, 1917, when 168 men died in a mine fire. I can't and don't want to even think about that. I would probably freak out just being in the mine, a mile underground. That's scary enough; they're very brave people for sure, the miners, then and now. The view from the memorial overlooking Butte was Butteful, ha ha—sorry. It was well worth the early morning workout.

I came back to the motel, made breakfast, and started loading up the bike. After I checked out of the hotel, I had about a 2-mile trail ride to Rocker from South Butte. I started off on I-90 West again, this time traveling for a little over 30 miles to Deer Lodge. Along this stretch of the interstate, I would come into some construction. This actually benefited me. Traffic was down to one lane, and it was the far left lane. They were paving the right lane, so I still had my shoulder, and now construction separated me from traffic. However, my shoulder was surely next up as it had those diagonal cuts prior to paving, which I had to ride over. The vibrations weren't too bad as the cuts weren't that deep or wide, a relief considering my bike issues.

I pass a town exit sign, 208, for Anaconda and Opportunity. I immediately think, I could use some opportunity in my life, maybe I should get off and find it. A possible missed opportunity, I instead got off at Deer Lodge and went to a grocery store to get a few things.

Riding down Main Street, I passed by the site of the last spike used for the completion of the Northern Pacific Railroad. I also passed the Old Montana Prison and Auto Museum. I don't need to visit any prisons; the view from outside is always better anyways, believe that. I also came to the historic Grant-Kohrs Ranch site.

I then had on my route the Old Yellowstone Trail, which was on the GART website. I found it and went about a mile in and ended up in a grassy field. Before I realized I had missed the trail, I stopped in some vast open field looked around and thought, Where the world am I? I turned around and found the trail. It's a walking-only trail. The trail had a barbed wire fence; you had to open it to continue. It continued onto private property, the land owner's cattle grazing area (the reason for the fence). I have no clue why this is included in the GART route; there is even a "no bike" marker on the trail sign, the circle with a line through it for bicycles. I wasn't at first happy about wasting an hour, but then I realized something: After all the stuff that has happened so far, what does this minor detour matter? Not a whole lot. I ended up just getting back on 90 West again at the north end of Deer Lodge. It was about a 12-mile ride into Garrison, where I was staying.

I've been listening to more music while riding lately. If I'm on a highway constantly hearing cars, I might as well hear some tunes in the background. It can be very motivating listening to music under these conditions. OK, I do sing along at times. I love it; I need it. Sometimes you just need that boost to get you through. I also have been shoving toilet paper in my left ear as it's so loud on the interstate. Some of the tires actually scream at me as they go past; that's another thing you don't realize until you're out there.

On I-90 today some idiot in a pickup truck hauling an empty flatbed trailer hit the gas and tried to blow a little smoke. They were in the passenger lane, luckily. The great thing was when he hit the gas, he also blew a tire on the trailer! Ha ha, it was perfect justice, and they deserved it for sure. I saw something come off the trailer and bounce, so I knew something had happened up ahead. They had to pull over to change the tire; they were two skinny punks in their early twenties. I passed them and just smiled and stared them down as I passed, head turning and all. I really wanted to say something, but they were still in a truck. I still had a little to go on I-90 and didn't want them to pass me again. I'll say if I had been forced to dodge or hit their blown tire, I probably would've stopped and said something. I already wanted to confront them and ask them why they felt they needed to do that. I won't put up with that and will usually make my thoughts known.

After all the excitement, I made it to my campground, Bernie and Sharon's Riverfront RV in Garrison. When I pulled up, I was greeted by a camp host before I could look for the office; that's service. Two guys, super friendly and very cool, started to help me. I originally was getting a tent site for twenty-nine dollars. These guys told me the cabins were thirty-four dollars. I was saddle sore, so as a joke, I said, "I'll take it if it has a padded chair." He just looked at me funny and said it has AC, ha ha.

I'll take it; say no more. Five dollars extra for a nice cool day and night of air-conditioning—let me weigh my options while I'm standing here in the midnineties heat at 2:00 p.m. I also got a fridge/freezer and two bare mattresses. I spread out my sleeping bag and used my own inflatable pillows. There's a heat wave going through here, and it did hit 101 degrees in Garrison today. This cabin was such a surprise, and I was so very glad I got it.

With the heat and absence of shade on the road, I'm cutting back to 40 to 60 mile rides the next few days. I'm starting to wind down my trip and have less than two weeks to go. It's hard to believe how far I've come and what I've accomplished so far. I feel this energy running through me while riding now. It fuels this rage/

adrenaline that's driving me. I still have setbacks, but mostly it's all positive vibes. Rain is coming this weekend, so we'll see if I get held up somewhere.

While riding today, one side of my rack popped out again; I had to zip-tie it together. I'm disappointed with the bike. Now with my rack mounts trashed, I can't take this bike on any more trips. Now it's only a day tripper, so I'm depressed and down about my bike. It's frustrating to no end: I had two good days in a row, and now there's another repeating issue.

Lately it's been going well though overall; it's harder to get down and depressed when I have this good weather and I'm seeing all these amazing things. Still, there are times when adversity confronts me. Like today, I am riding on a trail and hit a couple rough cracks across the pavement. My mirror falls off and falls right in line with my rear tire. Now my second mirror is cracked partially; I can see out of half of it still. I get pissed off for a little and get over it. There seems to be so many problems on this trip that these little things that used to anger me I now consider minor and petty. I'm on my bike, away from home, and don't have a time frame for my return. I need to remember that part too—the good.

I'm becoming worn down, I think, and I think it's from being in the sun all day. Ever since Nebraska or perhaps Iowa, there hasn't been a lot of escape from the sun. Then add in multiple days in a row. I'm also not allowing the time for my body to recuperate, I think.

Out here in Wyoming, and Montana, the Wild West, there isn't any place to stop unless you come into a town. And some of those towns are so small, they're just a road or two. It's hard to believe I'll be in Idaho in 2 to 3 days. I have under 1,000 miles to go, and it's somehow winding down.

I like the music on my bike. I like rocking out to the beat; at those points everything feels good out here and comes full circle, so to speak. It feels good; I feel good out here. Having been in the West for a little while now, I feel more confident with the knowledge and little experience I now have. But no prideful confidence here; I'm still humble to the dangers.

✪

8/16/23

DAY #50, RIDING #46

Miles—45.07 (3,196.69); Time—3:06 (271:20)
Beaver Tail Campground, Clinton, Montana ($28, primitive)

I started the day with something different: I didn't set an alarm. I woke up at seven and sort of rushed a little at first. Then I realized I had a shorter, easier day, but more than that, I needed to stop this thinking or acting like time mattered so much. I feel like I'm wired that way, like I always need to be on the move or doing something. It's like in my head, idle time is wasted time, but that is certainly not the case. It's just another daily struggle on my trips; this happens every trip, and I don't like it. It really didn't matter—I wanted to sleep in anyways. I'll do the same tomorrow as I'm splitting up one day into two shorter rides.

It would be another cloudless day, with a wide-open blue sky, at least at the start.

I got on 90 West right away to start my day; after 10 miles I got into some construction around the Gold Creek area. Actually, a guy in a truck drove over and was telling me what was going on. He asked me to get off at the exit up ahead because his crew was working where I would be riding. He was really cool, and I told him I had planned on exiting here onto Frontage Road. I had to at least go this far on the interstate to avoid a long detour, most likely climbing mountains and gravel roads. This was one of the times that riding I-90 was the only real option.

I end up taking Frontage Road for the next 25 miles. It's a lot more scenic but has more hills to ride. I'm out here for the riding, not just to do this as fast as I can. That's mainly why I still try to spend as much time as possible on the old highways before getting into this nonstop procession of lightning-fast vehicles. The land is diverse, and I have seen different landscapes. There are the farming and ranching areas, with their irrigation pipes and cattle grazing, making good use of the land. I also had two inspiring descents into canyons and down to the Clark Fork River.

On the way into Drummond, the sky starts to get hazy, and at first, I think it's a storm brewing up ahead. I arrive in Drummond, and the sky is almost fully covered by this dark haze. I stopped at the Conoco gas station, and the cashier tells me a wildfire broke out in Phillipsburg yesterday. Phillipsburg is about 40 miles south of my current location, and I've only got another 20 miles to my campground west of here.

Now that I knew what it was, it was really surreal being this close to a forest fire. I hear about them and see stuff on the news, but being out in the vicinity of one is another story, even as far as I was from it. I could faintly smell the smoke but don't think it affected me too much.

I would have about 17 miles to Bearmouth, where I'd have to get back on the American autobahn. The few miles from Bearmouth to my campground at Beaver Tail Hill have no roads in between, making I-90 the only option. I see more horses and cattle in the prairies; they all seem interested as I go by, and they like having their picture taken. The riding out here on Frontage Road between Drummond and Bearmouth is well worth the extra hills.

On the roads in Wyoming and Montana, there is nothing I enjoy more than dropping down into a canyon. I don't care how hard the climb is; it's always worth it. Sometimes I pause to soak in my surroundings and look ahead and behind. Other times I continue riding and just roll into my reward. Out here the canyons almost always also have a river going through them. That clear water just magnifies the beauty.

One thing is, I don't really have any shoulder and I'm white-line riding most of the day. I ride in the roads out here. I'm also always paying attention in my mirror and listening. In one video I made, I'm riding down the middle of the road going between 25 and 28 miles per hour. I notice a dump truck coming up a ways behind me, so I start to get over. For whatever reason, I veer into the gravel. "Shit, shit, shit," I say. I gently and calmly apply my brakes and I come to a stop. Eventually if you road ride, you might go off road at some point; same applies to trails. If you do, it's exactly like being in a car: stay calm and tap or gently press the brakes and coast to a stop. Nothing sudden, no fast moves—that's bad, and you don't want to crash going this fast. I also don't want a face full of gravel.

The mountain colors blow my mind; all the brown and reddish rock is a unique thing that I love about the West. The jagged, tall sheer cliffs, and the simplistic beauty of the West are hard to beat. Spending my entire life on the East Coast, I almost feel like I'm in another world out here. Everything out here blows my mind. I want to explore and hike out here. I make a promise to myself: I must come back at some point.

I arrived at Bearmouth and hopped on 90 West. I had a pretty good hill to climb entering Missoula County, but it was almost the end of my day already, and it was still very early in the day. I would only actually be on the bike for three hours to go roughly 45 miles.

I arrived at the Beaver Tail Campground and got a primitive site. It was a really nice campground, with a walking trail along the Clark

Fork River. After I moved around trying to get a consistent signal, I set up my tent.

I really am getting used to having music at camp; with my new power bank I don't worry about running out of power.

I could make it without a phone or map (most likely), though of course it would be more difficult. I have my entire route on paper, just in case something like that happens. I'm solo and I have huge anxiety issues, so I need a plan, I need a fallback option. It may be overkill, but that's why I spend so much extra time writing things down. What happens when you lose a signal and can't load a map? Some might be stalled by this, while I will be able to keep going.

I went for a relaxing walk around the park and ran into some turkeys. A good-sized male stood his ground, silently letting me know he was the protector of the group. I walked down to the river, and it was another great use of these sandals. I walk on the trails, everywhere when I get to camp in them. One of the first things I do is take my shoes off at camp. It was a hot one today, and I'm relaxing standing in the cool water.

It's been hot lately, but I think I'm starting to adapt to it. I'm down a couple thousand feet from Yellowstone, and that's very helpful on my lungs.

I had a very good day riding today and continue loving the terrain out here. Then something kind of crept up on me and made me cranky and miserable, thinking negatively and having thoughts that were just no good to have.

More of my complaining: The trip is costing more than I expected, and it's starting to add up. I'm staying at too many hotels and need to toughen up, I tell myself. I think about how I haven't had a real meal on the trip so far. I've been eating ramen noodles, peanut butter and jelly, and instant oatmeal nearly every day. With these thoughts, I start to spiral into the darkness.

I feel like a light switches, and my entire mood changes almost instantly. But the worst part is I have absolutely no clue how or why. It's something I just try to manage as best I can. I mean, what else can I do?

Montana's ten-dollar fee for out-of-state campers is starting to get to me after a few times paying it. I wish I could buy, like, a monthly pass or some discounted multiuse ticket. Out here lately I'm always paying the same price as an RV; I don't remember encountering many hiker/biker rates recently. Don't get me wrong, I'm still grateful for these and a place to camp. My problem is I see the bills adding up, and then I try to make it back by skimping on things, stretching things out, or compromising on things I want or could use. It's another mental roadblock that I need to figure out.

It was weird, it felt like this wave of sadness and misery just swept over me. I have these thoughts of How can I keep going? How will I ever go back to feeling OK? Do I have the strength—or, it's hard to say, desire—to go on? At this point, honestly I'm probably thinking about life more then my trip, if you want the truth. When this is over, what will change in my life? How will my life change from what it was? How do I find lasting joy and happiness when all I can see is the same path that I've been walking my whole life?

I want off this emotional runaway train. I want change. I want to be set free. I want to be liberated from being held captive by my own thoughts about my limitations. For so long I've felt chained down, like I can't stay happy. In the early days after I quit drinking, I had a guy tell me I was addicted to being miserable. Wow, I really thought about that one, and it's stuck with me. He was spot on, I think. The worst part is how quickly my day changed, and it happens more often than I'd like to admit. I also think my isolated, solitary lifestyle is severely wearing me down mentally. I don't want to be alone anymore.

✪

8/17/23

DAY #51, RIDING #47

Miles—40.79 (3,237.48); Time—3:22 (274:42)
Granite Peak RV Resort, Missoula, Montana
($38, water and electricity)

After the thoughts and feelings that just overwhelmed me last night, I was looking to rebound today; I had to. I would have another short day, with some time to explore Missoula or anything else I came across. Also, it was another day of not setting my alarm, considering I only had around 40 miles today to make it to Wye and my campground. As much as I needed a better day, I would also need to keep my head in the game. If I have a bad day or night, that's OK, but I need to be resilient and accept that the next day is a brand-new start.

I started out my day on my new thrill ride, I-90, from the Beaver Tail Campground to the Clinton exit, 10 miles to the west. From here I would stay on Highway 10 for a 15-mile downhill cruise into Missoula. Also known as Frontage Road, this route would once again wind me through some of the most peaceful, serene landscapes I've seen. It does follow a lot of 90 since there are mountain ranges both north and south of me—not a lot of spare space. I guess it's the only realistic option when making roads, so for now I have I-90 beside me.

I did get to ride along some amazing mountains and go down a couple of canyons. I could see the Clark Fork River, but it was on the opposite side of the interstate. South of me is the Selway-Bitterroot Wilderness, and to the north, I'm between the Lewis and Clark National Forest and Lolo National Forest. The combination of these landscape features out here blows me away.

All is going great; it has been a really good day so far. Then all of a sudden, my front tire slowly goes flat. I tried pumping it up and it seems to hold, so I ride on. Eventually it gets to be too much. I get to Canyon River Golf Club to start the Kim Williams Trail. I find a good, shaded spot to stop and change my tube out. After the tube switch, I get everything packed back up and load up my bike to start the Kim Williams Trail. I start the trail in this nice-looking golf club, and the trail takes me into Missoula. It's a pretty rocky trail but not too bad for the tires I have. It's such a sight-filled trail; it goes within a few feet of the Clark River and then becomes a pine-filled riding haven. The trail goes right by the University of Montana and right past the Washington-Grizzly football stadium.

I have to stop because my tire is running low again. Outside the football stadium, I pump up my tire and see an REI is in town. I decide to go there since I get free tube changes from being a member. Maybe they can find what I can't. On my way, I also pass a baseball stadium. The Missoula PaddleHeads is a team in a nonaffiliated league, similar to our hometown Lancaster Barnstormers. I enjoy passing and seeing stadiums and would like to see a game if I stay here.

I get to REI, but the guys there also can't find anything in my tire. I am slightly concerned, but they change it, and we wait a few minutes to see if it leaks. It doesn't, so I take off and go to Target to get some supplies. I start on my way to my campground, which is only 8 miles away in Wye. I take West Broadway to avoid I-90 and notice my tire losing air again. I pump it up a few times and make it to camp.

I take out the tube, pump it up, and wrestle around with it, bending and twisting it. It seems to be holding air or perhaps the loss of air is so slow because of the lack of the weight. Basically, I have no clue—I've looked now twice, and REI couldn't find the problem either. All I can assume is something about the tire is still causing me trouble. But now I can't ride back down into town or REI.

It's getting late, and I'm going crazy in my head trying to find a way to solve this tonight. For some reason, I have this absolute need to fix this tonight. I try hard but ultimately can't help myself. This is one tendency I *absolutely* need to fix; I need to be able to walk away from things like this and realize I don't need to deal with everything right away.

On the advice of an employee, I tried Uber for the first time. I was worried that I couldn't take my bike along but was told there was options for that. I doubted that but downloaded the app anyway.

I eventually get it figured out, and a guy shows up. Of course, I can't take the bike. I didn't want to pay for two taxi rides, so I took my tire off. Of course, I get a waiting fee now, and this is exactly why I do everything on my own as much I can. The world seems to nickel and dime consumers to death. Thirty-four dollars, later, I made it the 8 miles to REI, again.

Once again, they couldn't find anything wrong; I would've tried a bike shop, but they were all closed at this point. So I ended up buying a tire they had in stock. I got a solid bead Vittorio tire. It's only 35 millimeters wide, so it's also the skinniest tire I've ever ridden. I just hope it holds up. This is now the third front tire I've had on my bike during this trip. I called the guy who dropped me off on his phone, and he came and picked me up for a slightly lower rate in cash this time. A Middle Eastern guy, in his midthirties, I'm guessing.

We started talking, and it just seemed like he was maybe unhappy with living in this area. I remember him asking me about where I live, and how it was there. It's very expensive living here in Missoula, I'm told. I don't know I picked up the vibe that he needed an escape; I certainly know the feeling. Back at my tent, I couldn't help but total up expenses for my day; deep down I know I cause majority of my stress with my half-manic ways sometimes.

When I bought the three tubes in Nebraska, I failed to realize the Presta stem length. They're extremely short and stick out just barely enough to get a grip on to inflate them. They were the only ones at the store back then. They were very annoying, and as frustrated with them as I was, I was glad to donate them to REI. The bike mechanic told me REI donates equipment/gear to some place I forget. I still could've used the tubes, but with everything going on, I make rash rush decisions. I donated them mainly because I don't want to try to hold on to this short, stubby valve while trying to attach my pump. To get a true seal, the pump had to be against the rim; that's how short they were. I bought three new tubes to replace my donations. This added a little to my mental struggle against wasteful spending for the sake of convenience.

I did feel like I was losing it for a while today. Lately I'm feeling like a piece of string that's been rolled around into a tangled-up mess and tied tight at the ends. I got an email with my new credit card bill, and that didn't help. I ask myself, When will my mental suffering end? I know I'm probably in store for some hard times mentally up ahead. Who am I kidding? They're here now. The worst part of all this is the fact that I'm not naive enough to know that majority I cause, it's self-induced.

I usually don't complain about tent sites, but here, man WTF. The ground is graded so the water drains down toward the tent area! My whole tent site is even graded at a slight angle, and the overflow parking is literally five feet from the tent pads. A couple times, for some reason I had lights from the parking area shining right into my site, very annoying. Anyways, even with that and everything I worried about today, I was glad to be here. A lot of places don't allow tent camping, so it can sometimes be difficult finding a tent site out here.

Here I am again complaining and doing the why-me thing. I need to just understand this is life and, for God's sake, lighten up; I'm on the trip of a lifetime. *Do not waste this opportunity!* In the back of my mind, I keep thinking, I miss the East. But do I, or am I just lost, feeling empty and unfulfilled inside? Do I just need the comfort of home, something familiar?

★

8/18/23

DAY #52, RIDING #48

Miles—28.76 (3,266. 24); Time—2:26 (277:08)
Motel 6 University, Missoula, Montana ($175)

Today would be a new day, and it was off to a good-enough start. The weather wasn't good—there was a rainstorm later in the day, and there were supposed to be high winds along with that. The start wasn't bad as I rode 12 miles on Frenchtown Frontage Road to the town of Huson. The ride was another Western gem, with nice-looking farms along the way. The skies now had this ominous look that gave up any intention of hiding the storm later. I wasn't thinking that I made a mistake because I wanted to keep moving today.

The plan today was to go to Saint Regis, get close to Idaho, and make my Montana exit. I had to get on 90 West in Huson because the side road ended, and the connecting road went into the Lolo National Forest. Certainly not a road I want to be on, riding at least. I get on 90 West and start riding on my big clean shoulder. The wind was picking up and getting heavy.

All of a sudden, I notice my rear tire going flat. Same as last time—a slow leak. I catch a break and have a construction zone up ahead, with traffic detoured to the far-left lane. I stop and change out my tube, with two full lanes essentially to myself, one lane and a shoulder. Then there's a gravel area; that's where I change the tube, far, far away from traffic. Once again, I can't find the tire-deflating culprit.

I got it changed out, packed up my gear, and took off. The workers were really cool and waved me through. There was also a cool-looking BNSF train riding along the freeway. It was a cool scene, even if the weather wasn't. By now the wind was bad, must have been at least 20 miles per hour. I was being blown around and had to ride at an angle again to counter the wind. Of course, it was mostly blowing me toward traffic. To top things off, my rear tire was going flat again.

I just passed an exit at Cyr, but I also just crossed a bridge with no shoulder. You want to talk about crazy/scary riding? Ride a bridge on I-90 with no shoulder! Even this one made me shake inside. It was a short bridge, and I could see far behind me to gauge traffic. But still, even if no one was coming, the next person was doing at least the speed limit of 80 miles per hour. Now that's wild, and this wouldn't be the only bridge like this I'd have to ride across. No cars came behind me, by the way.

Anyway, I can't turn around on this side; I'm not going back over that bridge and certainly not riding the interstate against traffic, no way. I may think crazy, but I act rationally under pressure, when it's needed, anyway.

This incoming storm was an hour and a half away. I crossed over everything, all traffic lanes, very carefully to the east side of I-90. This direction had a shoulder over the Cyr Bridge. I got off at the Cyr exit. I used this bridge at the exit for cover and started calling places, looking for a ride. I had already changed my tube and inspected it and hadn't found whatever was causing the flat. With that and the storm coming, I just decided to try to get back to town.

While I was standing under the bridge, a guy in a truck asked if I need help. I told him my issue, and he offered a ride to Alberton. Alberton was the next exit east and had a restaurant and a motel next to each other. He was going east, so I got a ride to a much better spot. Not bad for only waiting there about thirty minutes under the bridge. I thanked him, and of course he wouldn't take anything.

I continued my searching and calling for a ride into Missoula. I was going to go to a bike shop this time. If I couldn't find a ride, at least there was a motel where I was now at across the parking lot.

I think it was some outfitter I called that gave me a number for Tommy. He drove around with a guy and transported people's vehicles. If you were canoeing or whatever in the water, he'd move your vehicle to the end point. Then when you finished up, you could load up and leave right away. Tommy was super cool, and he had a Grateful Dead background on his phone (an insignificantly important fact). I told him what was going on, and he asked me if I was that crazy dude on the interstate riding his bicycle in this weather, ha ha. He was actually still talking to me on the phone when he showed up at the restaurant! I had told him where I was before on the phone; he was already driving on 90 East. What good luck. I packed my bike inside his hatchback and squeezed in the back. I had to go in butt first, then get the rest in. I had my ride.

I rode around with them for a little while they did their work. I was OK with it of course; I loved getting to see these side roads and terrific views along the water. After they were done, we stopped by his house in downtown Missoula. After a short stop and a few calls around to local bike shops, I found one that was close and motels close by as well.

Tommy dropped me off at Hellgate Cyclery, and I thanked him for all the help. He was doing transportation for work, so I gave him twenty-five; that was all he wanted. I'm glad to have met him, a really cool dude. He did also really help me by picking me up as I had called a few places before I got his number.

The guys at Hellgate Cyclery, specifically the one who helped me (wish I could remember his name), were absolutely the best. I told them about my day and what was happening with my tire. I picked up a tiny sliver of a wire from a blown tire on 90 somewhere. He showed it to me; it was sticking out of the inside of the tire, and I still could barely see it. He had solved the mystery of my deflating tire. I couldn't find it, and neither could REI, and I'm sure now the same thing happened in the front. Wow, was it super tiny. I then asked him about folding tires, and he told me so much I didn't know. I was very glad I came here as I got so much more than my tire fixed.

I ended up with a nonfolding Schwalbe 700 by 40 and was very pleased all around. I also booked a hotel while I was waiting on the tire. So that was nice: I had everything in line, and I was ready to leave. I packed my bags. I then noticed I couldn't find my helmet. I went back in the shop, and the guy told me he didn't remember me coming in with one. I called Tommy, and he also didn't have it. I realized I must've left it in the truck of the first guy, the one who picked me up under the bridge. Damn! It's a bummer when I just forget stuff like this when my brain is overloaded with thoughts about how to solve a problem. It's not the first time I've left gear at random places on a trip; I did it with Giro gloves in Ohio on a prior trip.

They had the same exact helmet at the shop, the Giro Fixture, so that was good. Then of course I absolutely needed a mirror as well. I'm so grateful for everything Hellgate Cyclery did for me. The time the guy took with me was very helpful and appreciated. I learned some valuable tire information. If you're in Missoula, this is the shop you need to go to. I 100 percent recommend them.

Oh well, what can you do? At least I got here before the storm and people helped me out tremendously today. Now I'm ready to go onto my motel and decompress. It's easy to say "Oh well" now that everything is fixed; it's been a few hours now, and I'm calmed down. Wow, was I a semimess back on the interstate, with the tire low. First, I was in a completely empty area, Cyr, with nothing close for miles. Not terrible yet, but the anxiety was starting to build for sure. I knew I'd be OK once I got to Alberton, with its motel.

But man, was I trying to stay calm and not get worked up. While not an ideal situation, it was not too bad on the grand scheme of things that could happen. I was still slightly panicked, though, on the inside. It was getting harder to remain calm, not terribly hard, but I was feeling uncomfortable. For me, the thoughts and anticipation of knowing what's going to eventually happen is worse than the actual event itself. I think a lot of it was being broken down alone and in the middle of nowhere, with the storm coming in. Not to mention I was in grizzly territory, although my grizzly thing was not on my mind at the time and I realized the low likelihood of an encounter.

I was mentally breaking down, I think, letting the adversity win over my determination and will. I had thoughts of being sick and fed up with my trip and its never-ending problems. The last few days and today were completely breaking me down inside. In fact, the last few weeks had been tough, with some good problems along the way. Having to deal with all these problems alone, for me at least, is like carrying the world on my shoulders. Sometimes I wonder if I bit off more than I can chew. My confidence is shrinking. Something's got to change and change fast.

✪

8/19/23
DAY #53, RIDING #49

Miles—71.01 (3,337.25); Time—5:21 (282:29)
St. Regis Hotel, St. Regis, Montana ($72)

Waking up in my hotel, I slept in a little bit. I didn't set an alarm; I needed the extra rest. I also needed a turnaround from the past few days. With the help I got yesterday, I had a lot of reasons to feel optimistic. Everything was fixed, and the bike was looked over; that also felt reassuring. Today I wanted to get to St. Regis, and I knew I'd have a 70-mile day. Once again it was mostly downhill, with a few good, short climbs. I decided to start off on 90 West since I rode the first the first 30 miles yesterday.

It was another picture-perfect day to start off, and the landscape would turn into maybe my favorite on the entire trip. Before I got off I-90, I went through another construction zone, but they weren't working on the bridge. So for a few miles, I had basically two lanes to myself again. The views of the Clark Fork River with the tree-filled hills—well, mountains really—is jaw-dropping. I was loving this area, and it would only get better from here.

Once again, it's hard to describe how much I love this terrain. These mountains in the distance—they're like nothing I've ever seen. It's amazing, and here I am, never really knowing where I am but not lost. I'm really just trying to fully immerse myself out here. It just seems so peaceful. This is exactly what I needed early in the day.

I got off in Tarkin and took Frontage Road / Highway 10 again. More mountains and more just incredible riding. Canyons, hills, the river, going mostly downhill—this was unbelievable and a perfect combination to ride in.

In Superior, I had an opportunity to look down at the town from a higher point. There were people tubing down the river, and I could hear an announcer. There were also a lot of people watching from the bridge over the Clark Fork. Not sure what was going on, but there were also some local vendors selling things along the main road. Something neat to come across, for sure, even though I'm not sure exactly what it was—just a nice little surprise.

Here at Superior, I would also get back on 90 West to ride into St. Regis. After a short 13-mile segment, I arrived in town. I had planned on staying at a campground but passed a sign in town for a $65 motel. My tent site was going to cost $45. Easy choice for $20 more. It was at the bar/restaurant right off the exit; I had to go to the bar to book my room. It was just a small 4 or 5 room motel on the backside of the building.

When I got into St. Regis, I immediately recognized the hazy sky—wildfire. It wasn't too bad when I first arrived, but within a few hours, it got bad. Even I will admit it was a lot to deal with. I could taste the smoke and feel my eyes burning. I also couldn't see more than maybe 5 to 6 miles down the road. There was a fire burning 30 miles east, and it was the River Road East fire. It was discovered the day before and had already burned 12,000 acres. It's also, as of this day, 0 percent contained. It's surreal being this close to a wildfire; this one was a lot worse than the other one I went through.

It creates an odd sort of scene: Some people are trying to find out if the highways will close down. Some don't even seem to notice and are going about their business as usual. The closed highways could mean extra hours on the ride home as the roads are few out here, I understand from what I was told. Now I'm very glad I'm in a hotel, and it was also very hot outside today, on top of everything.

One of my planned side trips was to the Hiawatha Trail. I found a cheap hotel a few miles away from the trail and only about 30 miles west, in Saltese. The weather coming up called for heavy rains for a couple days straight, plus a late shower tomorrow. So for $65 a night, I found a nice little spot in the middle of nowhere in western

Montana. I absolutely don't want to be stranded out here in a storm, so Mother Nature will let me know when I can leave Saltese.

While riding on Frontage Road today, all of a sudden, I saw something black flying on my right side. At first, I figured it was a bird; I really didn't get a good look. I did look down though, and thought, Where the hell is my cell phone? I realized what that black object was now: my cell phone holder just randomly broke and flew apart on the road. My phone was lying there in the roadway! Luckily, I found the parts of the phone holder, that held the actual phone. I ended up using a rubber band to hold those two pieces together, pinching my phone in between. Wow, all I could think was, What if I had been looking to the left at that moment? I don't think I would have found my phone if I hadn't seen that black object flying on my right.

Today is definitely better than yesterday. I'm liking the new tires and how they feel. I've been mostly declining in elevation lately, and I'm hoping I won't pay for it later. I'm thinking, maybe I'm just slowly coming down from the Continental Divide into the Pacific Northwest and the ocean. I'm definitely in a better head space today. I don't feel pressure, and best of all, I don't feel the anxiety I did yesterday. I don't ever again want to be like I was yesterday.

I love being here, but I'm getting tested physically like never before out here in the West. It's certainly taking its toll both mentally and physically.

For instance, last night at the campsite, I was trying not to freak out, but I sort of was. My mind was absolutely racing a mile a minute, like uncontrollably. All I could think was, My tire needs to be fixed tonight; I've got to do this right now. And of course it didn't, but here's where I struggle: for whatever reason, I can't let it go and wait until later. Physically I can, but in my mind, I can't. I have this mentality that things need to be fixed immediately on this trip. It creates so much stress that I just don't need. Then usually other things will all snowball into each other.

I'm out here solo, so I need to somehow get over it and deal with it all. Or just do whatever I can to keep it together. No matter how I feel, I still need to function daily out here, and that can be tough. I need to remain mindful of how fatigued I am. I'm getting close to the end, and I can't burn out before I finish. It's both mental and physical burnout, but the mental burnout is what I need to keep an eye on.

I know when I'm tired, I need to keep pedaling to reach my destination, but how do I reach my mental destination?

8/20/23
DAY #54, RIDING #50

Miles—58.83 (3,396.08); Time—5:33 (288:02)
Mangold's General Store and Motel, Saltese, Montana ($65)

Today I decided to do something off the GART route, something I had read so much about—the Hiawatha Trail. Specifically, I had read about that it was one of the most scenic rail trails in America. There was no way I could pass it up, especially since it was right along my route. The weather forecast also had rain tonight and the next few days. The motel in Saltese was only a 25-mile ride from St. Regis, and it was another 8 miles to the Hiawatha from the motel. It was a perfect setup for me.

The smoke in the morning was still pretty bad, and I hoped I would start to ride out of it. There was a newer trail, Route of the Olympian, from St. Regis—31 miles to the Hiawatha—and an exit at Saltese. I started on the trail, but the first 5 miles were very rocky. I assumed the entire trail was like that and got off as soon as I passed a road to exit. Later, very much to my regret, I'd find out the first few miles from St. Regis were rougher but then it got better. I would've really loved to have ridden this trail. Instead, I got to enjoy the views from I-90. It was a short ride to Saltese and my destination: Mangold's General Store and Motel. The owner running the place was really nice, and I would enjoy the time there. Definitely stay here if you pass by, and bikers, this is an ideally located very well priced motel.

This area near the Idaho border is a dream ride. This is easily my favorite landscape; I know I have a few favorites. The mountains and incredibly tall trees that swallow up the views along the trail mesmerize me. The beautifully flowing St. Regis River is incredibly clean looking and adds to the visual appeal of the area. I feel like I'm in heaven out here; every second is some new visual treasure. I haven't been in scenic terrain like this; everything is mind-blowing. I'm not even on the Hiawatha yet; this sensory pleasure is happening in the first 25 miles to Saltese!

I at least started riding out of the River Road East wildfire a little bit. But there are other fires around. Actually, there are a lot of wildfires going on right now. There are a couple big ones in the Spokane, Washington, area, which is only about 100 miles away. It's crazy to be out here experiencing firsthand the effects of these fires in real time. I was glad to be out of the smoke of St. Regis, and I arrived at my motel, but my room wasn't ready; I was way early. They let me drop off my bags, though. I then took off for the Hiawatha and my first taste of Idaho!

This is a perfect place to stay, and a great spot for trail riding. I took the NorPac (Northern Pacific) Trail the 9 miles there; that was the next trail on my GART route anyway. It's a great trail, though a little rocky and bumpy for my full weight. Well, more because of my issues. It's not that bad; I'm just paranoid about encountering more problems. The trail is more suited to mountain bikes and wider tires, but I was fine. Not sure if I'll take this trail tomorrow, plus the Borax Tunnel on this trail is closed, permanently, so I might not even have a detour on the trail. There's a possibility it might collapse in on itself. I took a harder route to my destination; I had a short gravel road and a steep incline to the East Portal of the Route of the Hiawatha. There was another trail, the Route of the Olympians, I wanted to take back. I wanted to ride two different trails; that's why I took the harder NorPac there.

I got to the Route of the Hiawatha, and though I knew about the fee, I was still not happy about having to pay forty dollars to ride a trail. On weekends you must buy a bus pass that gets you a ride back to the top of the trail. It's a 15-mile, constant 2.2-percent downhill grade. I could've coasted the entire route. It is located in the Bitterroot Mountains, near the Look Out Pass ski area and is in both Montana and Idaho. It has 9 tunnels and 7 high trestle bridges!

It's billed as America's most scenic rail trail, and I believe it. It started out going through the 1.6-mile Taft Tunnel. What a start, and coming out the other end, I was in Idaho. Just incredible views, one after the other. The views from in between the incredible pines, looking across the valleys, were mesmerizing.

I left my lights attached for the entire trip as there were tunnels scattered all along the trail. My favorites were the trestle bridges. The tunnels are cool, but nothing beats the bridges. I stopped at every one and of course had to look over the side down below. The railings are only a braided steel wire, 6 separate lines running the length of the bridge. They also have 2-by-4 boards to stand on, and you can see in between them to the ground below. It's very inspiring and potentially nauseating looking over the edge. I feel both and love it all.

I'd say mountain bikes are preferred out here as some parts get rocky and bumpy. But I'm also riding a 35 millimeter tire up front too. I have zero issues, though, and notice maybe two other people with drop handlebars.

I'm also riding light out here with my pump and a tube bungeed to the rack. It's really nice not having to carry all my extra gear. On one trestle I pass Kelly Creek, and the views look like something you'd see in a tour book. I love seeing the pine trees coming down both sides of the mountain, forming multiple Vs as they descend into the valley below. The tunnels with the rock blown out are also a treat not to be ignored. After every tunnel, as I exit, I'm somehow greeted by a better view than the last. The absolute beauty of the day was confirmed by the one-hundred-plus pictures I took!

After finishing up, I got the shuttle back to the start, or close. I had to ride through the Taft Tunnel again. I started to leave and go back to the hotel. I decided to take the Route of the Olympians trail back to my motel this time. It was all downhill. Once again, I'm in love with this area. The trail terrain and its landscape are just perfect looking, to me. It's a relaxing trail to ride, that's for sure.

Tomorrow is a zero day. It's forecasted to rain almost all day, plus I paid for two nights at check in. Hopefully the rain only lasts one day, but it should help with the wildfires.

Today was such an amazing day; I need more days like this. I feel great today, seeing what I did. I was happy while riding.

8/21/23

DAY #55, RIDING #50

Mangold's General Store and Motel, Saltese, Montana ($70)

Today was a preplanned rain-out zero day. Such days are always bittersweet for me, but at least it did rain really good today, eventually. I say bittersweet because as much as I want to move on, it's vindicating for me when it does rain. It's always a good feeling knowing I made the right decision about something.

Being a creature of habit, I woke up at 5:30 a.m.! I made a cup of coffee and sat outside in a chair watching the darkness and eventually the sunrise. Outside my door was a walkway, with a covering overhead and a half wall. Perfect place to rest my coffee cup and kick my feet up. This would be my position most of the day, relaxing outside and covered from the rain. The sunrise made waking up at five thirty well worth it; it was beautiful to see.

After going back to sleep, eventually, I woke up around ten thirty to restart the day. It then started raining around noon and continued all day. I didn't get a chance to walk the main road, but I would squeeze in the half-mile road tomorrow.

There is nothing in Saltese besides the store/motel and a bar/restaurant at the other end of the road. I like it here; what else do I need? It's so quiet. I have two trails if it clears up, and the motel checks off my boxes—clean, quiet and cheap. It's got everything: TV, coffee maker, shower. It's a perfect place in which to sit out my rain delay.

I was sitting outside, and I saw a younger guy come riding in. After he settled in, he came out, and we started talking. Joe was his name, and he was from Montreal, Canada, of all places. He told me he was planting trees up north in Canada, part of a government replanting rule/law for logging crews. He told me it was basically a one-for-one up there—cut one, plant one—or something close to that. So after he finished, he bought a bike and took off. He was going to make a big loop heading south before going home. We sat outside and did our own planning. Not much else to do considering it was still raining. Just a good day to sit around.

Not sure how tomorrow will play out since there's rain at 50 percent almost all day. One storm, OK, but rain on and off all day with little or no chance of finding cover, I'll pass. I didn't do much of anything today, and it was actually really nice. I never left the hotel area. I just focused on looking over my route and maps and just looking ahead. I saw a Walmart in Smeltersville, Idaho, about 45 miles away. I figured there I could stock up and buy a new phone holder. My next campground was also only 50ish miles away.

It's always nice being able to resupply close to camp. If I can't fit everything in my bags, I end up having to put a bag or two under my bungee cords. You don't want to ride too far like that, for obvious reasons. I always empty out the boxes; I don't need to say anything about how big a food package is compared to its contents. I'm sure we've all gone through that disappointment before.

I'm also very excited to have longer trails back-to-back coming up. It's been a while since I could get lost in the wilderness along a rail trail, and I desperately miss it. I know it'll do me good. Also, I'm only a short distance from Idaho and leaving another state in the dust. I'll only be in Idaho for two and a half days, and it's all trail. I will be on another amazing trail in Washington before I wrap up my trip. I'm guessing I'm down to eight to ten camping days left until I'm done. The end is near and will be here soon. I'll just have to wait until tomorrow to make a decision about whether or not to move on.

⭐

8/22/23
DAY #56, RIDING #50

Miles—12.79 (3,406.87); Time—1:21 (289:23)

Mangold's General Store and Motel ($65)

Yesterday I decided I was going to wait until the morning to make a decision about whether or not to ride. West over the mountain, rain all day, and to the east, no rain. I looked at the radar and saw the green storm cloud has moved just to the side of Saltese. I was pretty much on the outside of the storm. Since where I was headed had rain, I decided to stay in Saltese another day. I've gone through enough tunnels and mountains to know how drastically the weather can change from one side to the other.

Joe, my temporary neighbor, decided to ride on as he was headed east. We decided, or he did, to take the Olympian Trail into St. Regis. It's a very nice but rocky trail. Maybe I'm just used to smaller rocks on the trails. It's by no means bad, just not ideal for a 35-millimeter tire. I'm also probably now being more cautious than I need to be. I don't know, I just call it how it applies to me. That being said, I think I live in a pretty special area for biking.

I can't even imagine having these trails out here for my usual everyday rides. The absolute beauty is like nothing I've ridden through, and it would continue to get better. If you live out here, I can't imagine it ever gets old. Everything out here, from the amazing trees to the abundance of green, is just so relaxing to me. Every turn offers some new gift to my senses.

I went about 7 miles one way with Joe until we both felt the drizzle. No way was I getting wet on an off day. I decided it was a good time to say our good lucks and goodbyes. I did warn him about the wildfire near St. Regis, but I figured given what he did for work, he'd be familiar with fires. The trail also featured a pretty cool-looking sketchy-siding trestle bridge. It was pretty high up, but I'm not sure what was more nauseating as I looked over the side: the thin wire sides or the two-by-fours with big gaps on the sides of the bridge.

It actually was a nice day here. Tomorrow, I have a 60ish mile ride to Cataldo, Idaho. I can't wait for the Coeur D'Alene Trail in Idaho. It's 72 miles and all paved and somehow looks even better than the Hiawatha on the views. The next two days are pretty good riding, but then I'm not sure about the eastern side of the Palouse to Cascades Trail. I guess I'll be doing a lot of on-the-fly riding. Based on my research, it seems to have a few detours, so I'll decide when I get there. Also, I hear the trail is very rocky and rough in the eastern Washington section.

I normally don't like making decisions on the fly; I like having a plan and being as detailed as possible. But the trail varies a lot in surface and obstacles such as missing gaps, bridges, and private property closures, all kinds of factors that prevent a through ride for me.

I'm waiting for the much talked about western cascades region of the trail. From what I hear, the western section of the Columbia River is breathtaking.

I'm sort of stressed out about having to navigate on the fly. I have two campgrounds planned, so hopefully I can connect those two dots. The trail website has detailed sections with detours, so I'll most likely just follow what they say. I'm feeling good and have got about a week and half to go. The anxiety is still high, but what's new? Bring it.

With the off days from the rain, I've had time to recharge and think, and that's put me in a better frame of mind. Two days of not doing anything has been better for me than I thought it would be. The next week is all clear of rain, so far, and I'm hoping to make the final push after this. Knowing that and that I only have a week and a half to go is crazy. I've experienced a lot of things on this trip, and I'm glad because I needed to get away from home for a while.

Back home, before the trip, my life was getting so chaotic and my self will was running uncontrolled. It was good to just get away from everything, but I don't even know what everything is because I'm such a loner and isolator. Maybe I had to get away from myself. Just get away to be able to slow down life, slow down Craig, and most importantly find Craig. Either again or for the first time.

Being out here can be chaotic at times, but the rewards are worth the price. There is more to deal with than I expected, in a good way. It's so nice being out here and not having to worry about much of anything. Stuff at home needs to be dealt with, but that's not here; that is three-fourths of the way across America.

Out here it's just me, my busted-up Diamondback, and the people I meet along the way. The people help me in a few ways, more than just with navigation. It's the camaraderie, the human contact—I think that helps me more than anything. It's odd, if I pass someone in public anywhere in my daily life, there's very little chance of me interacting with them. But put me on my bike or maybe on a trail, and that changes a little bit.

I'm doing a whole lot better now than I was a while ago. It was real bad for a while; I was honestly fed up with biking. Between burnout and being frustrated by various problems, I had a really bad temperament. All the problems adding up took its toll. But now I feel like I have a fresh start; what is there to worry about today? The bike is running good, it's currently sunny outside, I've got trails up ahead, and I'm riding out a dream. Everything's good; I feel good. I've found my happiness. And please enjoy this last week and half, I tell myself. After that it's over and I'm back home.

Maybe home is permanent, maybe home's temporary. So much of my life seems up in the air, and unknown.

I'm so ready for the Pacific Northwest. I can't wait for Bainbridge Island. Positive vibes, positive outlook. Be yourself, and just try to enjoy life. Follow and pursue your dreams and do what you want to do. Don't change yourself or your style for anyone.

8/23/23
DAY #57, RIDING #51

Miles—54.51 (3,461.38); Time—4:46 (294:09)
CDA River RV and Campground, Cataldo, Idaho ($25, primitive)

The storm moved on, and so did I. Since I did half of the trail to the Idaho border, and the other half was closed off at the Borax Tunnel—well, mostly because of the tunnel closure—I decided to ride the first 10 miles on 90 West. I didn't know if there was a tunnel detour, and knowing it was closed, I decided to just skip it. It was a good uphill climb to the border, and I exited at mile 0. I got on the NorPac Trail at Lookout Pass ski area. It's a cool place and must be an incredible skiing area. There are lots of ski lifts along the trail there; it's also where the Hiawatha Trail outfitters keep their bikes, book their trips, and have a small store.

The trail is amazing; the views looking out over the valleys offer multiple landscapes I never want to forget. From Lookout Pass, the crest of the hill, I could've coasted the 20 miles I had to do on this trail. Goodbye, Montana, and hello, Idaho, my eleventh state, along with Washington DC. Ten states down, and I can't believe it. It still doesn't seem real.

This is my first time in Idaho. This trail makes Idaho easy to fall in love with and doesn't disappoint. The lookouts offer a vast, expansive view of the beautiful fir and pine trees. I just absolutely love the trees out here. There are such scenic areas looking into the mountains, and I get the same feeling about the trees. The way they look with their tops dotting the mountains and landscape combines for a view I could watch all day. Once again, I just can't accurately describe their beauty; I'm not a good enough writer to do this any justice.

Another thing about the trail: part of it is actually a road; a car came up the trail alongside me. The trail was gravel and hard-packed dirt. Some parts had deeper gravel, washouts, and larger rocks. Nothing terrible—I just had to pay more attention and go a little slower downhill.

I came down this long stretch of trail, then I saw it, and right away I knew the only thing it could be. Standing right in the middle of the trail was a huge moose! I couldn't believe it, and I was really excited to actually see a moose in the wild. It was massive and antlerless; I kept a distance of probably seventy-five yards. I wanted to make sure it wasn't going to charge or act funny/aggressive. By the time I got my phone out, it had already casually walked into the woods. By the time I got to where it was standing, Bullwinkle was nowhere to be found.

I finished up the NorPac Trail in Mulan, Idaho. This was where I would start the Coeur D'Alene trail. It's 73 miles, fully paved from Mulan to Plummer Junction, Idaho, and then a few miles to Washington. This would end up being my favorite rail trail of the trip. It's some of the same landscape, but my favorite trees are still everywhere. It does follow the highway for a little bit but also the south fork of the Coeur D'Alene River.

I also went by some towns every 10 or so miles, it seemed, which was nice. Well, I say that now since I can easily remember how hard it was not too long ago not having any places to stop. I don't stop in many towns, but the trail offers great views into them. I was planning on stocking up big-time at Wally World in Smeltersville later anyway.

One of the things I was thinking about while writing this book is, How do I continually describe something similar multiple days in a row without repeating myself, or how do I not get boring in my writing? I really don't know, so I try to keep it in mind and not repeat myself too much. I'll keep it short on the Coeur D'Alene. What I've already described, plus its many views and crossings of the river is what makes this trail special. The waterways in the last few states are the cleanest-looking I've seen. The crystal-clear reflections really make the rivers stand out to me.

These two trails, and riding them back-to-back, are like a dream. I'm a liar—I can't say which I liked better, the NorPac or the Coeur D'Alene. This is exactly what I needed after nearly three weeks on the roads.

I stopped at Walmart, which was also conveniently located on the trail. I was out of everything, so this was desperately needed. I went inside and got enough to last me a while, that's for sure. Outside at my bike, I unboxed and stored everything in my bags. Tortillas, a jar of peanut butter and jelly, two types of Clif bars, Pop-Tarts, Nutri-Grain bars, a big box of oatmeal, and a big bag of Skittles. I had run out of room by now, so I had ten packs of ramen noodles bungeed around my sleeping bag on the back. I keep my sleeping bag in the center of my rack bungeed down. Luckily, I only had 8 trail miles to ride with this tied down.

Remember what I said about stocking up close to camp? Awkward load, and I just gained twenty pounds to finish my day. About the weight: I have been thinking of getting rid of one of my water bottles. I've never used two full bottles yet and could use the extra space. I would later decide against this idea.

I'm a little nervous about this Palouse to Cascade Trail. Once again, I don't think my tires are wide enough, from what I have read and heard. With the few tire changes now, I'll just have to wait and see and go from there. Take the trail as it comes. I do think I'll skip the trail going West into Tekoa, Washington, the John Wayne Trail. I've heard from a lot of people that the trail is rough and wider tires are almost a necessity. After this trail, I'll probably take the road into Tekoa. There's a cool bridge there, but I'll just have to wait and see the trail conditions.

Well, another state down. Goodbye, Big Sky Country, it's been a wild ride.

✪

8/24/23

DAY #58, RIDING #52

Miles—69.38 (3,530.76); Time—7:04 (301:13)
Baymont Inn and Suites, Spokane, Washington ($117)

It was a colder start to the day than normal, with temperatures in the midforties at 6:00 a.m. when I woke up. I did sort of wonder if I would have warm enough clothes for out here. And while it would get cold at some points, I never bought extra clothes. I just made do with wearing a couple shirts at once. Usually, I'd wear a long-sleeve under a regular shirt, and that would be enough. I had another 40ish miles to go to finish up the Coeur D'Alene Trail at Plummer Junction. I was ready to go and looking forward to the rest of the trail.

The trail eventually makes its way onto the Coeur D'Alene Tribal Reservation. There are a couple bigger lakes right along the trail that are incredible by themselves. But the Chatcolet stood out the most by far. It's easy to say that when the trail cuts out on to the lake and has a bridge over the middle. The trail around the Coeur D'Alene Bridge was such a beautiful area, and the bridge taking me over the calm waters was special. Between the lakes and the Coeur D'Alene River hugging the trail, it's easy to put this trail at the top of my all-time top rail trails.

At one point, while riding around the corner of the lake, the tree-dotted mountains ahead of me were battling for my attention with the huge lake only ten feet to my right.

Before leaving the trail, I'd pass by a bunch of sheds and garage-style buildings on the water. I could only assume they were buildings for ice fishing, which would probably start in a couple months. I also went by an area burned down by a wildfire. It was a somewhat eerie feeling riding through a place that had so much damage from fire, and I could still smell a very faint charred wood smell. I just can't say enough about how much I enjoyed this trail and how inspiring it was on a bike ride.

After leaving the trail, it only took a couple miles for everything to completely change. I decided to take a road ride into Tekoa, Washington, to the Palouse to Cascade Trail. The Palouse region is 100 percent different, and the changes come quick. In the blink of an eye, I'm in a flat, farming area. The landscape surrounding me turns into the golden color of wheat. It looks like I'm also entering a semi deserted, dry area. Goodbye green, and my favorite pine and fir trees. Hello to a new brand-new terrain, and region of America. After a short distance I saw a sign announcing my arrival in Washington! My final state, I have made it.

After a short ride I arrived in Tekoa, Washington, and the Palouse to Cascade trail. There was a really cool trestle bridge at the start of the trail. But immediately after that, I began to think riding this trail was a mistake. Bigger rocks, some ruts, and deep gravel were the trail surfaces to start. I only made it about 5 miles of the 16 to Rosalia City Park before I got a flat. I stopped; I had picked up a thorn, another goathead.

Now here's where it all went downhill. I start to dig out my tube and tools. I get my pump and notice the front face part is missing! I dig through my bag, emptying it out, scouring everywhere, and I can't find it. Now I have no way of inflating my tire, and I'm in the middle of nowhere, on an isolated trail, and I'm very doubtful I'll see anyone out here on the trail. So I start to walk. There's no shade anywhere, and the sun is shining unobstructed by the clouds. It's 5 miles back to Tekoa, or 12 miles to Rosalia, where I planned on camping.

I seriously started walking to Rosalia! I thought, Fuck it, that's the way I need to go, and I'm going that way. I'm so screwed up in my head at the moment that I actually decided to do that. I was going to walk almost three times the distance, compared to turning around.

I know I'm starting to get into a very bad head space, feeling overloaded and twisted up upstairs. I feel the sun's heat; I think it's affecting me and my thoughts. I do feel my thinking becoming slower than normal. I don't understand why I do completely illogical things, like in this instance, going completely against everything I preach about making smart decisions. To me, this signals some mental health problem; this is not normal or good thinking. I'm blindsided now, and my mind is racing, and in this instance I decide to make the wrong moves. This is exactly what I mean by making dumb mistakes that can have tragic consequences. I wouldn't have made it before dark to Rosalia.

What the hell was I thinking, really? I'd love to know because it's easy now looking back to see what I did wrong and should've done instead. But in this moment, whether I know it or not, I'm having a mental breakdown, which is combined with and aided by my dehydrated state.

I called my mom and asked for her help to look up transportation. When I get like this, I ask for help but usually have little intention of listening right away. It's almost like I just want to vent or complain to someone, but I disguise it as asking for help. Maybe I'm also secretly looking for comfort when I'm an absolute wreck like I am now, but I'll never admit that in the moment. Then after being difficult and rambling/venting with my mom, I feel the guilt raining down.

At this point it usually goes two ways for me. If I can get a grip and control my guilt, I only get mildly upset, call, and apologize. Often, I let it go and start beating myself up. Name-calling, thinking I'm dumb, prideful, stubborn, undeserving, et cetera. I let myself go; I start to dig myself a hole of depression and guilt, and I fall in. I hate this place, but it's also unfortunately a familiar place. I really wish I knew the underlying reason why I act like I do in these instances. Knowing the right choice but still dragging myself through the difficult or illogical is what I want to understand about myself.

I eventually wise up and start calling taxis. I finally get ahold of a woman with a van who will come scoop me up. She was located in Spokane, though, 60 miles north. I'm still sort of in panic mode, or I just have mental blinkers on. Because my mind is set that I need a bike shop, even though it's all the way in Spokane. Why didn't I stay closer? Well, there were no places really, but I probably could've found something. Once again, I just can't explain my reasoning or logic here. In my defense, I had to be able to get somewhere to buy a pump. If the pump part is not in my bag, what use is a ride? And the closest place I could buy a bike pump is Spokane. I just can't explain my reasoning or logic here. I walk for a few hours in the sun, pushing my bike along the way.

She eventually arrives and finds me on an isolated stretch of road. I am very glad to see her and glad about the fact that at least the day is almost over. I also know I'll be paying a very high taxi fare. The ride with tip was a high price, but she did have a van that made it very easy for bike transportation. At least the hotel was cheap since I booked sort of late.

I plan on taking an off day tomorrow in Spokane. All this due to a piece of a missing bike pump. Also, I never found the part.

Before I got picked up, I had to make a video diary entry. I was so close to losing it, I needed to vent. Here's the condensed wrap-up of it.

I'm sitting on the side of the road in Fairbanks, Washington, waiting on my taxi. Just incredibly mad at myself—I'm so pigheaded and stubborn. I could've walked 5 miles to Tekoa, but I decided to go on with a flat. I'm immobile with my bike, but yet in my head all

I can think is go, go, go. I was actually going to walk the 12 miles to Rosalia! I wasn't going to include this because I'm embarrassed by it, but I can't hide truths here—I did walk 5 of those miles! After that I said, "What the fuck are you doing, Craig? Really, what are you doing?

Who in their right mind is going to walk 12 miles with all this weight when they could've turned around? In my mind I had no place to stay in Tekoa but I could stay at the city park in Rosalia. But it really wasn't that. Why can't I ask for help from strangers? What's the big fear of people that I don't know? Why can't I ask a stranger for help? I have no problem posting on Facebook looking for help. I even walked by a couple houses and didn't stop to ask for help. When I do some soul-searching, what tells me to not stop and ask for help? Something prevents me from doing this, and whatever it is, is in full effect. Do I have that much pain inside? Am I scared? I've got some deeper issues, and this will exacerbate everything. I'll beat myself up over this for a while, and it doesn't need to be like that.

I really wish I knew how to do something about it. Man, this is freaking tough, and I feel like I created all this; well, I did. But this feels like such a huge problem. I keep thinking, Why didn't I turn around? Why did I continue on that trail? Why do I have this need to follow the GART trail route? I'm committed to the trail. Bullshit, I didn't ride part of the Cowboy Trail, and I hopped off other trails because of conditions. I don't even know why I do these things. I thought I knew myself, but I don't. I thought I did, until I got put in certain situations and saw how I reacted.

I didn't but got really close to losing it out here. There's something going on with me; what are my underlying issues? Watching this video, I'm lost, broken, confused-looking, and having a semi–identity crisis. I'm stuttering and have a lost, empty look in my eyes.

I don't want to be like this. All the breaks I've caught on my past trips are catching up to me on this trip. I've never had as many problems as I do now.

This has been so tough, and to be here all alone magnifies everything. Now is the time I could use someone with me. When I get down, I can get all the way down. I probably need someone to reassure me, give me some hope and confidence. Bring me back to life. I'm hurting right now. As much as I have lost, I need to keep putting one foot in front of the other. There's still no quit in me. Today has been a day to remember. Today has been a day not to forget but to learn from.

8/25/23

DAY #59, RIDING #52

Miles—11.76 (3,542.52); Time—1:46 (302:59)
Baymont Inn and Suites, Spokane, Washington ($150)

Today was a recuperating day, I'll call it, mostly a mental recuperation day. I decided to stay put since I needed a pump, and the closest store didn't open until 10:00 a.m. Nothing wrong with the tire, so we just replaced the tube at the shop. The owner was closing his shop up, and everything was 20 percent off. I got my new pump, and I bought a good multi-tool also. Every multi-tool I have had has been some cheap thing that was included in something I probably bought off Amazon. Having a nice quality feeling, the Crankbrother's multi-tool is a nice difference. I got all fixed up and went rolling on my way. There were a couple things in town I wanted to see before the rain came.

After visiting the bike shop, I saw REI was up the street. I had to go there because I knew they carried the mirror I like the most and I wanted it. On my way to Riverfront Park, I passed the big indoor carousel and came to the Spokane River. There was a really cool rock formation just under the water, and it created a nice-looking effect and mini waterfalls. There was also another bridge over the river with an even more incredible view of different falls. I believe this was the Upper Falls. The water came over the dam, separating into a couple channels mandated by the rock. It provided a really great view of that and the other bridges and buildings in the background.

After passing the Spokane Arena, I came into Riverfront Park. I would love to have gone to a Spokane Chiefs Western Hockey League game, if it had been the season. I hopped on the Centennial Trail, which was paved. It's a relaxing trail that follows along the Spokane River. I would get to visit Gonzaga University and ride through their campus. I stopped at the McCarthy Athletic Center Arena and really liked their Bulldog mascot statue. It's a huge Bulldog with a pretty seriously angry look, greeting visitors. They also had a really cool and very nice-looking baseball field. Gonzaga was super busy today; it was move-in weekend on campus.

After leaving the Zags behind, I crossed the river on a trail bridge. This brought me into the campus of Washington State University, Spokane. Not much to see here; this was mainly just buildings.

I really wanted to ride south a little and visit this Japanese Garden, but it was now starting to drizzle. Rain was forecasted for about an hour. So I just ended up going back to the hotel. Maybe I'd try to stop tomorrow, before I left town.

It ended up being a dreary rainy day, so I didn't leave again. The room had a nice, covered balcony I could hang out on. So that's what I did: I brought out a chair, kicked up my feet, and drank coffee. I also worked on a map for tomorrow, and while I was at it, I created a backup map for the next two days as well. Tomorrow would be a longer day to get back on track. My plan was to go to Ralston Memorial Park, just south of Ritzville.

There are problems every big city faces, and Spokane is no different. I do notice a lot of homelessness here. More here than I normally see in the bigger cities. That is one sad situation by itself, but I have noticed a way worse problem while riding around town today. The hard drug use I have seen around town in a few short hours has been disheartening. I'm talking about hard drug use—glass pipes and smoking off tinfoil. If it's like my county—meth is the culprit. The hardest thing to believe is that it appeared to be almost tolerated. People getting high, huddled together along the walkways and trails, where families walk, among everyone else. They don't even hide behind buildings, under an overpass, or in a hidden private place. There doesn't seem to be any fear or shame associated with this open drug use.

I'm not by any means surprised about drug use in a city or anywhere I go. I don't see many or any police around but also very much know just arresting people does no good. It's a different part of the country, with different thoughts, laws, and ideas from back home.

As I'd get farther west in my trip, I'd find people more open to things and ideas, in opposition to the narrow-mindedness I'm used to like back East. I like the seemingly less-uptight, carefree attitudes and beliefs out here. People seem to have an independence, a sort of freedom I can't really describe but think I feel. This is a way different area physically, politically, and ideologically.

Here in Spokane, for some reason, I'm more cautious walking around. Sitting outside, I see I'm in an area that requires more alertness when I'm outside the hotel. Not too bad, just a feeling I get here.

✪

8/26/23

DAY #60, RIDING #53

Miles—75.09 (3,617.61); Time—4:42 (307:41)
Ralston Memorial Park, Ralston, Washington (free, primitive)

I actually got a taste of slowing down in the morning. I had a choice to make: leave now or wait for breakfast an hour away, at 7:00 a.m. I kind of wanted to just get ready and leave, but I also wanted to start slowing down, so I waited for breakfast. Now, for a lot of people this wouldn't have been a decision, but I honestly had to make myself slow down enough to do this.

I needed to occupy my time, so I got a shower and watched the local news and weather report. Soon enough, it was seven and I was eating breakfast.

Since I usually budget-hunt hotels, a majority of the time it's always the same continental breakfast. But I'll say the waffles from the cooker that almost every hotel has come in handy for a good, tasty snack on the trails. Out in the West, since I'm finishing early and not on the bike too long, I usually skip lunch. I eat lunch first thing at camp and then dinner later. This slowing-down thing isn't so bad.

After getting back from breakfast, I started talking to a neighbor on the balcony. He was a truck driver, and I was asking him how it really was in some of the big cities out here in Washington and its surrounds. The big cities, Seattle and Portland in particular, are partly lawless, it seems, and can be a mess trying to drive a truck through. He said some parts are actually like you see on TV and some parts are ok. This is by no means anything political or a reflection of taking a side. But this is America—we're not a chaotic, lawless country. We can't allow any group of people to run wild with no fear of repercussions. It appears that some parts of these cities are out of the local government's control, and that's a part of America I don't understand. I really hope to avoid this in Seattle. But I'm no stranger to cities and watching my back or having to be aware of my surroundings in them.

I finally left around eight thirty for my ride that would end in Ralston, outside of Ritzville. It's a hot, cloudless, sunny day, and it topped out at ninety-three degrees at camp in Ralston Memorial Park. I started on my road map with a paved ride on the Fish Lake Trail. This was a beautiful trail that followed Marshall Creek for a little bit going south. I also passed an area that was burned out from a wildfire. I wondered how long ago it was because I could smell the faint hints of burnt trees lingering. There were a lot of still-alive charred trees, along with the dead ones. I eventually had to get off the trail for a bridge that was out up ahead. I wanted to get back on since a long running trail continued off Fish Lake Trail. I had heard and read a little about the Columbia Plateau Trail. I was told the surface is similar to the Palouse to Cascade, so I decided to not even try that trail.

I then came to a gravel road on my map. I would've been on this road for a while and didn't want any part of it. I looked up Washington bicycle laws for the interstate. I'm allowed on the interstate everywhere except for two sections. At this point, I just decided to get on I-90, eventually. I did have to ride on Highway 904 through Cheyney. There was a wildfire not too far away from Cheyney, but I didn't really notice any effects from the smoke. I strapped myself in and got on 90 West for about 30 miles.

The time went quickly as I averaged around 20 miles per hour the entire way. I had an uphill climb for the first 10 to 12 miles, and then it was downhill the rest of the way. I heard a lot of people ask why I go east to west, because of the wind, but I like the way I'm going. Living two and a half hours north of the eastern terminus in Washington, DC, ultimately makes the decision easy. I'd rather go this way, and ever since Yellowstone and the Continental Divide, I've been gradually going down in elevation to finish up. Plus, come on, when does the wind naturally blow with you, against your back and not in your face or sides?

The ride was mostly nice and pretty easygoing. Most of my shoulders were clean, and only some parts were trashy with debris. Going through those parts, all I could do was try to steer away from what I could. At least I had a shoulder of between six and eight feet to ride on.

With about 5 miles to go on I-90, I started to hear a clicking sound. I pulled over and looked at my rear tire because I'd heard this sound before. It was the spoke coming loose again! Luckily, again it wasn't broken, and this time I didn't hear it before it unthreaded itself. Nothing I could do, so I continued to the Ritzville exit.

Then, while I was riding, something happened that almost made me crash, on I-90 of all places. The screw that was drilled through snapped now. My rack, with all its weight, dropped and pinched my tire. It sent me sideways with a quick jerk, and I somehow managed to stay upright.

I was then riding in the low twenties, and my rear tire all but stopped. I think the only reason it didn't seize to a full stop was my speed.

Wow! Now that's freaking scary with traffic moving at least 75-plus miles per hour. I thought I was definitely crashing on the dirty, rocky shoulder. My heart was racing—that's for sure. Also, thanks to my buddy Jordan in Livingston (Dan Bailey's), I had zip ties to keep me going. That's twice now you saved me, Jordan. Thanks.

I get everything ready and made my way to the Ritzville exit for a 10-mile ride to my campsite. My camp was a small-town park in the middle of nowhere. Ralston Memorial Park is awesome, though, for exactly what it is: a place to camp in the middle of nowhere. It has green grass, water, and picnic tables. An oasis in this vast remote location.

When I got off I-90, it looked like I was in a barren foreign land. A sci-fi movie set. The crops were gone, and literally as far as I could see were flat dirt fields. Everything was dirt or cut crop fields with their golden dry color. Literally nothing but dirt, everywhere, 360 degrees. The ride had so many rolling hills, I was so glad to see the park eventually. Nothing huge, but too many in the 10 miles I rode.

The park is really nice and well kept. There is a leveled tent pad, a small playground, and a really well-done Veterans memorial. There's not much left of the town—a couple houses and a big mill.

It's mostly barren farmland here. Wheat is the crop I've been seeing the most of in the Eastern Palouse region.

After setting up at camp, I texted a phone number to see if the sprinklers would come on tonight. Eventually a guy showed up to shut them off, and we ended up talking for a bit. I asked him a little about the roads and such out here. He also opened up the building across the street so I would have access to a bathroom. He was really cool and helped me out. He said he heard the story about my flat out here. I posted on a Facebook page "Friends of Palouse to Cascades" about trying to get a ride or someone close with a pump.

At camp I took apart my tire and fixed up my spokes. Yes, I actually found two that had come unthreaded and needed to be fixed. I was actually good at doing this by then, and I tightened up my rack with zip ties.

I don't get a signal out here so no map-checking or music tonight. It's hard for me to believe the scenery out here. It's wild seeing just endless fields; I don't see trees or anything around. It's 7:30 p.m., and the sun will be gone in another twenty minutes, ending another day on my journey. The weather should be good for the next couple days, and I think I can get to the Columbia River by then, unless I have more breakdowns, but I sure do hope I'm done with all that. I've dealt with enough problems already.

I still don't know how I really feel inside about riding after this. The past two weeks have really pushed me to my limit, it feels like. It would've been so easy to quit and give up when major trouble came. It's been a heck of a ride physically and mentally so far, but I'm still going. Sometimes I think I'm being put through some kind of test, to see how much I can take. I keep saying I'm done riding after this, and part of me honestly feels that way. I'm feeling depressed and beaten down by all these breakdowns. What I've had to go through to get things fixed and keep rolling. Sometimes in my head I question if it's all worth it. Is all this stress and anxiety doing me any good? Will I ever get back on my feet? If so, how? Why do I seem to love misery so much? Why have I accepted feeling this way? Most of all, why do I continually beat myself up and feel like that's an OK thing to say, feel, or think? I've got a lot of work there, in that regard. I thought this trip would help me with some life problems or shed some light on things. So far it hasn't done that.

Maybe the miracle just hasn't happened yet…

8/27/23

DAY #61, RIDING #54

Miles—55.17 (3,672.78); Time—4:10 (311:51)
Othello Inn and Suites, Othello, Washington ($90)

Last night I woke up in the middle of the night and stepped outside my tent. There was a good amount of stars visible, and they offered up a wonderful starry night. But the real action was the coyote howling. It sounded like a Saturday night howling competition between a few different packs. It was really cool to hear, and I'm definitely glad I woke up and stepped outside for a couple minutes. It's these experiences that I really enjoy. Basically, the things I can't experience at home; I want to see everything out here I can. After listening for a little bit to the chatter, I fell back asleep. One of my trip regrets was not getting a video for sound; this was *very* cool to hear. I've heard howling but not from so many directions.

I woke up as the sun was rising. The sun's rays shining through the clouds was an inspirational way to start my day. I really enjoy seeing the sunrises and sunsets out here. The open land and endless views make for some memorable sights.

As I was packing up, I did a final check to make sure everything was tightened up. I almost always do a check before I leave, usually just a look at the spokes and my rack. I noticed this morning my rack was broken at one spot. Nothing too bad, a tube broken near a weld. I ended up zip tying it together to hold and didn't have any more issues with it.

I started off on my ride and came to the Palouse to Cascades Trail a few hundred feet up the road. I looked at the trail and decided it would be a day of road riding. Bigger rocks than what I wanted to ride over were all I needed to see. It looks like a great trail, but you definitely need wider tires. I wasn't about to test anything again—no more taking somewhat reckless chances. No more "Well, I hope I don't have any more problems out here."

I decided to take a few roads on my way to Othello. First it was 14 miles on Lind-Ralston Road, and I had a nice downhill ride of a couple hundred feet. At first, I encountered farms, with a few wind turbines in the distance. I did have a couple of small hills, and the landscape was far from flat. It must be harder and dangerous to run farm equipment out here. There are a lot of rolling hills in the land. We do have some of these same issues back home as well, but out here it stands out more to me. On this section of road, I start to see fewer farms and more desolate land. A lot of sagebrush dots the landscape. I see absolutely no trees or shade anywhere in sight.

I got to see some whitetail deer along the road, not to far off in the distance. They're hard to take pictures of; as soon as I stopped, they took off. They're a little bigger here than they are at home but still as graceful. Seeing them run and jump away through the brush was cool.

Coming into the town of Lind, I saw a sign for something I could only imagine seeing. I was almost two months late for the Lind Lions Club Combine Demolition Derby. A combine demolition derby, really? That would be very fun to see, and I would've absolutely made time for it.

After riding through the town of Lind, I took my next road 23 miles west to Warden—actually, past Warden to Highway 17 South, for the final ride into Othello. I would take Lind-Warden Road from, you guessed it, Lind to Warden. I would have two big hills to climb on this section early in the ride. I would actually have to walk twice also. It was a pretty hot day; at 10:00 a.m. it was already 90 degrees, and it would reach a high of 97. It's a lot to ride in when you don't have any cover all day. Unless I went into a town, I wouldn't have any shade. The roads were sort of empty, which I liked, and I ended up almost following the trail anyway.

As I passed Warden and went into Othello, I started to see more farming again. I was also starting to see more green, a lot of irrigation and watering of the fields. I saw fields of a short green crop; not exactly sure what it was, but I saw a good amount of it around.

The heat is taking its toll on me, but I keep on going and eventually make it into Othello. I hear there's camping at the fairgrounds, but that's 2 miles south of town. Plus, I'm not 100 percent sure there's camping there. That's a chance I don't want to take. I end up getting a hotel in town; I don't see any campgrounds to stay at.

I'm trying to shorten up my rides out here to around 50 to 60 miles per day. The heat and sun all day is wearing me down. It also looks like I'll be doing some climbing again soon enough. I was surprised to see when I came into Othello, I was only 1,099 feet above sea level. I know I've had it easier by going down in elevation lately, but I didn't think I had dropped that much.

On the way into Othello, I got to see some bigger mule deer also. I liked seeing these again, considering we don't have them back home, and they looked a little different from the whitetails. I also stopped by Wally World and stocked up on a few things. I did that after checking into the hotel; it was less than a mile down the road.

It's tough out here. Because of this, I'm mapping the Palouse to Cascade Trail and making such maps every day. Exactly what I didn't want to do. It stresses me out and ends up taking a lot of time.

I spend time looking over maps instead of relaxing at camp. It's not hard, and I make it out to be more than it is. I guess it's more in my head rather than a real obstacle to overcome. In reality, there are only so many options out here for roads, and by now I sort of have an idea of what to avoid. I just hope it all works out and I get to where I need to be. I sort of feel weighed down by everything I need to do once I get to camp. Between setting up, posting on Facebook, writing my journal entry, possibly making a video entry, and now mapping, it's a lot when my ride ends. But I'm going to keep going and try to manage. The rewards will be amazing when I'm finished, I tell myself.

8/28/23

DAY #62, RIDING #55

Miles—54.59 (3,727.37); Time—4:07 (315:58)

Wanapum State Park and Campground ($12, primitive)

I set my alarm for 5:30 a.m. so I could get an early start. No hotel breakfast meant I could eat and pack in my room right away. Even with getting sidetracked and generally being slow, I managed to leave by 7:30 a.m. Later I would be glad I did leave early. There's definitely a reason to wake up early, and there are benefits to doing so, especially now. I'm in the final day of a heat wave sweeping through, and today is predicted to be the hottest of the past 3 days. It would reach 90 degrees before 11:00 a.m. and top out at a high of 100 degrees today. That's hot, even without the humidity in the air. I repeat to myself, Get me out of this heat and into the shade of the Olympic National Forest.

I know I've maybe been pushing myself a little much lately; I can feel the heat affecting me. I feel sick to my stomach, I get cold sweats, I'm peeing gold, and sometimes I have a hard time remembering or just plain old forget things. I don't think I'm drinking enough water, and that's my problem. These symptoms come and go and don't happen all at once. I've been experiencing these things more often lately.

Today I would take Highway 26 for around 40 miles. Riding into Royal City, I started seeing a lot of cattle farms and large grazing fields. I was definitely starting to transition to a different landscape and terrain. I started seeing more green, and the mountains were starting to appear back into the distance. I started passing other crop fields too; irrigation ditches and pipes were in regular use out here. I also passed a sign for Ephrata, which was a nice reminder of home. Ephrata, Pennsylvania, is one town away from where I live.

Coming into Royal City, I started seeing a lot of orchards around. Another part of the changing landscape of Washington. And very soon I'd encounter my third transition. Right before 26 West met the Columbia River, I took Beverly Burke Road to T8 Road Southwest, according to Maps, which ended at the Palouse to

Cascades Trail / John Wayne Pioneer Trail. This was part of the trail I absolutely needed to get on. This last road ended at the trail and had a path leading up to the trail.

One problem: it was a steep, high incline to the trail, like a good 20-to-30-foot incline. The gravel/dirt was deep; I could barely push my bike up. Actually, I couldn't continually push the bike. It was that steep. I had to go a little and hold the brakes to maintain what I had just done. Pick up the front tire (by the handlebars), step forward, brake, and repeat. It was a tiring process, but I made it up onto the trail eventually. I had all my gear still attached while doing this; it was a real workout. The only other bridge near was on I-90, and I was *not* riding that to my north. So I had to make it to the trail.

As soon as I got on the trail, I was rewarded immediately with a spectacular view of the landscape: the sagebrush scattered around, the bridge in the distance, and beyond the bridge a huge mountain. I soaked it all in while I caught my breath from my struggle to get up here. The trail was deep with rocks and not really rideable for me, long term. For the short distance to and after the bridge, I'd be fine, though. I would only need to be on the actual trail 3 to 4 miles until I could exit onto the road again.

Riding onto the bridge was incredible; everything around me was breathtaking. The mountains across the water, and endless views both ways down the river.

The water is a perfect color of blue and is as reflective as a mirror. I love seeing the landscape reflected on the water. It's a serene, peaceful scene, and I take my time on the bridge.

The bridge seemed to go on and on; I'd guess it's close to a mile long. OK, I looked it up, and it's only a half mile, but it seemed longer. I read an informative sign that told of a huge flood that came during the last ice age. It created the canyon walls and carved the landscape I was about to enjoy, which makes sense, because this is my third complete change of terrain today alone!

On my way to camp at Wanapum State Park, I rode down through a series of canyons. I had to ride the trail a little bit after the bridge to my first trailhead. Exiting the trail at the Army East trail head, I then had a beautiful scenic ride on Huntzinger Road. It was an awesome ride, little traffic, the Columbia River on my right, and eventually some steep canyon walls on my left. I came to the Huntzinger fishing pier and Wanapum Dam. It was a great day to be out here, and I was incredibly lucky with the wind. This is a very, very bad wind area, and miraculously I had none this day. There's nothing to stop the wind coming down the river, and the mountains funnel it through, not allowing it to escape. Today going to camp I was very lucky, as I'd learn later.

I got to Wanapum State Park, located along the Columbia River, in Vantage. They have two hiker/biker sites, and one of them is way better in my opinion. I had my choice, and I took the one downhill from the showers and bathroom. There was a tree growing close to the ground that would offer some protection from the wind. I chased away the grouse keeping a watch over the site and set up shop. I made my usual lunch and then sat around for a couple minutes. The bathroom, water, and showers were right next to me also. It was nice taking a cold shower after the heat all day. After that I walked down to check out the river.

There was a trail that could be used to access the river from where I was camping. I put on my rubber sandals and took off in search of the water. The river was a perfect cool temperature to relax in. The water was so clean, calm, and blue. Walking out into the water, I was getting the most I could out of this. I focused on the now. I tried to push everything out, the other people around, my troubles at home, the unknown feeling of indecision in my life; it was just me and the water. I swam around a little bit, and after I just sat down in the river for a while. It was a great way to wind down and end my day.

The heat was something to contend with today, and I think it's affecting my thoughts. I feel maybe I'm getting dehydrated still and it's taking its toll upstairs. Or maybe I'm way off. Who really knows? Today, for a short time, I thought, I'm not having fun anymore. I'm not sure exactly what brought that on, but I'm sure it's multiple things that have snowballed together. I don't like it when I get like this. It can quickly drag me in one of two directions. The bad direction is so hard to dig myself out of. When I go down in a depressive spiraling state of mind, it can happen fast. If I don't take control of myself, it can feel impossible to dig my way out. I start wondering, What happened to the guy who knows that nothing will stop him? Where's the man screaming with energy and the confidence in crushing the roads and trails?

I'm still having the issue with my left hand going numb while riding. It seems to happen when I'm climbing; I assume I'm gripping the bar too tight.

I crossed into the Pacific time zone a couple days ago; don't think I mentioned that yet. I still feel like I'm on Eastern time, though. Today marks two full calendar months on the road. I started on June 28 and today is August 28, and it's hard to believe. Even with cutting my days shorter, I should be done in about a week. It's those things that remind me how long I've been gone, not the 3,600 miles I have ridden so far.

Honestly, if you ask me, none of it seems real to me. Like, it's no big deal, just me doing my thing, having fun.

8/29/23

DAY #63, RIDING #56

Miles—42.12 (3,769.49); Time—5:14 (321:12)
Sure Stay Best Western, Ellensburg, Washington ($93)

I could feel the wind on the tent first, then I looked outside and saw the trees blowing too. Today would turn out to be one of my hardest riding days, and thankfully it would be a short day as well, riding a little over 40 miles. I woke up at 5:00 a.m. and couldn't get back to sleep. It was a beautiful sunrise coming up over the Columbia River. I'm never too disappointed waking up early. I like to take a little time to just lie there in my sleeping bag. Then I get to see a sunrise in a place I may well never go to again. Finally, I can leave earlier; I like leaving just after sunrise if I can. I was packed and ready to leave Wanapum Campground by seven thirty.

Overnight the rain went away and would be gone for the rest of the day. In its place was the wind, and it would be a major factor in my day. It must've been blowing at 10 to 15 miles per hour at camp before I left. I remember it was a pain folding my tent, having to contend with the wind at camp, and trying to pack things up. Also, adding to the wind, my first 10 to 13 miles would gain 1,500 feet of elevation. These two combined would make my day very difficult. The climb to Ryegrass took me over 2 hours alone. My climbing to this location ended at an elevation of 2,535 feet. The sky was a beautiful blue, with scattered clouds to offer spots of shade.

There was a really cool bridge over I-90 on the Palouse to Cascade Trail, just past the high point of my early ride in Ryegrass. Since the bridge is over the interstate, it's obviously at a higher elevation, which means more climbing. The roads only added 5 miles, but the wind was what I was thinking about. The trail was still not rideable for me at this point. I really wanted to ride that bridge, but the ride on 90 West was hard enough. That was where I had to decide to ride either 90 or back roads. Also, the winds doubled in speed to 25-plus miles per hour by 11:00 a.m.! I decided on I-90.

The landscape was barren, dry, empty, but also magnificent, and it went as far as I could see. The mountains shrank down into dirt-filled rolling hills. At one spot it looked like a huge mudslide ran next to the freeway.

For as dry and lifeless as it appears out here, the seclusion I feel out here is satisfying. It's quiet here, calm, everything I see at this moment has this undisturbed feeling, like the land out here only changes from land movements and nature taking its course. Not a lot of human hands tearing up perfectly good, beautiful empty space. The way it should be. The endless, empty open space is something I greatly admire about being out here.

I saw a sign along the road today that sums up what I'm trying to say: "Preserve Open Spaces." Three simple words.

Right around and slightly after Ryegrass, I came to the wind turbine area. This is a perfect place for these as the wind speed is currently at least 20-plus miles per hour. I have one picture alone in which I count twenty-one wind turbines! Shortly after I pass all that, I see the bridge over I-90. This incredible bridge spanning four lanes of the interstate, has five double sets of support arches underneath, plus one single support structure. The total length requires all these supports, that seemingly appear more than a couple hundred feet high. It's certainly a marvel to admire. It must be a big draw out here, or at least I hope so. The trail is very nice-looking; I just can't get on it yet. I keep on moving on as I can feel the wind picking up.

By now the wind is between 25 and 30 miles per hour, and I've still got 11 miles to ride. I decided to end my day in Ellensburg. The riding was absolutely miserable, and I couldn't wait for it to end today. The land is open, literally nothing around to stop the wind, so there's no escaping it. Mostly it was all blowing to my left, which of course was also into I-90 traffic. The winds are definitely strong out here, and I'm really glad I didn't have any of this yesterday. I had to literally ride at an angle to stay on my bike, and this was a hard angle, it felt like. I was also shifting my body around constantly fighting the winds; it wasn't fun at all. There were also a few times a strong gust would blow me a little closer to traffic than I'd like. I was certainly looking forward to getting these 11 tortuous miles to Ellensburg over with.

This is one of the days when my legs and thighs are actually pretty sore. Maybe I'm wearing down; I know I'm mentally fatigued. I wish I had the drive and energy that I did a couple of weeks ago—well, at least the energy. I think I need some sleep and rest. I feel like I'm doing too much and wearing myself thin some days. But here's my thinking: I'm seeing places I might not ever see again. Do I not explore a town or go off trail because I'm tired or I just got done with riding? No, I want to explore, I want to see America, and I want to look around these small towns. What's the point of traveling if you don't explore? I'll rest when I'm done; I'd rather see as much as I can.

Today was one of those days I'm talking about. I had a hard, exhausting ride today, but I got checked into my hotel at noon. So what, do I just sit around? No way, I go out exploring. No rest for the wicked. I was in South Ellensburg, so I decided to ride north to visit the Central Washington University Campus. Along the way were a couple of stops to make as well. My first stop, because the rodeo was closed, was the Zipper Bowl, which is someone's house with a skateboard bowl in the backyard, according to Google reviews. The house has some cool skater graffiti on one side; the other side has some really cool-looking birds painted on it. Just some neat place to see and ride by.

That took me close to my next stop, Dick and Jane's Spot. Now this house is very cool and very artfully decorated. The house and property are littered with amazing handmade art. There are statues made of anything and everything: odds and ends making random decorations, metal artworks, just a whole lot of really interesting stuff to look at. My favorite was a rolling hill background painted on the fence with the words "Are we dreaming yet?" spelled out in a word cloud belonging to a black cat.

The rest of Ellensburg was interesting. This town was thriving, and seemed to have an identity for itself. It seemed like a nice town, except for this wind. I stopped to take a picture with some bull statue on a park bench before making my way to Central Washington University. I rode through the campus and saw the football stadium and a few buildings. What I wanted to really see was the Japanese garden, but it was closed. It was a cool town, and I was glad I did go for a ride around.

I made it back to the hotel by four thirty and was ready to relax. I was watching the news and learned there were 30-to-35-mile-per-hour winds in Ellensburg today! Where they get the numbers from I don't know, but somewhere in Ellensburg hit a high of 63! Well, that was according to the local news. Tomorrow there will be high winds as well, so I hope I can ride out of them early.

⭐

8/30/23

DAY #64, RIDING #57

Miles—42.48 (3,811.97); Time—4:30 (325:42)
Airbnb, Easton, Washington ($120)

I certainly wanted to take advantage of having a hotel and have everything packed and ready to go in the morning. I did get my early start around seven to start riding. I needed to get an early jump on the wind, I was riding out of a windy area. I didn't want to work or fight the wind like yesterday; that was really bad and difficult. I decided to take the scenic Highway 10 route, since it mostly followed I-90. I was mostly far enough away that I wouldn't see it. It ended up being a terrific ride, and I'm glad I took that route. There were some winds of 10 to 15 miles per hour I had to contend with along the 25-plus miles to Cle Elum.

It was a good day to ride with temperatures only reaching the midsixties and a little cloud cover in the distance. This ride was incredibly beautiful, and I had a slight incline the entire way, with a couple good hills to climb. It's a big train area, and I would almost constantly see the tracks. Out here the tracks, both empty and with trains in sight, only add to the landscape. I'd see a few trains today, more BNSF train cars. I saw more houses along the road. It's not hard to wonder why someone would want to live out here.

I got to see some more mule deer, but not much else today. Heading north and west on Highway 10, I would get some close-up views from high above the turquoise blue waters of the Yakima River.

I still can't get over how pristine, clean, and clear the waterways look out here. Back home you can't see deep in the water; they look nothing like this. But we also have different stuff going into our waters with farms along the creeks and streams that flow into the larger rivers. Go swimming in a Lancaster County waterway, and you'll want a shower after. Just because the smell is home to me doesn't mean I need to smell like home.

The ride on Highway 10 was such an amazing ride. At one point I was down by the Yakima, riding along the river with steep canyon walls, then open fields on my sides. In other places on 10, I got a bird's eye view of the terrain below me. These views overlooking the changing valley are always my favorite. I love these views, offering me a preview of where I'm headed. Also, if I'm looking down into a valley, that almost always means that I'm riding down into that canyon floor.

I just feel like I could ride all day out here and never get sick of the views. Luckily, the trees and rock walls have created a little buffer from the wind.

I did see a good amount of dark clouds ahead of me, as I came into Cle Elum. It was here I planned to get on the Palouse to Cascade Trail, finally. I heard it is as good as it gets here in Cle Elum, and I can certainly attest to the fact it was a really big difference. I'll still have to watch for rocks and deeper gravel spots, but that's true on any trail really. I just don't want to get careless and run over something I shouldn't. No more problems, please, and I'll give my best to do my part. I'm of course talking to nobody, just happy to be back on a trail. Really hoping my major issues are in the past. I'm really glad I'm able to finally ride this trail that I've heard so much about.

On the way here, I was thinking I'm getting more burned out from the road and that everything that's been wearing on me is starting to now break me down. I start thinking how I'm just not having fun anymore and I don't want to ride anymore. I don't feel the energy or drive I felt through Wyoming. I don't scream with pride and achievement while riding. I don't feel the confidence I once had, or maybe it's something more. Either way, I feel like I have lost my strength and a little willpower. Really, I think all these bike problems are killing me. It's not fun riding and worrying about my bike. My experiences out here are being negatively affected by the fact I think a lot about what's going to break next or hoping my back end holds up.

Those thoughts have the potential to ruin my trip if I let them. It really sucks when you have so much faith in a product or company and then you feel as defeated as I do about this.

Honestly, I think my bike, and the fact I can't go backpacking with it anymore, is the root cause of this recent misery on my trip. I still enjoy riding, and I don't want to sound like my world is ending, but I tend to dwell on these sort of things. I probably make it sound worse than what it really is, but when something really bums you out, doesn't it always seem worse than it really is? How can you not dwell on things when you're alone and have no outside stimulation for months? All I can do is think, ride, talk to myself, and think some more.

The actual trail now that I'm riding is everything I've been told. So far, I'm loving it, everything about it. The pine trees along the trail, the views of the Yakima River, some great bridges to ride over, and just being off the road is doing me lot of good. I need to get back in the woods; I can't say how much it's already changing my mood for the better.

I booked two nights at an Airbnb because there will be rain all day tomorrow. It doesn't look like much rain, but it is supposed to rain all day long, which I don't want to ride all day in, especially on a trail. Combine the rain and the low sixties temperature, and it'll be a cold, miserable, wet riding day. I've just got to remember it probably won't rain here in Easton, but 20 to 30 miles west, where I'm headed, is worse. That is the hardest part to not get excited about, not having rain where I am but having a storm where I'm going and can't see. That will antagonize me during my stay here. There are also not a lot of places to stay for the next 30 miles, and I'm riding slower now because of the trail surface.

But of course, I'm sitting in my Airbnb, beating myself up over the cost of staying the two planned days. I do pretty good making a living but have a feeling I'll never be able to retire. Like a lot of people, I just worry about finances as it pertains to my future. Out here in the West, compared to the East, it seems everything is more expensive. I think part of me is so tightly wound I feel like I need to try to maximize everything. I try to stretch my money sometimes so far, I can lose my mind. Once again, I hate it and don't understand how or why I act and think like this. I believe a majority of it stems from not working; I'm not usually like this with my with money/spending. It becomes a daily struggle, out here and at home.

How much this trip is costing me is driving me crazy. On the other hand, I sometimes tell myself, What's it really matter? Part of me just doesn't care, feeling partly ruined in life financially anyways. I don't really want to go home. I'm not happy there. I despise and distrust the county government and authorities and feel I don't belong there anymore. I have applied for help and have mixed feelings about the experiences I've had. Sometimes I get the help; sometimes I get turned away from programs and don't understand why. My time runs out, insurance stops paying, or whoever is funding certain programs stops. The worst is when I find out there are help or programs but I don't qualify for some insignificant reason; that seems to be the most frequent scenario.

I think this is a big reason why so many people are suffering like I am. I feel like sometimes I reach out my hand for help, like they say to do, and the county or state takes their hand away in a cruel joke. At least part of me feels that way. A part of me wants to just give up and say f-it. I feel lost, confused, and alone mostly. I know I isolate, but I feel I don't fit in with most people. I'm probably wrong, but my thoughts tell me otherwise. I also generally avoid people if I can. This all leads to a depressing life, a life lived all alone, and the feeling of being unloved outside of family.

The fact that I've got a day of nothing tomorrow honestly drives me crazy. I feel like I've been getting soft lately and taking too many easy outs. I'm getting lazy, using my credit card too often and easily. I'm not happy with myself. I know I don't need to be here, so why am I? What, I suddenly can't get wet? Here I go again attacking myself. I don't know what to do or think most times anymore. I don't have high hopes for myself when I get home. I feel like I want to run away from the world. I hate depression...

8/31/23

DAY #65, RIDING #57

Airbnb, Easton, Washington ($120)

I had a strange feeling yesterday about today and the weather. In the back of my mind, I felt like I had made a mistake by booking this Airbnb. I got this feeling that either it wouldn't rain at all or the rain wouldn't be a factor in the day. Of course, it wouldn't end up raining in Easton until 6:00 p.m. This is the hardest part for me. I think by now you'll understand how that drives me crazy. It's a combination of sitting around all day and the absence of rain. It's mostly the sitting around all day; all I have is time, and my mind doesn't need that much downtime when I feel this way.

It is a nice place to stay; it's secluded and very quiet. The room is a converted garage, with no cable or Wi-Fi to signal into the TV, so all entertainment is on the phone. My options are few, mainly Amazon Prime and the SiriusXM app, unless I go digging for a streaming site for live sports. The room is located off a gravel road in a very rural area. There is a walking trail that goes a little bit down to the Yakima River. I hang out here for a while and enjoy the solitude of the immediate area. Well, as much solitude as I can feel with the I-90 in the background.

I sit out here and enjoy the moment. I tell myself that none of this really matters, these are the bumps in the road inherent to going on such a long trip. I know deep down I'm overreacting, overly stressed out, and absolutely off centered. I know I'm also doing good, all things considered. I'm healthy and honestly having a lot of fun. A whole lot, if not the majority, of my complaining and worrying is from another fear I have.

I only come clean with almost all my thoughts and feelings because I feel an absolute need for honesty in this book. If my writings are bullshit, then so am I. I also have a big need to always explain myself. I always think I'm misunderstood, and that causes me to almost always go into further detail than needed. This is a perfect example of my truths: all that rambling about money and other things is based on a fear. I think all or at least the majority of my worrying is from my fear of the future. I honestly don't think I'll ever be able to retire. I think I'll be dead before I'm financially secure enough to retire. The fact I'm forty-one now and haven't worked in over a year doesn't help. I have an associate's degree and almost twenty years' experience in my trade. But yeah, I have an absolute fear of my financial future.

I know I can't see the weather up ahead, but I think I could've ridden today. Most of the day I ended up sitting around, planning, looking over my routes, and getting camping spots lined up. One great thing is since I'm on the Palouse to Cascade Trail, I'm back on track with my route and itinerary sheets.

Although it was a struggle mentally today, I tried to limit the self-inflicted damage. I still did a little; I couldn't shake the thought of not riding at all today or feeling like I wasted the day. It did linger around for a while, and then it started to drive me a little stir crazy; that's when I walked to the river. I do have a tendency to let my problems brew up, then it boils over and starts to affect me. I have a very hard time not doing this. But it's unfortunately what I know all too well. So I sat in my own misery for a little bit today but also snapped myself out of it somewhat. I watched some new Woody

Harrelson movie on my phone that wasn't too bad. As bad as I made it sound, it wasn't the worst thing that could've happened today.

It's still hard not to think of today as a waste, and I'm made more aware of this by the fact I have five days of riding left, with two days until I ride through Seattle and take the ferry to Bainbridge Island. I'm really looking forward to that area. My dad's parents used to live in Port Orchard, and that's just south of there. I was very young but remember a few things. I remember a lake and an A-frame log cabin on the lake. But it's one of those things that, for some reason unexplained, I feel this calm, peaceful feeling thinking about it. I guess those memories, combined with seeing pictures of the area, make me feel this way. I was probably between the ages of five to eight the last time I was out there, so my memories are very few.

The Olympic National Forest is one of the last things on my trip I'm really looking forward to. From what I've heard and seen in my research, I can't wait to get there. Even if I'm only riding on the border of it. I'm also very excited that I'll be mostly trail riding the rest of my trip. There is a bright light at the end of the tunnel, even though sometimes it doesn't feel like there is. No matter how bad I feel inside, I have to keep going. The only way to get out of the tunnel and into the light is to keep putting one foot in front of the other. As long as I keep making progress and moving forward, I'll eventually get to the end. And make my exit out of the darkness and back into the light.

I'm feeling deflated, like a lot of fun has been sucked out of me. I worry way too much about bike breakdowns and the condition of my bike. These, combined with my prior issues, are taking away from me fully enjoying this trip of a lifetime. It sucks. I hate feeling this. I don't want to ruin my trip, but I don't know how to fully push away these thoughts. I don't know how to get back to just riding and enjoying myself. Now it seems like I'm just hoping to make it through a day without having any bike or gear issue. I 100 percent know that this is drastically affecting my mood.

Going back home concerns me, as I've mentioned. What am I going home to? What do I have to look forward to besides seeing family again? I hate talking and thinking like this, but it's how I feel. This bike trip is something I've been thinking and dreaming about for years. In this current moment, I couldn't care less. Not a fully true statement at all but close. I don't know what is going on with me lately, but I'll keep moving along in life. It's nothing new; it's how I've felt the past ten to fifteen years. Honestly, at times it can feel debilitating.

I feel like a tangled mess upstairs, that ball of string all knotted up that needs to be unwound and untangled. I hoped this trip would help, but at this down moment, I don't know if I am benefiting; maybe I'm regressing. I do feel better mentally on the trails versus the roads. I hate writing this because it makes me sound like all I do is complain and feel miserable out here. OK, maybe the miserable part is true at times, but how do I fight off the depression? It's incredibly hard to hate the way I think and feel but heartbreaking to not know how to overcome it. It's like my brain goes there even though I desperately don't want it to. The difficult thing is I don't even necessarily feel bad at all; I might be feeling great, then as fast as a light switch, it can change, and it can happen when nothing physically bad triggers these thoughts either. It's like it randomly just pops up in my head.

This is the story of my life: I wind myself up, and I don't know what to do. This is me fighting myself. Sometimes I'm my own worst enemy, and it's a tough fight. It can be a daily struggle sometimes, and this isn't anything new. This is a phase, a depressive stage; they're frequent, but deep down I know what's real and what's just feelings. I just can't shake the depressive thoughts and feelings that overshadow my true thoughts and feelings. But I guess that's depression.

I'm trying to overcome or at least find that balance between the light and the dark. I wonder if I want too much from this trip. This trip is for me, but am I making it too much about me? I think I get these big grand ideas of these awesome things that are going to happen or of things I want to do. And if they don't happen or fall through, I feel crushed; I put too much into it, and it causes me to concentrate on the bad things only.

So what if I can't camp at a certain place? As long as I keep on making my daily destinations, I'm making progress. I just tend to have a pessimistic attitude toward most things. Unfortunately, I'm comfortable like this, or maybe I'm confusing that with familiarity?

9/1/23

DAY #66, RIDING #58

Miles—72.11 (3,884.08); Time—7:11 (332:53)

Motel 6, Issaquah, Washington ($147)

It's a new day, and I finally get to get back on the road. With the depression sort of hitting hard recently, downtime isn't a friend of mine. When I get this way, it's best for me to keep busy. That means less time for my mind to wander to someplace I don't want to be. So as you can tell, I'm very happy to go and to be able to ride today. The day started off cold, with temperatures in the midfifties, along with scattered drizzling rain.

I would start my day with a 40-mile ride on the Palouse to Cascade Trail, which becomes the Iron Horse Trail. The trail in the Western Cascade Region was one of the most scenic and enjoyable rides I've ever done.

The endless lookouts and views over the valley seemed so tranquil. It was a totally amazing experience seeing all this, and the riding was also pretty good. The clouds were lying low and seemed to cover the mountaintops at some places. I love seeing the clouds scattered along the trees, especially when it looks layered like it did this day. I could see the bottoms of the trees, then clouds, and then the tops of the trees. The tunnels, lookouts, bridges, and scenery combine to make this trail section dreamlike in appearance. The trail also has the Yakima River running aside it, offering some spectacular views. I passed a couple big lakes that gave off a quiet, peaceful feeling.

Before the Snoqualmie Tunnel, it was in the midfifties and drizzling, with heavy cloud cover. The Snoqualmie Tunnel is 2.1 miles long and right on the trail in the Snoqualmie Pass / Hyak. It's the longest tunnel closed to traffic in America that you can ride or walk through. It seems to go on and on, but is also a fun, cool (literally), long, dark ride. You can see the light at the end; it's very straight.

Toward the end it started getting a little rough. I didn't have my fingers on the brakes, and I started to veer off into the wall. Not really sure what I was doing here, but obviously I wasn't paying attention.

I did some bumping and grinding on the wall. I got my hands on the brakes, but I was already headed for the wall. I know enough to know that when you're not in control of the bike, you shouldn't make any sudden jerky moves or else you might go down. I brushed against the wall and cut up two knuckles. Not bad, just some blood and a little skin missing. Worse was I got cut right on the knuckles, so it'll take longer to heal, and it did end up leaving a tiny scar.

While in the tunnel I'm thinking to myself about the past couple days. I've been dwelling on some negative thoughts and feelings lately. I need to forget about it all and enjoy my last few days, get back to how I felt in Wyoming, loving the ride and enjoying myself. Today I tell myself, I *will* work on my attitude and outlook. I don't want to complete this and be in a foul, depressed mood. That would be like doing this and just flushing it down the toilet. If you know me, I can definitely do that. So we're going to avoid that; today *will* be a turnaround day. Ultimately, I'm the one in control, and I need to take my control back. Oh, and I do have a video of me crashing into the wall.

Coming out of the tunnel, I was hoping to see some wildlife. I heard about a bear hanging out on the west end of the tunnel but didn't see it. Actually, I'm surprised I didn't see any wildlife today.

Coming out of the tunnel was like a brand-new day. It drastically warmed up, I'm guessing as much as ten degrees, and some of the clouds disappeared. It's incredible how the weather changes when you pass through the mountains. It's like I'm riding in a movie scene or riding through the places I could only read about before. I can't believe I'm seeing this on a trail. It's like I'm dreaming. Words can't explain the beauty out here. I mean, really, how can a place be so perfect-looking? The tree-lined mountains descending into the valley floor leave me floored.

Exactly how was I supposed to finish this trail before dark? I went 40 miles and was stopping every mile to, honestly, take pictures and soak it all in. To further explain, I took 134 pictures and 3 videos today.

I would be riding in forested areas with the trees lining the path, and then I'd ride through a blasted-out mountain. Riding through the incredibly hard work these brave people did by making the Chicago, Milwaukee, St. Paul and Pacific Railway is a definite bucket-list ride. I did pass two primitive camping sites; one I was planning on staying at until the weather changed my plans. When I came to the Alice and Carter Creek campsites, there was a posting up about a black bear frequenting the campsites. Part of me knew this was a possibility, and honestly, I was hesitant because of the bear. If I had to guess why, I'd say it is the fact that bears are capable of severely injuring or even killing me. I think this is what gives me apprehension about bears, no matter how small the chance of an encounter or, even more remotely, an attack.

No, I don't think this is something that happens regularly; I know it doesn't. I think it's the fact that a bear can do anything to me, and what can I do? Maybe it's a control/fight thing: I can't control a bigger animal, and it will do what it wants in the end—I have little to no say. I think I need to have a run-in with a bear to start to get over my fear. Being out here and seeing pictures of the grizzlies, I'm fascinated by them. As strange as it seems, that apex predator is now my favorite animal. Go figure, maybe it's a respect thing. These bears are magnificent and at the same time terrifying to me. The only way to conquer fear is to confront it.

That trail took me to Snoqualmie Valley Trail, and the beauty continued seamlessly. It took me longer than normal to finish these trails because of all my stops. I can't believe a trail that has so many amazing views is accessible to people every day. Going past lakes and two rivers gave me spectacular views from the valley floor. It was breathtaking scenery high up looking down, as well as looking up from the valley floor.

As I was coming into Snoqualmie, my trails ended in town. It was here I got sort of a reality check on my mental state. I heard on the news about a missing person, then today I saw two missing posters on a trail sign in town. One was a young man of twenty, and he was found a couple days after going missing. He unfortunately was found at the bottom of the falls. This could have been me, and that's scary. I have such strong views on suicide, but honestly how much pain can someone take before even their principles are gone? My stance will only help me for so long, and that is a little scary. But seeing this, combined with all the friends I have lost to suicide or addiction, is fuel for my fire to persevere. It sometimes takes a hard reality check like this to really, I mean really, know how good life is and how that is in no way an option in my life.

Getting back to my day, I had to take a 6-mile road ride to get back on the next trail. Something got mixed up on my map, and I ended up at this steep hiking trail. If you live in or know Snoqualmie, I'm at Denny Peak Park and plan to take that trail to the Preston-Snoqualmie Trail.

What in the world was I thinking taking this? Wow, this is a true hiking trail; I can't ride and am walking my bike. I also see signs for bear and cougar sightings. I need to be aware; I certainly don't need any cougar encounters, but from what I hear, I probably wouldn't see one unless it wanted me to. The silent stalker. Now this is another terrifying animal that I really want to see, maybe.

I was so very happy that Maps was right about this place and I came out at the Preston-Snoqualmie Trail. I thought, What happens if I don't come out at the trail? How far do I need to go? I'm already three-fourths of a mile in; that's a lot while pushing a loaded bike along a hiking trail.

Thank God, I made it out of the woods and to my next trail. I finished up my day with two 5-mile-long trails. The trails were named after the towns they arrived at. My first was the Preston-Snoqualmie Trail, and the second was the Issaquah-Preston trail. These were a great way to end my day. Two easy-riding paved trails. Unfortunately, I couldn't find any tent camping in town, so I had to book another hotel. It's really hard trying to find places that will even allow me to tent camp. Everything seems catered to the RVs. It stinks because it seems like bikes and tent camping aren't popular out here. I'm going to guess it's just the vicinity I'm riding through.

My problem is I'm not comfortable stealth camping out here. I'll do it in the East, back home, but out here I'm hesitant. The Midwest I avoided it because of farm and ranch dogs; some will get very protective. Out here it's the wildlife, but a lot has to do with the fact I have no idea about property out here, whether it's private or public. I don't want to wake up with any guard dog issues or possibly the farmer's gun in my face, so I pay to camp or stay where I'm allowed. I don't stealth camp on any private land.

Hotels from rain days are adding up; that I didn't anticipate. I try not to think about it, but it's hard with my situation back home. This is me, like it or not; it's how my mind works. Trust me, I don't like it either, but I have to find ways to cope. One way, I'm realizing, is writing. I just hope I'm not coming off like some money miser, I'm not normally like this at all. Normally, when I'm working, these thoughts are nonexistent. But once again, I know there's way deeper issues than money. Money is an easily identified problem, which makes it easy to dwell on because it may be the only issue I realize I have at a given moment. So it unfortunately gets full attention and becomes bigger than it is in reality. This allows me to avoid digging deep and trying to find the root cause(s) for all this internal suffering.

I'm beat, and it's ten thirty.

Once again everything seems nonstop—will it ever slow down?

9/2/23

DAY #67, RIDING #59

Miles—54.71 (3,939.79); Time—5:31 (338:24)
Fay Bainbridge Park, Bainbridge Island, Washington
(free, primitive)

Today was a day filled with ups, downs, and adversity, but I made it to Bainbridge Island, as you can tell by the chapter header. It started out great, with all trails. One thing about today is it's Labor Day Weekend, so I expect a lot of people to be out enjoying the nice weather.

My first trail was the East Lake Sammamish Trail, which had amazing views of you guessed it, Lake Sammamish. It was also a very wealthy area, in particular the Inglewood and Adelaide areas. Very nice new homes along the water. Also, the cars in the driveways were a giveaway to this area's wealth. The trail was really nice and paved as well. One thing, though, about the trail, was that there were these big metal barricades at everyone's driveway, I guess so people don't drive down the trail. It seemed like overkill to me as they were literally at every driveway.

This day, many of the trails, if not all, were paved.

I was now on my second trail (well, third if you count the Mary Moore connector), and the crowds were awake and out on the trail. I was now on the Sammamish River trail. It was one of the busiest trails I'd been on in a while. No worries, I totally expected the masses to be out today, based on the holiday, and I found out that

Washington University was having their first home football game that day. Seattle was probably always busy this time of the year, but given it was a Saturday and Labor Day Weekend, hopefully I could still see what I planned to.

After riding these trails, I got on the Burke-Gilman Trail in Bothell. This was also a beautifully paved trail and followed the west side of Lake Washington. Incredible riding, but the foot traffic was increasing. This foot traffic had somewhere to go, however. Like I said prior, this also just happened to be the Washington Huskies first home game. I rode by the Alaska Airlines Field thirty minutes before kickoff. I absolutely love being in these atmospheres; I really enjoy sports, and seeing these big college stadiums is impressive to me. The trail was wide and full of purple jerseys, with a few orange and blue Boise State jerseys scattered in the mix.

I think this is a really cool way to go to the game, a trail! There were a few partiers on the trail (it is college after all), and overall, it was a very cool scene. Being able to see the stadium from the trail was neat. It looked like a nice, big stadium, and I'm sure it was at capacity for the home opener.

Before crossing the Fremont Bridge to Queen Anne and Seattle, I wanted to see this sculpture called the Fremont Troll. It's a work of art under the Highway 99 bridge. It's an odd but cool-looking thing that had drawn a crowd when I was there. Then on the way back down the hill to the trail, it happened.

Going downhill the few blocks I had walked up, my back tire seized up again! I knew exactly right away what had happened. Honestly, I was expecting this to happen a few days before or really anytime since the last incident. I figured that the zip ties would eventually fail. Riding and just waiting for this to happen—the anticipation was the killer. Thinking about when the problem will happen again totally took control of my ride and living out one of my dreams.

I think I really need someone to air out my frustrations too; I don't have any friends that I talk to regularly. I've got friends, but I feel I've abandoned them. My depression and isolation have made me into some kind of new-age hermit. I go out and do things—well, hike and bike mostly—and when I do, I tend to avoid people. Something in my mind makes me feel alone in the world, and I can't shake it. It's even sadder how long I've felt and lived this way.

So when I get frustrated, my parents usually hear it, then later I feel this horrible regret that absolutely hurts me inside. Then that leads to the feeling of more depression. It's a seemingly endless cycle that I know all too well. I have to change this pattern of behavior. It's not that I'm saying mean things, and my voice never rises, not at all, ever. I guess I just flat-out don't have anyone else to turn to. I normally just express my frustrations to them, in the heat of my feelings, sometimes blinded to everything else. It's me venting, but it kills me. I don't even like writing about it, like a few other things too. But if I'm doing this book, I can't hold back; I need this to be real. Most of the time, though, I just keep it all to myself; it's easier and hurts less.

My bike broke down at the rear rack again. I found on Maps a bike shop 0.3 miles away, so I was going to try to make my way there. I was done with zip tie temporary solutions; it was time for a mechanic, one last time, I hoped. I would fix it temporarily, move a little, and then it would fail again. I had to repeat this process three or four times, and by then I was only a couple hundred feet away. However, it was not worth fixing anymore, as I would only get a few steps, and it would break again. I literally had both pannier bags in my left hand and the bike with my sleeping bag and frame bags still attached in my right hand. I was walking down the sidewalk and crossed the street while still holding all this gear. I'm sure this was a sight to see.

I walked into Cascade Bicycle Studio and was telling the mechanic my problems—bike, not personal, ha ha. This is a very nice and high-end shop; I've never seen these kinds of bikes or frames. Super lightweight, electronic shifting—this area has the wealth for bikes of this style. Man, would I love to take a test ride on one of these. I can't imagine how smooth and efficient the riding would be. They also have a specialized bike fitting machine and service. This I'd love to try; I wonder if it could correct the numbness I get in my left hand by changing my posture. I am or was at one point very happy with my bike, plus these bikes are not for my kind of riding; these would not be suitable for riding on an unpaved trail.

There were people hanging out after a group ride. Very friendly atmosphere. After everyone left, I was talking with the mechanic. Super cool, down-to-earth guy, but I forget his name. Don't get intimidated by the word studio and products on display; this place is great, and I definitely recommend them even if it's just for a bike fix like I needed. After all, at the end of the day bike shops this one included, are here to help. He got me fixed up and rolling again. He even put a sort of brace on my broken rack! After a little over an hour, I was off again.

Now I'm confident that it will hold for the remainder of my trip. I can't describe how relieved I am now. It feels like so much of my stress, anxiety, and worrying are gone now. I feel this immediate rush of relief and best of all, a true feeling of happiness. Thanks again to Cascade Bicycle Studio for the quick fix!

I'm honestly also feeling some relief from if not fear, then maybe apprehension. I know this is a solid fix for now, and I'm very satisfied with the rear rack again. It's literally a whole mental flip; I'm starting to feel like I'm enjoying my trip more.

Leaving the shop, I noticed this dinosaur cut out of a huge bush as I crossed the street. I went about a quarter mile and crossed the Fremont Bridge into Queen Anne. This was an amazing area along the Puget Sound, in Discovery Bay. I got on a couple short, connected trails that took me to Centennial Park and then into Seattle.

It was really cool riding past huge shipyards, a lot of ships, and a couple luxury cruise liners. It's amazing how big these ships are, and my mind goes to thinking, How do you build something so big? It was very refreshing breathing in the air. It was calming because I could taste and smell the salt water. This ride was enjoyable to all of the senses.

While still riding the Elliot Bay Trail into Seattle, I had some great scenery along the water. The few trails I needed to take to the Bainbridge Ferry were along the water, so I didn't have to ride through this enormous city. Honestly, I was very happy about this for a couple reasons: (1) it was just way easier and safer not riding in the city and (2) based on what I saw in Spokane and what I've heard about all the problems in some of Washington's big cities, I certainly didn't want to be a part of that or have my route go through a hostile political environment.

So I picked a few sights to see, close to the trail. I went into Seattle to see the Space Needle, and I of course had to see the Chris Cornell statue. Since it's the MoPOP and not Experience Music Project anymore, I feel no need to go inside. This museum used to have a lot of Jimi Hendrix memorabilia on display (and they may still). If I could see any passed-away musician in concert, no doubt it would be Jimi. I grew up on grunge and alternative music in the nineties, so Seattle is obviously a little special to me. I really wanted to visit the apartment building where Layne Staley passed away, the Bruce and Brandon Lee Memorial, and the Kurt Cobain house site, but they were mostly on the far opposite side of Seattle. Also, now time was a minor issue I had to keep in mind.

After riding the Seattle Waterfront Parkway, I arrived at the Bainbridge Ferry Terminal. I first went upstairs to buy a ticket but was told to go to bay 41. I would be able to buy a ticket there prior to getting on. I guess I went past the pay station, but I didn't see anywhere to pay. I did stop and look. So I ended up waiting in line and not paying for the ride. I went by what looked like a pay station but couldn't put cash or a card in the machine.

It was an amazing feeling of accomplishment being on the ferry. It meant that I was done with the American mainland! I had freaking done it and now just had a couple days to go. I got a little emotional and a little teary-eyed when I really thought about how far I've gone and what I've done so far. No matter how I'm feeling mentally, I need to cut myself a break. It's a matter of whether I can follow through on that, though.

The ferry ride was a lot of fun, and I enjoyed seeing Seattle disappearing behind me.

I was hoping to see some animals swimming around in the waters. I wasn't sure if I'd get to see orcas, sea lions, sea otters, whales, and seals; I didn't unfortunately. Wow, if I had gotten to see one of those, it would've been epic. Almost as cool as my grizzly sighting. Well, while the grizzly sighting was cool, it had me incredibly scared at the time.

My ferry ride ended, and I continued my riding on the island to camp. It was only a 7.5-mile ride, but it felt like a roller coaster ride, up and down. It was a beautiful area to ride, very, very green. I love the trees out here; there's something about the way the pine trees look. It's amazing; I can't imagine ever getting tired of the scenery and terrain. I also found a lot of blackberry patches along the road, and they're a lot bigger than the ones back home—delicious.

The road riding was OK, with not much of a shoulder. But the people were great, gave me plenty of room or patiently waited behind me. I started my day at 7:00 a.m. and arrived at the campground around six thirty! It was a very long day. I stayed at Fay Bainbridge Park, which is right on the water!

I was told it was sold out but they've never turned anyone away. When I got there, there were 4 or 5 primitive spots. I asked if anyone would mind sharing a spot, and the 2 groups of people both said of course. One group was a couple probably in their 50s, and the other a couple in their late 40s. Both were very friendly, and we talked about my trip. They were amazed I rode the whole way here with no sleeping pad. When I told what I wear riding, they all laughed in a good way, and then I told them I only had shirts, nothing heavy or made for the cold. The older couple was blown away by the fact I had ridden all but 4,000 miles with no padded pants/shorts or a sleeping pad. I told them that I prefer the cool ground after a long day and when my back is hurting, a hard, flat surface is what I need.

Alberto, part of the couple closer to my age, called me a dirt bagger. He said, "No, don't buy a sleeping pad. Man, you're a dirt bagger. Go minimal." They couldn't believe I had everything for a cross-country trip in basically two pannier bags. I had never heard of a dirt bagger; must be a West Coast thing. But from what Alberto said, I'm proud to be one, if indeed I am one out here.

Alberto, to me, was the absolute embodiment of the free-spirited, adventurous, freethinking Western attitude that I'm really feeling more and more connected to. I want what he has; I want that carefree Western attitude. He arrived with his girlfriend at camp in a canoe! It's not like that in the East, or at least conservative Lancaster County. If I said my thoughts and feelings about my thoughts and principles, I don't think it would be accepted back home at all. Maybe that's what's holding me down, that I don't belong in the East anymore, and need to head West?

The place was full, with a huge group that was a little loud, but the annoying thing was the kids playing at night and shining the flashlight in the tent camping area, not on purpose, just kids having fun, but thankfully it ended at ten, quiet time.

I'm down to 2 1/2 days! It's just strange to say that: 3 days of riding, and it's all over. Three days is all that's left. Wow, talk about having your mind blown. It's odd in a way to think about only having 3 days left because it's hard to realize I've been riding over 2 months by now. It doesn't seem real and certainly hasn't fully sunk in. It's like I'm just some guy riding with this naive outlook about my ride. To me, this is just what I enjoy, and I don't see it for the big deal it is.

All I know, I'd be a dirt bagger for life if I could. If I could, I'd just ride and write. Anything to be financially stable from riding my bike would be an absolute dream, either touring with a company or operating my own or even writing for a living.

I made a video on the ferry, and I was feeling it all so much I could barely talk. Wiping some tears away, choking up, I think what I had done was sinking in. I didn't know if I would get here or not. It's been such a hard ride so far; I didn't know if I'd make it to Bainbridge Island. Leaving the mainland of America hit me hard for sure. It's been over two months and a long, hard journey. Thinking of the few days to go, it's just mind blowing. Amazing what you can do when you put your mind to it and stick with it. I had more problems today, and it's just unreal. It's been hard, difficult, and rewarding.

All I know is, I did it! I have a couple hundred miles to go, and then I'll have ridden across America. One last leg, and that'll be it. I don't know what to say; it just means a lot to be able to do this. And to do this trip solo is just wild. I've just got to keep going—I'm almost there.

✪

9/3/23

DAY #68, RIDING #60

Miles—69.55 (4,009.34); Time—6:06 (344:30)
Dungeness Recreation Area, Sequim, Washington
($10, primitive)

Every morning I try to see the sunrise, if I'm up, especially when I'm on the beach, and this morning didn't disappoint. It was cloudy, but that actually added to this mysterious-looking sunrise. Simply put, incredible: washed-up driftwood, water crashing onto the beach, bringing the water up to my toes, the slight view of Seattle, and some other land in the background.

This was my first full day riding on the Olympic Peninsula, and it went really well, which was a blessing because as you can tell, I'm wearing down, mostly mentally though. So this was absolutely needed. I started by finishing up my road map from yesterday, 22 miles from my campground to the Hood Canal Floating Bridge in Port Ludlow. I would soon learn that the region over here is anything but flat. I had to climb so many hills over 22 miles and an 1,060-foot increase in elevation, with the same amount going back down. I would end up walking a couple times this day as well.

Starting out riding through Port Madison, I saw these really cool painted rocks. One was a funny-looking frog with big eyes and some nice red lips, and behind it was a painted ladybug rock. Today I would ride through a few Indian reservations. The first was the Suquamish Tribal Land, a nice area; I saw my first Indian casino out here. It was a very green, shady area, with beautiful, forested land surrounding me. I would also keep seeing blackberry and raspberry patches along the road. I had to stop almost every time and indulge on this fresh, tasty treat.

Right before the bridge in Port Gamble, I came to the Port Gamble Forest Park. This trail is the reason I love this area. A hard-packed dirt trail with lush green everywhere your eyes can wander. Washington's state nickname is absolutely spot on: the Evergreen State. Literally everything minus the ground and sky is green. It's almost like I'm wearing green-shaded sunglasses. I can't get over the trees out here, between the firs, pines, and the mammoth western red cedar.

Exiting the park, I came to this bridge going to Squamish Harbor. The bridge offered up some pretty views and, thankfully, wide shoulders, wide enough I felt safe stopping for pictures. I was very happy that the bridge was the way it was—starting out with a concrete shoulder, then transitioning to a metal grated section. I was so relieved that they had these wide mats over the metal to ride on safely. Riding over a metal grate surface is OK if it's dry, but when it's wet, well, remember my crossing into Ohio? That was like riding on ice; I had white knuckles, and I was actually scared. So I was relieved this surface was covered.

After crossing the bridge, I would start my second road map, a 20-mile ride to Port Townsend, and would have some tougher climbs with it. I had two big hills on which I had to walk a little. On those hills I'd walk to catch my breath until I could pedal again.

Out here it's been all paved roads with little car traffic. I did have to ride on Highway 19 North, but only a short section of it. I wanted to stay off highways and see the area from the regular roads. I passed the Olympic Peninsula Gateway Visitor Center and stopped for a little break. Not counting the big climbs, the riding out here is easy and allows for a relaxing cruise. I passed by some logging areas and wondered if they replace the trees they cut down. I hope so because this area of America is not the same with tree stumps littering the views of the landscape.

With a few miles to go, I entered Discovery Bay. Along the water I saw the first of a few signs warning about the toxic shellfish. It stated the clams, oysters, mussels, and scallops were unsafe to eat because of biotoxins. That's very disappointing because I remember

Opa (what I called my grandpa) literally digging out these shellfish with ease.

Shortly after this I would start the Olympic Discovery Trail. It's a long paved trail but breaks at certain spots requiring some road riding. There are plenty of signs saying how long the road detour is. It's one of the best-marked trails I've ever been on. The trail followed along Discovery Bay until just before Gardiner. Then it followed Highway 101 to cut over to the tranquil Sequim Bay. It was here I cut up north to my campground in the Dungeness Recreation Area. The trails are breathtaking; they're all tree-lined, or else green bushes hug the paved pathway. When not obstructed by thriving green flora, I have picture perfect views of the bays or water. What more could I ask for? A peaceful ride and more importantly a mind at ease.

It was a cold, dreary sort of day. I had cloud cover almost all day long. I also got a short drizzle of a rain shower for about ten minutes. It didn't help me feeling a little cold, then getting wet early in the morning, but it wasn't a hard rain at least. It was a chilly day with the temperature reaching a high in the midsixties. Everything, including the rain and clouds, combined to make a cooler ride all day, but at least there was no wind.

It's funny, in a way, I'm really the only one not dressed properly for the Pacific Northwest. I'm just wearing my usual two long-sleeve shirts. I see everyone out here wearing rain jackets and warmer clothing. Actually, I wouldn't mind a sweatshirt for the nights out here. It's been colder at night, and combine that with the cover from the trees. It was certainly a cool ride in more ways than one.

I 100 percent enjoyed my ride today: the views of the water, the forest, Discovery Bay, and everything else I came across. I also went through a couple Indian reservations, as I mentioned. You can definitely tell the wealth differences in the tribal lands. Some seem thriving, and some seem to not have as many businesses. I hope they all have the accommodations they need. I wonder how relations are today because we all know what we did to lay claim to the land. It's a sad story to me, but I see it as a cruel world. It seems like if someone wants something, sometimes they feel they have a right to it. And that "right" tends to turn to violence. Why? What does it matter? Like a great man once sang, "Imagine no countries, no possessions and the world will live as one." Yes, I'm definitely a dreamer.

On the way to my campground, I stopped at the Jamestown S'Klallam Tribe visitor center, right along Sequim Bay; it was this absolutely incredible setup. The view of the bay, a couple paved pathways leading to the water, and a playground were only a couple of the things that set this site apart. They had these totally amazing-looking totem poles, and the visitor center looked brand-new. This is a thriving community—at least appears to be—and there is also a casino just up the road to help pay for all this. From what I've seen, reservations with casinos tend to be more financially stable.

I really wish I knew more about these totem poles; they are just so cool-looking. I'd like to know about their significance and what they mean to the S'Klallam. Maybe because I feel more in tuned with nature, I have a big interest in the Native Americans' beliefs. With my depression and other stuff holding me down, I would very much be interested in some form of Native American healing. But of course, I would never pursue this beyond thinking and now writing about it; this is a sacred thing all their own, and that needs to be respected.

Just outside the town of Sequim, the trail went into a wooded area. Along this part, some of the trees I passed were enormous. It was amazing how tall they were and how high they went up before sprouting their first branches. Journeying through Sequim, I came up to a lady riding her bike. Her bike had a long storage space in the front that was trapezoidal. It had a front frame that held the storage area, and it was over a foot deep. She was going grocery shopping, she told me, and all together her bike was about seven to eight feet long. I've never seen anything like it, but it's certainly an interesting way to go shopping.

Coming into the Dungeness Recreation Area, I arrived at the campground. Shortly before arriving at the camp, I hit the 4K mile mark! It's hard to believe that at this point I've ridden that much. I understand how much that is on a bike, but it still doesn't seem real, like I didn't really do that much.

The campground on Voice of America Road is hard to beat. The area, first off, is absolutely beautiful, with the Salish Sea crashing in the background.

I found a good spot and set up my tent in the hiker/biker area. I love the separate primitive areas and this campground has us tucked away between the trees. There are 5 to 6 sites and a couple picnic tables. I really loved this $10 primitive campground. It has hiking trails also, with one going 5 miles out into the Dungeness Bay. It's called a spit, and it's like a little strip of land; also, the trail ends at a lighthouse. Since it's 5 miles one way, I won't have time to walk the trail. Tomorrow I will encounter something similar in Port Angeles, but I can ride that one.

After setting up everything and eating, I took a walk to find the water. I could hear the waves crashing in the tent area, and I couldn't ask for a better sound to hear constantly. Once I got to the path, it took me to the water's edge, and to the cliff's edge. The trail goes up to a cliff with a steep drop-off, with fencing, so there's no way to get down to the water. It's waves rolling toward me for as far as I can see. The water goes on until it meets the fading sun. Such a beautiful sunset—it's hard to believe that wasn't the best part.

I leaned against a fence post, closed my eyes, and just listened. I let the sea and its rolling, crashing waves take me away to an absolutely peaceful place. This was, 100 percent, no doubt, the most calming, soothing noise I heard all trip. I literally could've fallen asleep standing up listening to the waves crash and roll. The view of the sun setting on the rolling water, combined with the sound of that water hitting the rocks, took me away to utopia. I can honestly say, falling asleep to the sounds out here, I could hear this every night and not get tired of it.

I'm feeling a lot better mentally lately. It makes such a difference when I don't have to worry about my bike breaking down. Before almost every bump, I immediately cringe and think about the rear. There's no way to enjoy myself when I constantly fear when the next break will happen. I honestly believe this has been a huge factor in my thoughts and feelings so far on this trip. I'm now able to ride my way and not worry about a breakdown. I can make the bike work again; I feel confident in the fix.

It's crazy to think I have one more full day of riding until I'm done, in addition to a half day of about 35 miles.

I am in a really good mood today; my whole day went the way it was supposed to: just carefree riding, no worries, no rushing, and trying to be like a sponge soaking it all in.

A funny thing happened: I'm was on the road, and all of a sudden, there went my sleeping bag. I guess it worked itself loose from my bungee cords. Luckily no one was behind me. I just stopped, gathered my sleeping bag and chair, and put them back on the rack.

It's a cold night out here; I'm guessing because of the sea breeze but even more so the trees that cover the primitive camping area. As soon as I got back from my walk, I went in the tent; it was chilly outside, and I was tired.

Once again, lying down in my sleeping bag, I can hear the waves still hitting the rocks at the cliff wall. Just a perfect experience and something that I was in need of. The perfect way to end my day.

9/4/23

DAY #69, RIDING #61

Miles—70.98 (4,080.32); Time—6:28 (350:58)
Klahowya Campground ($17, primitive)

Today was a good day to ride. Well, the main reason was it would be my last full day. There wasn't any rain today, and there wasn't any in the forecast. From what I've heard and read, there is a lot of rain out here. Also, today half my ride was on the border of the Olympic National Forest. Any day it's not raining out here is a good riding day.

With the colder temps to start the days, I start out with long- and short-sleeve shirts, a beanie under my helmet, gloves, and of course pants—no more shorts during the day. I also had almost total cloud cover, at least in the morning. It would become a little sunny later in the day and warmer as well.

I had a later start today; I got to talking with a guy in our camping area. He was from Washington and just doing a few days' trip around the area. I've been meeting more people as I come farther west. I've actually come to enjoy it, meeting new people out here. I used to try to avoid people. I usually pick the farthest-away campsite, try not to make eye contact, just try to appear busy or uninterested in my own world, hoping I'll be left alone. But meeting people out in the West seems so different from meeting people in the East; they certainly have a different mentality. Basically, I feel more at ease and feel understood talking to the people out here. It's a nice change of pace, and I've actually grown to like it.

I had to start out with a couple-mile ride on Kitchen-Dick Road to get on the Olympic Discovery Trail. Yup, that's the actual road name from my campground to the trail, Kitchen-Dick Road. Starting off, on the trail at Robin Hill Farm, I passed a fence that had a bunch of bodybuilding trophies attached to it. Also, a crab made from debris washed up on the beach. I like passing these random things along the trail; it keeps things interesting. Out here I tend to see more than I did in other regions. It's fun to see how creative some people can be. I would see a couple spots along the trail where people had decorations and random things in their backyards. Yogi the bear in a chair smoking a cigar is one I remember, with a lot of other things there as well.

I would travel almost 20 miles from camp to Port Angeles, and there were also a few hills, of course. The trail is still all paved, and once again I can't say how well marked the road sections are, with signs announcing the road routes, along with the mileage for the road sections. Along the way, I'm doing a lot of climbing out here; there aren't a lot of flat distances on the trail or road. Being close to the beach and water, I figured I'd have a flat ride throughout this section. Nothing huge, though, just a fair amount of hills.

Most of the drivers are great out here, but I've got to say this is also the highest concentration of people not slowing down to pass me along the roads I've encountered. I get it; I'm not mad. But it's frustrating when someone can get over to pass but chooses not to. As a rider, you just have to expect anything and everything and just go with it. The ones that concern me are the trailers that don't get over. I just hope they realize their camper sticks out farther than their truck as they pass me.

These past two days have really kicked my butt. They've been long days, and I've done more miles than I probably should have. The past two days, I did 70ish miles, and that's probably pushing myself this late in the trip. But I'm here, and I made it, so I'll enjoy it.

The trail ride into Port Angeles was a sensational adventure. It wandered through a lot of wooded areas. I loved getting lost in the beauty of the trees again. The scenery out here is a real pleasure riding through, with a smooth surface and enough natural wonders to change anyone's mood around. There are a couple of nice bridges to ride across, which somehow add to the magnificence of this fantasy world I find myself in. Winding out of the woods, I come into Port Angeles East, Port Angeles Harbor, and the Salish Sea.

Coming into Port Angeles was surely a sight to see. The trail goes right along the beach, taking you into the city. This is a very big city, definitely the biggest one I have encountered since leaving Seattle on the ferry. Soon the beaches give way to the docking area for boats and the town. It's a very nice city, with plenty of shops and restaurants.

I did some looking around but wanted to keep moving. I wanted to get to the strip of land that I had seen yesterday. I also planned for a longer break. Out here I'm in no way rushing, and everything takes me longer. I do a lot of stopping for pictures and just looking around. I really love this region of Washington, and I can't help stopping as much as I am.

After riding through a good deal of Port Angeles, I arrive at Sail and Saddle Park on the Ediz Hook. I took this little skinny piece of land that curled into the harbor. It was a two-lane road and trail that eventually came to a dead end. At the end was the US Coast Guard Port Angeles Station. The strip of land hooked eastward, with Port Angeles Harbor on the southern side. The northern side consisted of a beach, Puget Sound, and eventually Canada. It's a fantastic ride that extends three to four miles one way.

I parked my bike, walked out, and hung out on the beach for a while. I was enjoying it all out here: the taste in the air, the scenery, and most of all the calming sound of crashing waves once again. Maybe because it's been so long, I'd have to think about my last time being at a beach, or I just have a new appreciation for something. Either way, I can't get enough of hearing this mood-altering, trance-like sound.

As I came back to my bike, there was an older lady in a van trying to tell me something. She asked me if I needed an empty bag. Strange, but being nice, I said sure and thank you. It was one of those grocery-store type bags. She told me her name was Lynn, her birthday was this month, and she'd be seventy-five. We got to talking for a little bit, and she offered me a bag full of snacks she just bought. It was a few small cashew bags, Cheetos, and popcorn. She said she didn't want them and was not sure why she even bought them. I thanked her and was glad to take them from her. We kept talking and had a good conversation. She told me how her son was a nurse, lived on her property, and looked after her. Lynn also told me that she forgets things and where she is sometimes. The only place she's allowed to drive to anymore is this beach. She told me a story about how she lost her van for a week until a neighbor told her son it was at the end of the road. We also talked about family, how it's important when life comes around and it's time for the kids to take care of the parents later in life. She was very nice but only seemed about 75 percent there.

This experience reminded me of some factors in my life. Anyways, I hope she made it home safely. Definitely a very nice person but not sure she should have been out alone. This is the kind of senior that someone probably could easily take advantage of when they're alone.

By now it's after 1:00 p.m., and I still have 40 miles to go.

Outside the main city, I came to Crown Park, a residential area. It was here that deer were literally eating in people's front yards, walking through driveways, even walking within a few feet of me as I took a couple pictures. It was really cool; even back home they don't get that close. I also passed through the Lower Elwha Klallam tribal land.

The trail surface is amazing; there's little to no cracking in it. It's paved and appears to be very well maintained the entire way so far. I would love it if we had trees like this at home, but not sure I'd trade them for ours. You can't beat the fall color change back home.

There's so much to stop and see out here. Once again today I took a combined 139 pictures and videos. Riding the trails, I don't make much progress before I pull over for something, usually a picture. It makes for a longer day, and today I'd finish up at six. But I wouldn't change any part of the day.

Most of my road ride was along Highway 112 West, the Strait of Juan De Fuca Scenic Byway. I also got on the Pine Spruce Trail for about 10 miles, toward the end of the day. It was on the northern border of the National Olympic Forest and, wow, was the trail amazing. I'd put it up there with the Coeur D'Alene in Idaho.

It was also around there where the sunny skies from Port Angeles changed to the cloudy skies of the Olympic Forest. I'll take that trade anytime.

What can I really say about the Olympic National Forest? How could anyone describe the natural beauty and wonder of it all?

I don't even get to go into it, though; I really just get a teaser of what it offers. My trip just rides along the northern border on a road ride. Everything is green, just different shades. I sound like a broken record, but the flora and fauna out here are maybe my absolute favorite. It's hard to beat the Evergreen State for incredible landscapes. The moss growing out here—everything just has a mystical appeal, like I'm walking around in some magical fantasy world. Sometime I need to get back here and explore this park. But for now, I'm more than satisfied by what I've seen.

One of the absolute gems of my ride today was riding along Crescent Lake. It offered up breathtaking views of the trees—the pines, the spruces—and the rest of the foliage. At the start I saw a sign warning me about cougars: "Be alert, and don't hike alone." Nothing about biking alone, so I guess I'm OK, I thought. There were a *lot* of people out here enjoying it all, and I'm not surprised. Can't imagine a much better way to spend this Labor Day Monday.

There was so much to see today; I stopped so many times. So many pictures and soaking-up of the landscape. I love seeing the haze coming through the trees or cutting off the tops. The views along the lake with the hazy mountaintops in the background, breathtaking. I could get used to seeing this every day; that's for sure. I also saw my first Pacific Northwest slug; wow, are they different looking out here. They appear to be wearing a helmet, with a mean grin on their face.

I eventually make it to the Klahowya Campground, and it's perfect. Very good spacing, lots of room, privacy, and I also have my own pathway to the Sol Duc River. Lots of trees overhead also. It's been a chilly day, in the high fifties and maybe up to sixty, but it'll feel colder out here with the tree cover. The river is very nice, the water is low, and the rock bed gives me a path to the water. I can hear the water up at my tent, and it's never a bad thing if that's the only thing I hear. The only bummer is the flattest spot has tiny rocks everywhere. I feel them lying down; there is no way I can kick them all away.

Oh well, I'm beat, and I'll still sleep on them. I'm not setting an alarm for tomorrow—well OK, maybe six thirty, ha ha. I still can't start too late, even if tomorrow is it. I can't believe it. It's been such a long trip, but it also doesn't seem like I've been gone that long. It's hard to believe tomorrow is it. I almost don't believe it.

I'll wrap this up with some things I had to say in one of my videos. Today was the final full day of my trip, and it's hard to say how I think or feel. I'm in a really good mood and think it's from a combination of things. It may sound funny and may not be true, but it's how I feel—the biggest holdup was my bicycle constantly breaking down. After the last fix, as with the other fixes, I got this instant relief. Now it's literally hardware through the frame and nuts threaded on the end. Did I mention because the nut is on the gear side of my lower frame and the frame's thickness, I had to lose my two highest gears? I had the limits changed, so I couldn't shift into the top two gears and have my chain hit the nut, now threaded on. I haven't had my top gear since my fix in Livingston, Montana, outside Yellowstone.

Another breakdown would have to be something catastrophic, and what's next, the frame actually breaking? I don't have to worry about the bike now; literally every minute I heard the creaking and rubbing of the frame and bike rack because it was only held in place by zip ties; I knew any moment it could break. The anxiety of knowing that it's going to fail at some point, but then it didn't—this went on for days, and it became very hard to deal with. Waiting and knowing, the anticipation, literally drives me crazy.

It's been awesome and so crazy to think about how this is almost over. I know what I want to say, but it's hard to come up with the words. I've got about 35 miles to go, that's it; 35 measly miles, and I'll have gone across the country, only having about a week off; although, I think some of those days I didn't need off. It doesn't seem like it's been over two months at all.

I'm beat. The riding out here is great, but there are so many hills. I know I'm also riding in a new position. I'm getting a sharp pain in my neck, and my back is really starting to hurt. For the longest time, I didn't notice any pain from riding, just tightness in my back, which has been an ongoing thing for many years.

I think some of what I'm doing is starting to kick in. All the complaining, and difficult situations—I think that just goes with something like this. Especially when you have no one to lean on, that's OK to a point. Then either you quit or do something to change it. Complaining is a form of venting for me, and I see it as OK, in small doses. But it's only OK if I realize it and make a change. If I don't, then I need to take some time and learn to accept the situation for what it is. If I don't, well, we've seen my dark feelings and thoughts by now. Emotions and feelings happen. They're natural; to try to control them is futile. Let them happen and flow, then after determine the best way to work with them. I believe you can't change the way you feel without some drastic change. So just embrace them for what they are.

It's been fun no matter what the past pages say.

9/5/23

DAY #70, RIDING #62

Miles—36.22 (4,116.54); Time—3:04 (354:02)
Quileute Oceanside Resort, La Push, Washington
($34, primitive)

Well, amid all the good and bad, the light and dark moments and feelings, I've persevered through it all. I have arrived! I finished my trip across the country on the Great America Rail Trail. I ended in La Push, Washington, with my feet in the sand of the Pacific Ocean.

It was all road riding today and mostly downhill, finally. Although, I did have one hill to climb, and it was a good one. I had to have at least one climb today to finish everything. It would be a slow pack-up today, no need to leave any particular time. I knew I only had 30ish miles, and being all on the road, it wouldn't take me long. I was sure I made extra coffee this morning and sat in my chair just a little longer. Not too long, though; it was cold just sitting around.

In the first 10 miles, I finished up the Olympic Discovery Trail. It was mostly all roads left, but today I would have a couple scattered, very short trail segments winding through the Olympic National Forest, which of course I loved; I wished there were more miles through this wonderland.

The roads were deserted, and I was very happy, of course, to see this. Only two cars came my way, and no cars came from behind me. The back roads were very nice and of course very green. I was absolutely in a state of pure bliss riding through all this again—the foliage, the landscape. The sun even came out to create the perfect ending to my journey. All day the sun was out, with some minor clouds, but this huge, wonderful blue sky was everywhere today.

The last 30 miles consisted of my last road map, my last destination, Quileute Oceanside Resort. The last 25 miles would have to be highways, no other options. I started on 101 West, and that took me to 110 West. All that would come to an end at James Island Lookout, a beach area and my campground. Along the way, I would take my time and soak up as much as I could.

I did get to see a few different sides of this area. I saw a bunch of signs about projects protecting the salmon and the rest of the native species. This has to be important for the people who depend on the fish, not to mention the wildlife. I also still see a lot of signs warning about shellfish biotoxins and high levels of paralytic shellfish poison, I'm assuming, preventing the consumption of all these tasty creatures in the Olympic Peninsula region.

One thing I would see more of was the logging of the lands. I passed lots of cleared-out acres along my route. It's sort of a bittersweet thing for me. I suppose I don't like seeing a huge empty piece of land where something beautiful once stood. But I also assume there's a greater purpose out there for everything that was there and the land; I hope so, at least. Riding through one of the few towns today, I didn't see much, and I loved it. The Beaver Fire Department and maybe a visitors' center—that was it. Riding with the tree-lined roads was enough of a sight for me. After making my way past the forest, I started entering the Quileute tribal area.

Turning on La Push Road, it was surreal to think how many hundreds of roads I had been on, and here was the last one.

This route was also on Highway 110 West, but once again, there was not a lot of traffic. The winding Sol Duc River gave way to the Calawah and Bogachiel rivers, and then those combined to make the Quillayute River. Although the rivers met in Mora, the waterway curled around to greet me at La Push.

Leaving the forest, I know in the back of my mind that sometime, somehow, I will be back. This area is truly an inspiring place, and I loved my short time here.

Entering the Quileute Reservation, I note it's certainly different from the S'Klallam Tribal Lands. There isn't much developed out here, and there are no businesses that I see. All I really remember is the resort and the convenience store at the resort campground. I like the less developed land out here but wonder about the people and their economy. Whatever the case, the land out here is absolutely amazing.

Arriving at the Quileute Oceanside Resort, I first checked in and booked my tent site. I got tent site 7, a minute walk over some driftwood to the Pacific Ocean and exactly the site number I wanted. Before unloading, I continued on to the end just up the road to James Island Lookout. I made a couple-minute video riding from the campground to the end. Of course, I had to record my final minutes. The views are of a tourist book, picture perfect. Rialto Beach, First Beach, and Jamestown Island area are all incredible to see. Jamestown Island sits just off the mainland, has a strip of land that extends close to it from the beach, but is not publicly accessible. Just off to the north sits Rialto Beach, and First Beach is the area that the resort sits on. This primitive camping is an absolute must, and they also have rooms in their resort.

I can also see this all from the spot where I'm standing, my final destination, the end. I run down to the beach, fall to my knees, and rest my hands on the sand. I've done it; I'm at the Pacific Ocean. I've completed my first cross-country trip, solo at that. I get my picture taken by some kind tourists and try to understand, or feel, what I've just done. However, at this current time, I don't grasp it at all. I just understand I'm done, it's all over.

I tried to make a video, and the first thirty seconds were me just stuttering and repeating, "I don't know what to say." I really didn't at first; I guess I was in some sort of shocked state. I definitely wanted to thank everyone for sticking with me through all my problems and complaining. Wow, 4,100-plus miles, 70 days, 62 days of riding, and it just doesn't seem like I did all this. Not sure how long it'll take to actually fully sink in. I'm so glad I did this and stuck with it. Don't ever give up on anything you care about. Do you really want something or not? Adversity will happen, no doubt, but for me, I can't quit. If I did, it would be more than quitting the trip; it'd be a monumental failure. A failure I would surely drag into the rest of my life. I'd say that's the main reason I can't quit—it might actually slowly kill me inside. Bottom line, if I had quit this trip, then I would have taken it as me being a failure, and that's extreme, but it's how my mind works. That can't happen, so I can't quit; it's just not acceptable under any circumstances. Call it motivation. Call it depression creating action. I don't know, but it's who I am. No giving up, no matter what.

I go and find my campsite and do my last camping setup. I love this spot. It's at the end—no neighbors, close to the water, and bathrooms are accessible. There was an empty RV site, so I charged my phone there as well. The landscape out here is serene and peaceful. The rock formations in the water, and of course James Island, create a landscape anyone could fall in love with. Everything combined into a panoramic scene: water, sand, sky, driftwood. It creates a space that will make you want to spend a few days out here.

I have today and until early afternoon tomorrow. My dad is driving from back home to pick me up out here, and he should be here around noon.

It's hard to write about feelings and what this all means to me right now because not a lot of this trip, if any, has sunk in yet. I don't have a huge sense of accomplishment or achievement. Right now, it feels like another successful trip down. It's hard enough to believe I've been gone two and one-fourth months. I do know I accomplished something; I am 100 percent aware of what I did. I just don't feel like it's a big deal, at least currently. Don't get me wrong,

I'm very proud of myself for sticking with this trip. I never gave up; I made it through thick and thin, the hard times, and the joyful, carefree times.

Every single event, no matter if it was good or bad, played a very significant role in my journey and led to it ending right here, right now. I had to have the bad to go with the good. To borrow a thought from a book that means so very much to me (*The Book of Joy*, by the Dali Llama, Archbishop Tutu, Douglas Abrams), "How do we know joy without hardship? You don't know what's good if everything is always good, because then good is normal. So, you need the bad (adversity) to know what joy and happiness feel like, and vice versa." I was also told by a friend once "Hardship is the pathway to peace." Now that is a true-life statement; just think about that one.

I can hear the Pacific Ocean waves crashing, and I love it. Once again, what a way to fall asleep.

So what other benefits did I think I'd feel or get, besides the feat itself? I didn't have any expectations coming out of this, just hope. Hope that it would give me more confidence or the ability to apply that confidence in my life. Maybe help me to not avoid people like I do. Maybe even something in a group setting, slow steps, though. I think if any change is going to happen, it's going to be gradual. I don't expect anything. I didn't do this trip to have some guaranteed change in my character, feelings, or life. I did this trip because I had the free time, and it was on my bucket list.

I did this trip to get away from everything, to find myself. Maybe also to help shine a light on myself, on the inside. Originally, I wasn't sure I was coming home. I didn't want to go home. I thought maybe I'd just pack my stuff and go. I still have the desire to leave. I need to understand what's going on, what's been holding me back all these years—these are the answers I'm seeking. Why have I abandoned my friends and even some family? Why have I put up a wall around myself? Why do I live in a world of complete isolation? Most importantly, how do I break free?

The answer I'm looking for is the one to this question: How do I begin to start to break down the wall? How do I learn to be sociable again, and meet new people? Where do I meet a woman I can settle down with? Where does someone my age who doesn't drink go to meet new people? How do I let go of the doorknob to unlock the door so I can let people and the light shine in?

Sitting on the beach, making my final video, I'm surprised I'm not feeling more emotional. No tears, nothing at this point. It's a little strange to not really feel any overpowering emotions. But I assume it'll take a little time to fully kick in. My lack of emotion tells me I don't understand fully what I've done. Right now, I feel like I'm just sitting on the beach at the Pacific Ocean, on any ordinary day. But wow, what a wild ride—all the pain, the problems, the anxiety, and my worries combined to make the trip what it was, incredible. I'd take no substitutions. All the work going into this, the day-by-day routing when I realized I knew nothing about the West. I needed all this to happen exactly the way it did, even though in certain moments, I might have begged to differ.

I know where I am and how I got here, but the gravity hasn't sunk in, not even close. It's weird, I don't know how or what to feel right now, and maybe I'm not supposed to. I feel great, happy as hell, but why don't I feel the emotions of it all? Is it because I feel disconnected from the world most times? Am I even capable of having happy feelings? Can I allow myself to feel happiness for myself, or will my mind and depression not allow me to do that? I just rode 4,100 miles, 70 days, and I'm feeling like, OK what's next? Like it's no big deal.

I want to know what causes my sense of, well, let's call it "Who the f cares?" syndrome. I can think of two reasons I think this way: (1) OK, so I rode across America; it's what I enjoy doing. Who the f cares? (2) My depression won't allow me to feel good about myself for this accomplishment. I'm thinking, Big deal; who the f cares" in sort of an Eeyore-sad state of mental being. I believe this syndrome, as I call it, has multiple routes to the same ending. I believe it starts with my feeling of being withdrawn from life at times.

Bike packing and going on these adventures, whether for a weekend or on a seventy-day trip, is what I do; this is the real me. When I finish a trail or trip, it really is no big deal because I see it as just a hobby of mine. Just another trail, just another trip. It's me. It is crazy to think of doing this trip solo. How someone reacts alone, with no one immediately to help, is certainly a true way to tell what a person is made of. Can you walk the walk, or will you crumble? Can you handle the pressure of it all? Can you remain calm while broken down in the middle of nowhere or climbing a mountain with no shoulder in Yellowstone Park? I'm not putting myself up high, but it takes a certain type of individual to work through seemingly mile-high problems alone and come out on top. Now that is a true gift, one I need to bring into my personal life.

This was really tough, with a lot of huge mountains to climb and a lot of huge mountains to ride down. I saw a lot of cool animals and a couple scary animals. Seeing the transformation of America was the best experience of the entire trip. Starting in Washington DC, riding into the farming land of Ohio, Indiana, and Illinois, to the Midwest, and then the mountains of the West. There is so much to see still here in the great USA, I don't know if I need to leave the country.

I'll someday be able to look back on this trip and say how fulfilling and adventurous it has been. It's just that today is not the time; everything hasn't sunk in. Later I'll feel the excitement and sense of accomplishment. I have no doubts on that. Hopefully, this is the start of change in my life too. Hopefully it will give me the confidence to apply it in other aspects of my life that have been lacking or neglected or even abandoned. I hope this produces a lot of changes and ramifications down the road for me. I desperately need change in my life. Life was a pretty good shit show back home, and like normal, I was running full throttle with little sense of direction. Getting away and doing this was needed.

Life is good right now; at this moment, I feel tranquil and at peace. The sun is setting behind me, and my time on the Great American Rail Trail is complete.

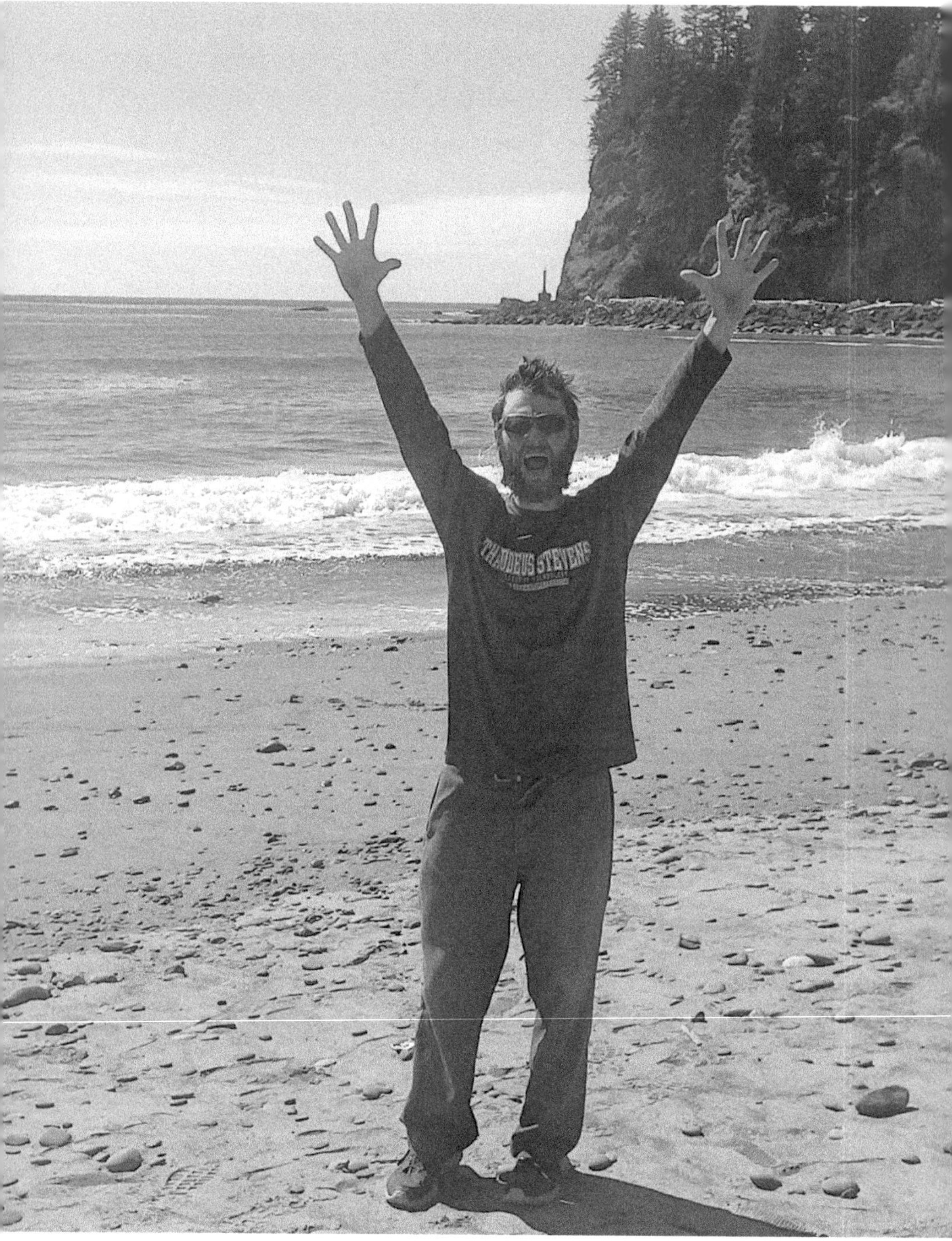
THADDEUS STEVENS

9/6/23 to 9/11/23

THE DRIVE HOME

One last thing not to be missed if you ever get to visit La Push is the sunset on the beach. It's absolutely breathtaking and one of the best sunsets on the trip. The dark blue clouds with the sky behind them are only one part of it. The red and yellowish outer edges of the clouds, where the sun is shining down, create this contrast of colors that puts this over the top. I couldn't ask for a better way to cap off my last night. Waking up the next morning, I would encounter a cloud-covered gray sky. It was cool out in the morning, but of course I still enjoyed a morning walk on the beach.

I hung out at the campground until my dad showed up, which was around noon. It was really good to see him, and I was relieved that he had made it out here. I mean, it was great seeing family again. I've been away for longer stretches, but something about here and now made this special to me. Well, it's not hard to figure out what was different about this meeting; it was the trip, of course.

I was already packed up and ready to go. I didn't want him waiting around, so I was all set. I took off some pieces of my bike so we could just set it in the back seat. With the drop handlebars, all I really needed to take off was the rack and front tire. We wrapped an old towel around the chain and pedals for obvious reasons. Everything fit in the car for the adventure back to Pennsylvania. We did spend some time on the beach and drove to the James Island Lookout. He's been in the area before, so a little bit of it was familiar to him.

After a little sightseeing, we took off for the ferry back to Seattle. One of the things I wanted to see, well my number-one thing, was the Jimi Hendrix Memorial in Renton, Washington. It's actually close to the hotel I stayed at in Issaquah, and I was considering the 10-mile one-way ride to get here at the time. It was a pain with traffic to get there, but after being there, it was definitely worth the frustrating road congestion.

The memorial site is beautifully done, with purple flowers around the outer edge of the big circular grassy area. Inside the center is a big stone memorial with a few blocks inscribed with some of Jimi's quotes. My favorite one here is "Straight ahead, woman and child, man and woman. The best kind of love to have is love of life. Pass it on." In the center is a guitar, and he is buried with some relatives at the domed marble memorial. It's a very nice resting site for one of the greatest guitarists ever, and one of my favorites of course.

After leaving, we made the short drive to Issaquah and actually stayed at the same hotel I did when I came through. Day one down, and I know we were both glad to get out of the Seattle traffic.

On the second day after completing my trip, I still don't feel any different. It still doesn't seem like I did anything special. Maybe I'm distracted currently; I'm sort of in a state of shock. It's a very strange feeling being on a bike for so long and now, all of a sudden, being in a car. It feels strange sitting in a car seat, and it's a really weird feeling being the one going 70 to 80 miles per hour. I keep telling myself that sometime it will kick in and I'll be able to sit back and enjoy what I've done. But secretly I wonder if my depression will rob me of this feeling I want to experience. Is it possible to do something this difficult and after say, "OK, so what? What's up next?"? Will I ever feel any sense of accomplishment? The pride in myself is there; I'm glad I did it. So when will I feel happy for myself?

For now, I try to focus my time in the moment, enjoying the time with my dad. Also, this is my first cross-country road trip. Although, with my dad having already driven one way and me having been out for over two months, it's a fast-moving road trip. I know the coming days will be long and eventually probably will become very boring. I love the sights of the West, but after four to five days of all-day driving, it's going to get boring. We will get on each other's nerves at some point. We will disagree on directions, food, and what to see. What would you expect from being in a car for so long? Nothing bad at all, just too much car time, I guess. I imagine there will be long drives after we lose the mountains and get to the all-too-familiar farming lands.

I became a little miserable on the second night. We had a long driving day from Issaquah to Livingston, Montana. We literally drove all day, with a few stops for gas and sightseeing. But mostly it was all driving, and I think we were both burnt out.

Tomorrow we were both looking forward to, I know. It would feature a welcomed new place for my dad to see and drive through. We were going to follow the 90 East to Sioux Falls, Iowa, so I suggested a short detour through YNP. A drive through YNP is exactly what we both needed. Actually, tomorrow would turn out to be quite the site-filled scenic drive. We would go through Yellowstone and then through the Big Horn National Forest.

September 9, Friday, our third day driving, was just a perfect day. They must've known we were coming to YNP because the skies were blue and the day was so much better than any day I had in the park. We did hit a few showers on the way in but nothing that lasted. We got to YNP early, around 9:00 a.m., and had to remember we only had so much time there. So we were really just planning on a driving tour, with a few stops scattered in between. We missed the Grand Prismatic Spring, but we did get to see Old Faithful, which was a test of our patience; we must've just missed the last eruption because we waited almost forty-five minutes.

One of the things we did that I couldn't on my trip was drive on some of these loop trails and roads. One I distinctly remember was Fire Hole Canyon. It was a short loop that started in the canyon and went down along the Fire Hole River. I know we both really enjoyed this as we had to get out and do a little walking to see it all. Somehow, we managed to see around seven bison combined.

These animals are incredible; they're huge and impressive looking. I couldn't believe how big their heads were and of course the size and spacing of their eyes.

When we were getting ready to leave, we pulled into the Fishing Creek Visitors Center. On my side, five feet away, was a monstrous bison! It was casually walking away, and luckily, nobody noticed it. I can't imagine how stupid someone would have to be to want to get close to these animals. Their size and horns alone would make you want to keep your distance. They seem docile when they are grazing, but we've all seen the videos of these wild animals. That's the keyword people forget or just don't care about: these are *wild* animals. Leave the animals alone; in the end they're the ones that suffer the real consequences of human contact. I read a quote, and I absolutely love it: "The wild, without wildlife, is just scenery." Please don't ruin the wild.

We got to drive to Canyon Village, which was very cool to see. I didn't make it here on my trip, so I was happy to see it now. We got to see the High and Low Falls. The Grand Canyon of YNP was incredible, and I'm very glad we took a quick drive here before leaving. The views from atop of the canyon were out of this world. The way the mountains worked their way down to the Yellowstone River was a sight to see. We made one last stop on our way out of the

East Entrance: we had a break to watch the waves crash in Lake Yellowstone. I was glad my dad got to experience Yellowstone, and of course I was happy to see it again. This is easily my favorite of the national parks I've been to.

One thing I got from driving through YNP was the beginning of an understanding of what I had just done. Heading toward the East Entrance, where I did a *lot* of climbing, it really started to hit me hard. Leaving YNP and staying on Highway 20 East, we followed my route. Driving what I rode is what it took for me to say, "Wow, I climbed this?" especially driving through the park, seeing the mountains and hills I climbed, and pointing out my memories as we drove past them. On some of the hills we drove over, it blew my mind to think that I had ridden my bicycle over the same path. It's still hard to believe I biked the mountains of YNP and the surrounding area. And driving the long, winding roads was the only way I could fully appreciate what I had done in this amazingly scenic area.

After riding through Cody and Greybull, we took Highway 14 East through the Big Horn National Forest. The first 15 miles were some of the most scenic miles I have seen from a car. The views coming into the land offered a preview of what was to come. Driving through the canyon was something that could easily make a bucket list. Add to that the layered colors of the rock walls and scattered brush along the lower elevations. Even though it's obviously a slower drive, it's worth it. We were both very glad we took the scenic byway. We continued on Route 14, the Bighorn Scenic Byway, back to 90 East and got a hotel in Buffalo, Wyoming.

We didn't really stop anywhere, and after a full day of driving, we were getting tired. No matter how awesome the landscape is, it's hard being in a car over two full days, considering what we both had done to get to our meeting spot. My dad is like me in more than a few ways. I see similarities. As with every father and son, some are good and some not-so-good. Trying to give directions is a challenge for me. I'll tell my dad where to turn and how far, and a little later he'd ask, "Where are we turning?" It drove me crazy, but I'm sure he'd tell it differently.

What can I say? My Dad and I had probably the classic long-distance drive. We had good times, we had different ideas, we laughed, and we were quiet at times. Like I said, all that's expected driving five days across the country. I wouldn't have done it any different, though, and that's really the only thing that matters. We both wouldn't change the way we did things, but doing it again? We'll see…

As much as I don't want to talk about this, it needs to be included. On the way back home, I got incredibly depressed and wasn't sure what to do really. I guess being a passenger, not driving, being in the car that long, combined with preexisting conditions, drove me to a place mentally I never want to go back to. I get in these moods, and lately it seems anything can trigger me to think and act like this. I can't take it and don't want to feel this way, but once again it's life to me; it's normal. I hope this changes because now I want to get home so I can pack up and leave and run away. Feeling this way feeds my depression, like I want to give up when I get home. I hate the way I'm feeling and feel worse because I'm sure I'm not making things fun for my dad. Currently thinking about the future, specifically my future, scares me and leaves me feeling unsure and uneasy.

Sometimes I feel I just don't belong or don't know where exactly I fit in. I don't want to give up but feel like taking that easy way sometimes. Sometimes I feel like walking into the woods and just not walking out. I feel like the cartoon ostrich at times, just wanting to stick my head in the ground and hide. When my depression takes control, I just want to disappear and run away. Right now, I want to run and not look back.

One of the things my dad wanted to see the most was Mount Rushmore National Memorial. I must say, I wanted to see it but didn't expect it to be so big. I know that sounds very odd, but pictures don't do it any real justice. It's hard to fully appreciate the magnitude of this monument unless you can see it in person. It's such a sight to see; I'm very glad we went and stopped here.

While we were out here, we also drove through the Black Hills and some of the Bad Lands. Once again, the natural beauty out here was exactly what the doctor ordered. One way to help me escape my moods, even if temporarily, is to get out and experience what nature has to offer.

Driving through these regions just blows my mind. The flora, the fauna, and everything else is so different from where I live, and I tremendously enjoy it. All I see is dairy farms, farms of all kinds, and certainly not the endless open space. Out here I'm in a foreign land, a place so opposite from where I live, and I can't seem to get enough.

Tomorrow is the last day of driving, and then I'll be home. I can't lie, the last couple days have been boring. The Midwest and the prairie lands are great but don't do it for me like the Western mountains do. We have seen some cool things, but I'm getting restless. It gives me time to think, and right now I'm not sure that's a good thing. I keep thinking, What am I going to do, and how will anything change now that I've completed my journey? How will I react to the same old apartment and town that I don't want to go back to?

There is to much pain I feel in my heart and body as I think about staying in the New Holland area. I don't even want to be in Lancaster County at this point. But scariest of all, I don't think I care or have feelings; it's like I feel numb to these thoughts. Even writing this makes me sad inside (what's hard is reliving these thoughts when I don't necessarily feel that way currently at this writing). It makes the depression seem so much more problematic. It's hard to even write this because everything just seems so damn bleak currently. I wish I knew what to do. Once I get home, I'll need to sit down and really think about what I want and how to go about achieving it.

★

9/12/23

HOME, NEW HOLLAND, PENNSYLVANIA

After getting home, I wrote the final entry for my book. I also made my final video, which was sixteen minutes, and this is the easiest way to include them. I'll paraphrase them in two parts.

✪

Last Writing 9/12/23

DINING ROOM TABLE, APARTMENT

I finally made it home last night but ended up being busy until 11:00 p.m. I just couldn't help myself—cleaning, washing, and putting things away. I wanted to do a video and write, but I did neither. So here I am, the day after getting home.

The ride home had its ups and downs. We did get to visit the Hendrix Memorial and drove to Mount Rushmore. We saw sections of and animals in YNP that I didn't see before, we went through the Bighorn Forest, and so much more. These scenic byways out West are just incredible and fun to drive through as a driver or passenger.

With my anxiety and whatever else is going on, I need to have some sort of plan. I need to at least have an idea or game plan in places I'm not familiar with. I like to say it's because I want to see the best sights and such. But it probably comes down to some form of control. I'm fine with unplanned trips, but I think I'm going to miss something I might've really wanted to see if I do.

I think anyone driving together for 8 to 10 hours a day for 5 days will get frustrated with each other at some point. It might be almost unavoidable, mostly because of the trips both of us took to get out to Washington. My Dad had a long five days coming out, I know that. Add in the fact that both of us are probably stuck in our own ways, and it created some memories for sure. Don't get me wrong, I love my dad and enjoy our time together. He also drives me crazy sometimes, and if you ask him, I'm sure he'll tell you the same about me. I guess that's family, and at the end of the day, none of it matters. The only thing that matters is that I wouldn't change any part of the drive home.

Now that I'm back home, I'm not sure how I feel. One little part is glad to be home, but the majority of me wants to leave immediately. I still have the feeling that I don't belong in this county or maybe even state. I certainly want to get out of New Holland. After the incident here, I feel a need to leave, almost like I don't feel safe here. After those events, I don't like driving at night and dread any police contact. My thoughts vary, but my anxiety runs off the charts when I think about any form of interaction. I sometimes wonder if there is a place out there for me, if and where I belong or fit in. I don't feel that fit here, and that's not a new feeling for me.

I feel different now, like my eyes are opened up to the real world. Well, I feel I've known what the real world is like for a while now. Now, I'm doing what I want in my life. I'm not letting outside issues affect me or my plans. No more worrying about what anyone thinks; it's time to try freedom, real freedom again. Do I think leaving on a two-month trip was the right thing to do at the time? No doubt, this getaway was exactly what I needed. I needed to get away from myself and the run-and-gun lifestyle I had at the time. I feel I was on the verge of a breakdown. Pressures were getting to me, and all kinds of outside issues that don't mean much controlled my thoughts and part of my life. I had to get away and do what I did. Everything was there for me, and I had to take this opportunity.

A lot of things in life happen only once or a couple times, if you're lucky; these are extremely special opportunities. If you don't take advantage when they present themselves, you might never get the chance again in your lifetime. So no matter what, listen to your heart, and do what makes you happy. For me the time was right, but the circumstances surrounding it all made my decision to leave all the easier.

Now I need to be able to keep my head up above water and not go back to that sinking, drowning feeling inside. Sink or swim, which one will I choose? Yes, I do believe we have a choice in how we react over time. The immediate feelings and emotions are natural, but it's how we react to them, how we deal with them, that matters. No change will happen in life without action. I can't just complete my trip and hope that now all is well. No, I have to take and use what I have gained, how I felt during this trip, and apply that in my life now. It's much easier said than done, and I know this will be a huge undertaking for me.

I know I have to change. If I don't at least try, how will my life get any better? What benefits will this trip have in my life if I choose to sit and continue this downward spiral into my depression? How do I break out of my so called "misery comfort zone," as I call it? I can't answer that, and I think it's still a long journey to find out. I do think that trail has an end to it. I just need to continue walking to find it. Any step forward, no matter how small, is still progress.

Stay true to yourself, do what you think is best for you, and run with it.

✪

FROM MY VIDEO

Right away my first comment is a common one: I don't think I want to be here. It seems like a reoccurring theme. I think of it in light of everything out there in the country I've now experienced and more than that, what I've gone through here. The hard times I've created for myself and some of the other times I have a strong opinion about. Some things in life I don't know if I'll ever fully accept. Maybe they're my feelings now because I just got back. I'm sure there are multiple reasons for me wanting to leave, and I might not even realize all of them. But in reality, I probably won't leave, mostly because of family. I'd feel like I'm abandoning my parents. Bottom line, I probably just won't, no other real reason, no excuses; it's just the way it is.

I went through a very rough time before I went on the trip, and that is also the reason I had the time. I went on this trip searching for something, or maybe I just needed to get away. Turns out it was both. As far as my goal, it's more than just riding across the country. I needed to do some searching deep inside, and I was hoping to find some answers and clarity in my life.

Right now, I don't feel I gained much of those. I do think the rewards that might come from doing this trip are somewhere down the line. I think going through this alone and having to work through all the different situations have grown my confidence and inner strength. I think, I hope, I'm pretty sure.

I'm not naive—I've been through enough life experiences to know that if I'm given those things, confidence and inner strength don't just magically appear. If I'm rewarded with that, it's because I've continued to work for it. Riding across the country, or 4,000 miles, doesn't mean a damn thing if I choose to remain stagnant in my life at home. It doesn't mean life will get better or worse, and it doesn't mean life will change at all. It's just an accomplishment, a feat. I'm proud of this; it's something no one, including myself, can ever take away from me. My point is, unless I make changes myself, my life will never change for the better. No action means no relief. When have you ever felt better mentally over time by doing nothing?

Everything I went through on this trip can lead to one of two outcomes. If I continue to be down in the dumps all the time and stuck in my ways, this trip won't do anything for me. It just goes back to a trip across the country instead of the higher purpose—namely, to get away from it all and do some real thinking about my life. What I've been through, what I want out of life, how I'd like life to play out, and what I need to do to accomplish that. I don't want to keep going through life the way I was. I can't; I need change. I need to break out of my isolated state, which at times I did struggle with on my trip. Early on I did try to avoid almost all interaction; it's something I need to work on.

I don't know why I react the way I do in certain situations that have something to do with either interacting or asking for help. My tire incident in eastern Washington more than showed this glaring problem. What are my underlying issues? Why do I act and think the way I do? Going through this, I thought I'd come back to more change. Maybe it hasn't happened yet, or maybe I'm crazy for thinking something is going to or even supposed to happen.

I went through this trip feeling great, mostly. Now that it's over and I'm home, I don't know how I feel about anything. I feel like I'm back to the same old rut, spinning around in the hamster wheel of life, stuck. This is the depressing part I wish I didn't feel or could better control.

I've also had thoughts of going back to school. I already have an associate's degree, but I'm really thinking about transferring my credits to a branch campus in Harrisburg. I've been in talks with the professors in the mechanical engineering program but need more information. I think this would be a good move, but going back to school at forty, that's a tough decision.

Coming back and sitting in my apartment, I still get this feeling there's not a lot here for me anymore. It wasn't the easiest forty years for me; a lot of it has been stuff I've created. A lot came from my past alcohol problems, which fortunately haven't been a problem since January 28, 2017, the day of my last drink. Even that doesn't guarantee me anything, but it sure does make things more manageable. I'm at a crossroads, and I don't know which way to go. I just got back. I need to take some time to digest everything; I don't want to rush life choices right now. I have so much to look over, and read; I think in a day or two, reliving my trip will help me. So much stuff happens on a trip like this it's hard to remember it all. Thankfully I kept up with my daily writings.

I need to go through it all and comprehend what I did. If I don't, it might all go to waste. Some form of change must come from this trip. If I don't take anything from all this and don't change my life, then it just becomes a bicycle adventure. I'm in need of a life-changing adventure; some form of change *must* take place. This is too big to not affect me and my life. Anyone struggling in life that has gone on a journey like this, has engaged in any form of getting away, hopefully understands what I'm trying to say.

I don't want this just to be a sightseeing tour. This was intended to be so much more, and it turned out to be. Some of the moods I went through widely varied. In Nebraska and Wyoming, I was screaming at the top of my lungs on my bike because I knew I was in control. I knew I was going to do this, and I knew there was nothing that would stop me. What happened to this attitude along the way? Is it all because of the bike breaking down, or are there other issues contributing? I certainly know it's both, but that's the stuff I want to find out. I don't know how to find it, though. I tried seeking help but never felt understood or had enough time or other circumstances intervened.

I don't know what to do with myself. I'm restless; I already want to go out and do something. I'm not talking about a day hike here. I'm talking big, time consuming, adventures. I don't want to do anything else, just go on these trips. Is that too much to ask? How can I do that? How can I make money to sustain that sort of lifestyle?

I would enjoy being a tour guide. I planned this by myself. I've proven I can handle myself on tours, so why not a group of people? In today's world there's so much money going around; look at the internet and these influencers. There's so much money out there it makes my head spin, but thankfully I have no idea about that stuff. I have Facebook, and that's it. But in today's world, it's there if you want it. I just need to find a way to tap into that. Of course, then I'd have to be interesting, and I don't see myself as that. Being self-sufficient from my bike would be a dream come true.

I used to think, Can I do something like this? How can I afford it? Now it's like, Why not? Why not go, why not now, why not tomorrow, and what do I need to do this? That's my current mentality, to keep moving. I've gotten a taste of real adventure, and I want more.

Before I was using all my vacation time for bike trips, so it was usually limited to a week or two at most. Unfortunately, I need to save up and get a new bike. My new bike will not be a Diamondback;

that personal allegiance is over. Back to doing some more research into something that will suit my needs.

I'm stubborn; if you knock me down, I'm going to get back up. I'll continue getting up until I physically can't. It's like life—life can beat you down, but you've got to keep fighting. If you can't fight back, just keep moving forward, making progress. As long as you're making progress, it'll eventually work out. Perseverance is a major part of life. Never, ever give up.

10/15/23

WRAP-UP

With all the writing I have done so far, I wasn't quite sure how to start the ending of my book. I might as well finish the way I started, just rambling and writing. It seems to do the trick for kick-starting my thoughts.

It's been a month since I returned home, and honestly not a lot has changed. I've continued my pursuit of a possible return to college—initial talks, open house, and a tour of the labs. I want to see which of my previous college credits will transfer. Then hopefully I can get an idea of a major deciding factor: time.

From my previous GART trips and with the time I had, I knew I had to complete what I started, but I had to start at the beginning. I knew I'd be tested; I knew I could break down in the middle of nowhere. I knew about the dangers out there, and I thought I was ready and prepared.

You can do all your research, be great at fixing your bike, but you can't prepare for how you'll react. How will you react to a flat tire on the interstate, with winds at 20-plus miles per hour and an oncoming storm, in a remote area? What do you do upon seeing a grizzly bear watching you ride your bike 10 to 15 feet away? Will you give up climbing a mountain to an elevation of almost 9,000 feet when you feel like there's no air to breathe? You just have to know yourself, how you react to adverse conditions.

As you know now, I might have started to lose it, I might get worried or even scared, but I was out there alone. I had to solve every problem, or be able to seek out help. There was no "Well, someone will come along and help." Although sometimes you luck out with that. My point is I couldn't count on that happening, even though a majority of people will help if you're broken down. That puts a lot of stress on my shoulders, not to mention my mind.

I'm not some great mechanic; most of my "fixes" usually end up at my local bike shop. I can do basics, and I'm good at improvising if needed. I think of the bike like a car: if it's in good condition, I don't expect major issues on a long trip. I do maintain and do daily checks on some things, mainly keep everything important clean—derailleurs, chain—and check the tires every couple of days. Barring any crash or anything else major, I wouldn't expect a major breakdown of the bike.

For someone like me, who, as you've read repeatedly, can get twisted up mentally, the physical challenges are one thing, but the true hard challenges are mental. While I didn't do the greatest on this trip, I think I did do a good job managing it. I was in a real bad place mentally going into this trip, and I thought just getting away and doing what I loved would help me. It did help some, but like anything worth something in life, it must be worked for. If I don't put any effort into trying to change my life, how will it ever be different? I can't sit around and wait for a miracle.

I got to meet a lot of great people, and I'm also starting to see how interacting with people is not as bad as I once thought. Seriously, some of the help I was given and/or offered was amazing. There were people out there that were actually interested in what I was doing, and that was not something I was used to. Strangers showing a genuine interest and caring for me is something foreign to me.

Even a little over a month after my trip, I don't feel it's that big a deal. It was just me doing what I enjoy. I know what I accomplished, but inside I guess there's not a huge sense of pride in having done it. It's a "Just another adventure down; OK, what's next?" feeling.

It was a busy summer for riding, and I did a few trips. Well, after spending 6 months in county prison, having everything dropped 3 days before a court date, I had to get away and fast. I was released in March and completed a round trip of the 165-mile Delaware and Lehigh trail a month later. A month after that, I rode the 325-mile OTET, both ways as well. It was on this trip when I stayed at the primitive campsites in London, Ohio, and met a group from the Wounded Warriors. They were doing a fully sponsored trip on the GART. After talking with them, combined with my own thoughts, I knew when I got back, I was going to start to prepare to ride the GART in its entirety.

I got to see so many incredible things along the way and experienced so many new things it's hard to wrap everything up. The rodeo in Cody, the juvenile grizzly watching me, seeing a moose in the middle of a trail in Idaho, the beautiful trees of the Pacific Northwest, Yellowstone, and so much more. Being from Amish and Mennonite country and having lived there all my life, I just sit back and think about it all. My elevation at home is around 400 feet, and yet the elevation in Yellowstone was 6,000 to 9,000 feet. The mountains of the West, riding through the seemingly endless cornfields of the Midwest, the crop dusters covering those fields, all the beautiful state parks I got to camp in—I just try to absorb as much as I can because it was a lot.

Of all the sights I saw, the gradual transformation of America from my saddle was the absolute best. America the beautiful indeed; I'd be hard-pressed to venture overseas considering all the natural wonders we have right here. Seeing the landscape take different shapes and also riding through all that change was incredible. I took, by my count, 3,365 pictures and recorded 88 videos. There were times when I got extremely frustrated with the terrain—I still don't want to ride gravel roads again—but overall the riding was fine. There were sketchy times with no shoulders, and I also had shoulders 6 feet wide. I can now say I've ridden on the freeway with a posted speed limit of 80 miles per hour! I've climbed 9,000-foot-tall mountains, I've braked going downhill to maintain 25 miles per hour, and I've let it open and cruised at 34 miles per hour down those mountains—there was a lot of white-knuckle riding for sure.

Of all the things I had to fight through, the toughest was fighting myself. Getting stuck in my moods, thoughts, fighting depression, anxiety, and then still being able to function enough to continue alone was tough at times. Not knowing where I was most of the time was an odd feeling, but I sort of love the feeling. I had no clue where I was but knew where I needed to go. That's one fun part of exploring—not really knowing or caring where you are. Then, suddenly, a town or something amazing comes out of nowhere. I generally wouldn't know my exact location unless I looked at my GPS on Maps. But for sure the hardest challenge on my trip was overcoming or at least maintaining/balancing all the unrest going on upstairs.

Well, I don't want to go into details—but I did seek help again, eventually. I've been dealing with all this alone for so many years. I couldn't tell you how many—perhaps ten or more?

One thing I had no concerns over was alcohol. While I'm still aware of it, it has been almost seven years now. I don't use drugs, never was my thing. I was trying not to break down and buy a pack of cigarettes, and I didn't! I quit this year but got stressed and bought a pack on the two prior trips, as I mentioned. I did buy pouches on this trip; I figured I wouldn't use them at home, but I might buy a pack of cigarettes at home. You know the one last pack excuse? I know myself. I'm happy to say no cigarettes and no single Black & Mild either.

Like I said, nothing happens without change; if I want my life to get better, then I better change. Going to see the doctor and potentially going back to college—I'd say that's a good start. Will I change where I live? That's still up for debate, I guess. Maybe I'll find change through this book; maybe somebody will read this, and my life will change through that. I hope you've gotten something from my writing. Maybe you find similarities, or maybe you think I'm crazy, just complain, and repeat myself. Either way, thanks for reading. Reach out and say hi; I'm not hard to find, and I'd like the feedback too.

I'm no one special. Whatever I can do, so can you. We all probably underestimate ourselves as to what we can actually do. I do all my own planning, mapping, everything. I literally pore over so much to get the info I need. It probably took me over a month to plan everything for this trip, and I think I severely rushed it. I just wrote two hundred pages for a book. I exposed myself mentally; you know some of my issues and look at what I accomplished. It takes work, but if you're dedicated to something and stick to it, you *will* accomplish your goals. The biggest obstacle is usually yourself, and once you overcome that, the rest is downhill.

Who tells you to not try something? Society or social norms? Screw them. Be yourself and do what *you* want to do. It's your life, not theirs, and in the blink of an eye, you're forty-one or whatever age and wondering where the hell the time went. If that opportunity in life presents itself, grab it right away. Listen to your heart and not your brain, sometimes.

It's hard to believe I've written all this alone. Now wrapping it all up, I've got to say I've had this dream to do a long ride and write about it. It was supposed to be about my adventure but soon enough became so much more than that. The book became about me and my personal struggles. Thinking and looking back, the trip wasn't really scary at all (which is easy to say after the fact). You know what's really scary? Being in your early forties and exposing yourself to the world. I still have to work, I still have to live a life, and now I choose to write about myself, my struggles, expose some secrets, my convoluted thoughts and thinking to the world. And the world will ultimately judge me one way or another. Now that's freaking scary, especially when one already has acceptance issues.

But at some point in your life, you can't be scared anymore. At some point, you'll have to stand up and face your fears. If you don't, you'll never have a chance at true freedom; living with fear isn't living free. And at the end of the day, that's what I want, mental freedom. If I can ride solo across the country and write a book, imagine what you can do.

Finally, I want to thank everyone who took the time to read my ramblings. I hope you got something out of it.

I'm not quite sure this book has a point or any meaning. I guess maybe this is my way of explaining myself or me just getting some stuff aired out. Bottling everything up is not on the road to healing; I learned that years ago. If you liked my book, got something out of it, or want to tell me to stick to riding and not write anymore, I'll listen to it all.

If you see me riding out there say hi. Who knows maybe I'll even start riding with people. Thanks again to everyone I met along the way, anyone who followed along with me daily on Facebook, and everyone out there who understands the feelings expressed in this book or has felt the same way.

THANKS

I want to say thanks to a bunch of people who helped me, who became friends, or whom I've known for years, in no particular order. First, of course I want to thank my mom: without your help and support throughout the years, I wouldn't be the person I've become. Dad, feelings and deep talks were never our thing, but we both know what our thoughts and feelings are, and that means everything. Bob, I can't say thanks enough for all the support throughout the years you've been involved in my life. The rest of your side of the family, Aunt Judy and Mo, I know how you enjoy following along; thanks to both of you and of course everyone else on the Connelly side. I want to thank Aunt Missy, who followed along and sent me all kinds of local stories during my journey.

Thanks to all my friends and family back home, those I still see and those I haven't in too long a time. The two new friends I made in Ohio, Karen and Larry—that was a heck of a way to meet two people, but I'm glad I did get to know you, and thanks for meeting up for the ride. Bob Texiera, it was great having our campsites side-by-side; man, I still can't believe that starry night we shared in Montana. Joe Pepin, my new Montreal friend, it was fun spending the rainy day together, hanging out, and riding a little bit. Jay Waters, a fellow GART through rider, thanks for all the help answering my questions about the trail. Tommy, fellow Deadhead in Missoula, thanks for the ride. Ray B, thanks for being understanding and letting me go on this trip, all things considered.

Jordan and the crew at Dan Bailey's Outdoor Co. (Livingston, Montana), the help and the fixes were awesome. Our talks were great, and I'm glad you didn't have to drive out to scoop me up on Highway 89. Finally, thanks to the rest of the bike shops that helped me along the way, Wheelzup at Canal Place (Cumberland, MD), Ernie's Bike Shop (Massillon, Ohio), Endless Trail Bike Shop (Omaha, Nebraska), Hellgate Cyclery (Missoula, Montana), and Cascade Bicycle Studio (Seattle, Washington).

★

myamericansolitaire.com

★

ABOUT THE AUTHOR

Craig Martin, a lifelong resident of Lancaster County, is an adventurer at heart with a passion for bikepacking, hiking, and hockey. His love for thrill and adventure is evident in his explorations, both physical and mental. A dedicated fan of Pittsburgh Penguins and Baltimore Orioles, he also enjoys attending concerts. His book, *American Solitaire: My Exploration Of America and My Mind*, reflects his adventurous spirit and love for exploration. It's a must-read for those seeking inspiration to achieve their goals. Craig's experiences and insights make his work relatable to a wide audience, from teens to adults of all educational backgrounds.